# Advance Praise

Always defying categories, psychiatrist and urban activist Mindy Fullilove takes us on a geographical and historical journey to Main Streets around the world. With stops for a bowl of soup or to pop into a toy store, we follow her through her own phantom tollbooth. This is as much a guide for the perplexed (or depressed) as it is an astonishing study of the built environment and its effects on our health, communities, politics—and our future.
　—**Maura Spiegel**, PhD, Co-Director, The Division of Narrative Medicine, Vagelos College of Physicians and Surgeons, Columbia University

What if we could ignite our collective creativity and renew our democracy by repairing our cities? What if that repair could begin with one street; a place of complexity, sociability, and busy-ness? What if it fed mind and body, laying a table of earthly and spiritual delights? Welcome to *Main Street*, you will want to stay.
　—**Gerry Kearns**, Professor of Human Geography, Maynooth University, Ireland

We see a genius at work as Mindy Fullilove pulls from public health theory and her training in medicine to develop a unique and essential intersectional approach in understanding how to build democracy and a just city for all. The story of *Main Street* is the story of this country and countries around the world. As urbanists think about the future of cities, communities, and connections in this new world, *Main Street* is the place to start this analysis, not only for understanding the commonality that anchors us all, but also the way to approach relationship building and theory development. Organizers, researchers, doctors, architects, and politicians, by reading this book, will learn how to build the city in which everyone prospers.
　—**Nupur Chaudhury**, MUP, MPH, Host, NupurSpectives

Synthesizing her observation of over 100 cities and conversations with leading thinkers, Mindy Fullilove's *Main Street* provides a novel perspective that guides us to see the social geometry of what makes a community vibrant. It should be required reading for students in urban sociology, architecture, urban planning, and community health.

—**David Vlahov,** PhD, RN, Yale School of Nursing, Yale University; Editor, *Journal of Urban Health*

The doctor is in...examining community life. With the eye of a natural scientist, with the warm wit of a country practitioner on house calls, psychiatrist Mindy Fullilove prescribes the renaissance of Main Streets for the ills of industrial decline. You will not see your neighborhood, nor your neighbors, the same way after reading this book.

—**Helena Hansen,** MD, PhD, Associate Professor, Departments of Anthropology and Psychiatry, New York University

Reading *Main Street* from the perspective of an urbanist, planning practitioner, and educator whose professional career was birthed during the anti-war and civil rights era of the '60s, I was moved by Mindy Fullilove's ability to blend memory, issues of racism, environmental justice, climate change, and the "psychology of place" into a coherent and integrated whole. *Main Street* builds on Mindy's previous works, and, while it focuses on the corridors that connect us on a daily basis, she has treated us to one of the most important books about our contemporary towns and cities since Jane Jacobs' *The Death and Life of Great American Cites*.

—**Ronald Shiffman,** FAICP, Professor Emeritus, Graduate Center for Planning and the Environment, Pratt Institute

How can Main Streets create democratic spaces that support our common life? How do their complex systems work? Take a stroll with Dr. Mindy Fullilove along the arteries that nourish us, our neighborhoods, and nations. Filled with personal stories, landscape scrolls, and unfolding expert and local perspectives, we learn how these inclusive civic settings offer the possibility to repair our fractured cities. With insights from 178 cities in 14 countries, *Main Street* is both a resource and inspiration for students, planners, and community activists.

—**Karen E. Till,** Professor of Cultural Geography, Maynooth University, Ireland

# MAIN STREET

# Also by Mindy Thompson Fullilove

*The Black Family: Mental Health Perspectives*
(editor)

*Homeboy Came to Orange: A Story of People's Power*
(with Ernest Thompson)

*The House of Joshua: Meditations on Family and Place*

*Root Shock: How Tearing Up City Neighborhoods
Hurts America and What We Can Do About It*

*Collective Consciousness and Its Discontents:
Institutional Distributed Cognition, Racial Policy
and Public Health in the United States*
(with Rodrick Wallace)

*Urban Alchemy: Restoring Joy in America's
Sorted-out Cities*

*From Enforcers to Guardians:
A Public Health Primer on Ending Police Violence*
(with Hannah L. H. Cooper)

How a City's Heart Connects Us All

# MAIN STREET

## Mindy
## Thompson
## Fullilove, MD

*Foreword by Andy Merrifield*

 newvillagePRESS

Published in the United States by New Village Press
bookorders@newvillagepress.net
www.newvillagepress.org
New Village Press is a public-benefit, nonprofit publisher
Distributed by NYU Press

ISBN:    978-1-61332-126-3 (paperback)
         978-1-61332-127-0 (hardcover)
         978-1-61332-128-7 (ebook)
         978-1-61332-129-4 (ebook institutional)

Publication Date: October 2020
First Edition

Library of Congress Cataloging-in-Publication Data

Names: Fullilove, Mindy Thompson, author.
Title: Main street : how a city's heart connects us all / Mindy Thompson
    Fullilove, MD ; foreword by Andy Merrifield.
Description: First edition. | New York : New Village Press, [2020] |
    Includes bibliographical references and index. | Summary: "How do Main
    Streets contribute to our mental health? This question took social
    psychiatrist Mindy Thompson Fullilove on an 11-year search through 178
    cities in 14 countries. From informal observations, Fullilove discerns
    the larger architecture of Main Streets. She describes the myriad ways
    that Main Streets are shaped for social interactions and how they are a
    marker for the integrity of civilization. Her illustrated book shows how
    urban centers are essential for gathering people to share information
    and to tend civic and commercial tasks that benefit all. She addresses
    ways cities can cure, not only ills of an inequitable, post-industrial
    culture, but malaise of a post-pandemic culture seeking reconnection."--
    Provided by publisher.
Identifiers: LCCN 2020022604 (print) | LCCN 2020022605 (ebook) | ISBN
    9781613321263 (paperback) | ISBN 9781613321270 (hardcover) | ISBN
    9781613321287 (ebook) | ISBN 9781613321294 (ebook other)
Subjects: LCSH: Community development--Psychological aspects. | Community
    psychology. | Central business districts--Social aspects. | City
    planning--Psychological aspects. | Urban health.
Classification: LCC HN49.C6 F85 2020  (print) | LCC HN49.C6  (ebook) | DDC
    307.1/401--dc23

All photos by the author except where indicated.
Cover illustration and design: Carol Hsiung
Interior design and composition: Rich Brown

For Michel Cantal-Dupart

*Merci les villes!*

# Contents

# List of Figures and Tables

## Chapter 4 – Circle

## Chapter 5 – Line

## Chapter 6 – Tangle

## Chapter 7 – Time

## Chapter 8 – The Great Mistake

## Chapter 9 – Exiting Regularity

## Chapter 10 – Status Quo

## Chapter 11 – Planning to Stay

## Chapter 12 – What Happens Next

## May I Have the Envelope, Please?

# Foreword

MY FIRST ENCOUNTER with Mindy Thompson Fullilove was on the page and it came with a *Wow!* Actually, it wasn't so much on the page as on the front cover of her book *Root Shock*—a blurb from the legendary urbanist Jane Jacobs. I mean, a blurb from Jane Jacobs! *Wow!* Jane had only a year or so left to live, but one of our savviest urban scholars ever had this to say of Mindy: "By practicing good science in a fallow field, Fullilove illuminates her chosen subject and also transcends it." Jane knew a good egg when she saw one.

Mindy does practice good science because, unlike most other urbanists I know, in a field where PhDs are a dime a dozen, she's a *real* doctor, a trained medical doctor, a fully qualified psychiatrist. Yet a peculiar breed of doctor at that. Indeed, rather than cash in on all those expensive years of medical school, setting up some cushy private practice in a rich part of town (the fallow field Jane talks about), Mindy has done something more novel and noble instead: toiled for public betterment in a poor part of town.

By 1992, in a cramped Washington Heights office, she belonged to a small yet dynamic multidisciplinary team called the Community Research Group (CRG), part of Columbia University's School of Public Health and New York State Psychiatric Institute. Their laboratory was right outside the doorstep, on the gritty upper Manhattan streets. All around her, every urban epidemic imaginable swirled, from AIDS and crack addiction, to mental illness-related violence and multidrug-resistant tuberculosis. Walking to work, Mindy said, meant negotiating sidewalks littered with crack vials. Unsettling as the experience was, it was somehow inspirational, too. Some epidemics weren't yet imaginable.

In those years, just as the banks and Wall Street piled up speculators' profits, New York was grappling with fiscal crisis and deindustrialization, with decline and hard drugs. Yet Mindy and her co-workers were dealing with an urban rot really rooted in the fifties, with its large-scale urban renewal programs. James Baldwin had called this urban renewal "Negro Removal," since of the one million displacees, 63 percent were African American. Other policy nostrums during the sixties and seventies further threatened life and limb of low-income urban dwellers, both black and white. One was "Benign Neglect," the not-so-bright idea of Richard Nixon's urban affairs advisor Daniel Patrick Moynihan. Nothing "benign" here. This was the *purposeful* running down of disadvantaged neighborhoods, those too much of a public burden to fix; "Malign Neglect" critics termed it, emphasizing the active pathology of the process. Its partner in urbicidal crime was "Planned Shrinkage," Roger Starr's brainchild, "planning" the elimination of "bad"—read: poor, minority—neighborhoods across America.

The paradigmatic case study of Planned Shrinkage was New York's South Bronx. It was too costly for fire trucks to keep putting out all those fires, so let's shut down the stations! Mindy's colleague and mentor, epidemiologist at CRG, Rodrick Wallace, argued that Planned Shrinkage unleashed a "synergism of plagues." It wasn't one plague in particular but a whole accumulation of them, each conspiring together to have a catastrophic effect on inner-city neighborhoods; a complex mix of how bad urban policy creates bad environments, and how bad environments became toxic for people with few resources to cope. The cycle becomes vicious, urban decay a contagion, a public health nightmare.

Starr himself poisoned the air every time he put ink on the page.

He launched tirades against "community," insisting the principle doesn't exist in urban America. Since there's no such thing, blocks could be blasted and people moved on at whim. He cited a report on Boston called "Grieving for a Lost Home," which "found that 26 percent of women relocated were emotionally disturbed two years after the move." "Were they not 'emotionally disturbed' before moving?" Starr wondered.

Mindy was in serious disagreement with Starr. In her scientific work, she'd spent a lot of time talking to people who'd lost their homes through various urban policies. "What they had described to me," she says, "was a wrenching feeling of disconnection, accompanied by disorientation at first, followed by alienation and nostalgia." Yet this was nostalgia "in the psychiatric sense," she stresses, "a profound and even life-threatening grief caused by the loss of home. I labeled this *root shock*." She'd borrowed the language from gardeners. They use the term to describe how carelessly moving plants from one site to another, severing roots, is deadly. Plants can't tolerate the transplantation, and neither can people. "It was a regular part of people's stories," Mindy says, "that old people died when the neighborhood was uprooted. They couldn't take the move."

My own brush with root shock came when I was five years old. Needless to say, I didn't know it then, hadn't experienced it directly, but Mindy would later help me piece it together. It was 1965 when my grandmother and grandfather were shipped off to Cantril Farm, a brave new housing project on the fringes of Liverpool in the UK. There were several problems with this shipping off. For one thing, my grandmother, grandfather, and my mother's younger sister Emily were all shipped off *whether they liked it or not*; they weren't given a choice in the matter, just a letter in the mail. The letter told them that their house was condemned, that it was deemed a slum, and they would have to move out soon. Their little inner-city row house on Holden Street in Toxteth—their prim and proper, if poor, little row house, on a block rich in social relations and mutual support systems—was deemed squalid by urban "experts."

Yet even before it was finished, Cantril Farm was falling apart. Tower blocks were leaky and damp, there was little sound insulation between apartments, communal corridors smelt of urine and lacked lighting, and elevators were frequently broken. There was no public transport, no doctors' surgeries, no stores, no nothing; a high-rise wilderness set in a wilderness, a fallow field in a fallow field, cut off from anywhere, from any memorable past and any discernible future. It was row upon row of austere breeze-block towers, homes for twenty thousand wounded denizens, mushrooming on land the council acquired at a snip. Little wonder my grandmother didn't last long in this wilderness, nor my grandfather. Both died a few years later, of broken hearts within a broken community. Soon after, my thirty-something aunt Emily developed ovarian cancer. She was dead by forty. As a five-year-old I knew nothing; later I heard words describing this life-and-death form: *alienation, alienated life,* initiated by nameless, faceless professionals. Now, though, I know it was *root shock.*

My first encounter with Mindy in person came around 2015, at New York's New School, where she'd just begun teaching. I'd been invited there by the architect Bill Morrish, Mindy's new colleague, who we'll see cameo in *Main Street.* Bill asked me to talk about the plight of capitalist cities and I probably said more than he'd asked for, maybe even spoke too downbeat. I wasn't seeing much intrigue or novelty in urban life anymore, nor much democracy. Our cities were increasingly unfair and uninteresting, flattened by familiarity, even as those glitzy skyscrapers went up.

Past decades have seen colossal urban expansion. At the same time, the parameters for human expansion, the expansion of the self, have diminished, dwindled for many denizens. Cities gorge on capital and wealth. The rich plunder urban land as a lucrative financial asset, expelling a *residue* of people priced-out, displacing and uprooting them. It's something of a global phenomenon, happening almost everywhere. I said that maybe we could see this growing residue as a sort of *shadow citizenry* of disenfranchised people, who carry within their being *shadow passports*, unofficial documentation expressive of a phantom solidarity.

I wasn't sure what the audience would make of such a flight of fancy. I'd brandished the idea partly in jest, as a provocation, and partly as a metaphor, to get people imagining. But then, afterward, somebody approached who'd been listening intently, knowingly. Introducing herself, it was Mindy, and, all of a sudden, from her own secret sleeve, she thrusted before me a real-life shadow passport! Another *Wow!* Immediately we became soul mates. The thing looked like a genuine US passport—same size, same thickness, bearing on the same bald eagle seal. And yet, it was bright orange colored, and inside its back flap, swashbucklingly dressed, was a Puss-in-Boots mascot, with the accompanying caption: "*Sound Mind in a Sound Body in a Sound City.*" Here, then, was my first glimpse of the elicit travel papers of the University of Orange, in Orange, New Jersey, Mindy's hometown.

Situated in a multi-racial, multi-ethnic community, since 2008 the University has been open to all comers, to people for whom "official" paying universities are firmly shut, beyond budget. Its faculty, including Mindy herself, is wholly volunteer; the classroom isn't so much about teaching as sharing experience, a dynamic dialogue between student and instructor, discussing civic engagement and community participation. Students earn "Be Free" degrees by taking classes, voting in elections, attending town meetings, and volunteering to do something in the community, even if it's just sweeping trash up off the sidewalk. With each community duty fulfilled, the holder's passport is stamped. Each stamp counts as a credit toward graduation. With this, shadow passport bearers learn how to scamper through the brambles of life.

The University of Orange figures prominently in Mindy's more recent book *Urban Alchemy*. The educational project is one element in Mindy's magical bag of tricks, conjured up to ward off bad urban karma. Mindy comes from the East, yet she acts more like the Good

Witch of the North, knowing that behind every evil spell lies a counter-spell to undo it, one that can change the course of the hurricane. She knows that while there are plenty of evil spells fracturing neighborhoods, other counter-spells can unite neighborhoods; that while evil spells create division and hate, counter-spells spread joy and love; that while evil spells turn life into a dark puzzle, counter-spells unpuzzle, make life collectively human and thrilling.

One of Mindy's best spells is no hocus pocus. It insists that communities discover what they're FOR, find something that might bring people together in a positive sense, affirming the creative, not merely denouncing the negative. Part of this magic is earthily unmagical; it asks communities to look within themselves, to see what they've already got, to reclaim their hidden assets, not just wallow in their more obvious deficits. It's as easy, and as complex, as ABCD— Asset-Based Community Development. Find solidarity, celebrate your achievements, no matter how small or seemingly insignificant.

*Urban Alchemy* witnessed Dr. Mindy becoming more poetic and impressionistic, more personal and, as such, maybe even more political than before. She edges her science toward social science, her philosophy toward spiritualism, all the while waving her characteristic Good Witch wand of generosity and compassion. Such is the timely spirit that infuses her latest endeavor, *Main Street*, a companion volume to her two previous works, the fulfilment of an urban trilogy, pursuing once again the theme of what's wrong and what's right about urban America. I say this thinking of Scott Fitzgerald's passage from *The Crack-Up*, that "the test of a first-rate intelligence is the ability to hold two opposed ideas in mind at the same time, and still retain the ability to function. One should, for example, be able to see that things are hopeless and yet be determined to make them otherwise."

This seems to me the agenda Mindy has now set herself, under the awful presidential watch of Donald Trump. Never has modern society been so full of conjuring tricks as today, carried out by self-serving politicians. They've cast spells the likes of which we've never seen before. They've become sorcerers of collusions and conspiracies, of tricks and deceptions, of fear and loathing, of fake news and endless, unbelievable, sleights of the economic and political hand that have become, alas, all too believable. *Main Street* thus appears as an anti-hate manifesto, the kind of counter-magic we need to help transform us back into thinking and caring human beings.

Mindy's text was written before one of those hitherto unimaginable epidemics, Covid-19, assailed the world, killing and upending social life as we once knew it. But with its priority accorded to acts of human kindness and community solidarity, it's hard to underscore just how crucial *Main Street*'s program is during any crisis. Implicit within its pages is the message that those old inequities, the short-term greed and divisions that pervade our society, that have been manufactured by our leaders, can no longer cut it; business-as-usual economic distancing must never return. As of this writing, not a few of Mindy's Main Streets will likely be on the brink of collapse, if they haven't collapsed already. (An early victim was her beloved Irish pub, Coogan's, in Washington Heights, shutting its doors under New York's March lockdown, never to reopen.) Some of the wonderful characters she introduces to us, too, may even be no more. And yet, Mindy shows us why these Main Streets lived on so vibrantly in the first place, and why it is vital for our public health that we keep them in life.

At a time when presidents and prime ministers bully and sprout lies, *Main Street* assembles an array of gentle voices and honest testimonies—from Mindy's friends and family, mentors and colleagues, poets and philosophers, clergymen and cardiac patients (like Mr. Glover). We listen up as Mindy scours the Main Streets of a hundred and seventy-eight cities in fourteen countries. Her avowed mission is nothing less than "to discern the contribution of Main Street to our collective mental health." "When we go to Main Street," she says, "we take in fashion, culture, and sociability. We shop, mail letters, get library books, and have coffee.... Sometimes we take our laptops to be in the flow and in the know while ostensibly working. This makes us happy. It is a Machine for Living."

When Main Streets disappear, the center disappears, Mindy says, and people are propelled into a "centrifugal crisis." Main Streets are intricately ordered microcosms of a bigger macrocosm; their mutual survival is dependent on their coexistence. "When parts of a region have collapsed," says Mindy, "this has consequences for the region as a whole....We ignore the reality that the prosperous parts also suffer when segments of the city are allowed to fester. There are useful parallels to what happens to people in the aftermath of a stroke, when they might ignore the affected part, acting as if it were not there."

Main Streets form capillaries of a living, breathing, palpitating organism. Mindy's Main Streets are full of cells and soft tissue where streets are arteries that need to flow to nourish the entire body politic. But Main Streets need independent structuring as well, a particular set of architectonics in order to function healthily. They'll require clear demarcations, specific relationships to surrounding buildings, and definite borders—borders that are open and porous, that loop and curl into backstreets, that have walkable links and accessible transit connections all around. Main Streets need to be discrete though not *too* discrete: they can't be ghettos hacked off from the rest of the city, engulfed on all sides by busy highways.

Mindy has drifted through a lot of Main Streets, walked them, observed, talked to people, ordinary people as well as professional practitioners. While she got to pace many miles of New York's Broadway, ate French patisseries as a *flâneuse* in Gay Paree, sipped çay in Istanbul, and chilled in Kyoto's dazzling Zen temples, her real concern is Main Street, USA, the more modest main stems of provincial America. There, she paints her canvas as sensitively as Edward Hopper, touching up with a few hues he'd left out. There, she has us journey to, amongst other places, Baltimore and Brattleboro, Charlottesville and Cleveland, Memphis and Minneapolis, Salt Lake City and St. Louis. Many more of her Main Streets are closer to home, in New Jersey—in Asbury Park and Englewood, in Jersey City and Livingston, in Maplewood and Newark, in Tenafly, and, of course, in Orange.

She even pays homage to Sauk Centre, Minnesota, with its daddy Main Street of them all, the Main Street Sinclair Lewis used for *Main Street*, his 1920 allegory of the narrowness of small-town USA. "*Main Street* is a frustrating book," Mindy writes near the end of her own *Main Street*. Carol Kennicott, Lewis's protagonist, "is perfectly good and perfectly inept," says Mindy. "But the narrator's deeper impatience is with the status quo and its ability to suck the life out of good people who want to make things better."

The status quo will never suck the life out of good people like Mindy; she's no Carol Kennicott. She has the right tools, knows the real facts of the matter. Maybe she's more like Robert Frost, whom Mindy cites, with his tree at the window: it's all about the inner and outer weather, about putting our heads together, about the fate of the imagination. Still, after I'd finished reading the manuscript of *Main Street*, I was reminded of the artistry of another intrepid reporter who'd likewise prowled the everyday American landscape: Robert Frank. Frank captured postwar America in a series of black and white photographs assembled under the rubric *The Americans*. He took pictures, Mindy mainly uses words. (She has some great graphics in *Main Street* nonetheless.) But Frank's little camera similarly snapped a beautiful and sad poem of America. There's a famous introduction to Frank's collection, written by Jack Kerouac. Jack gave the Swiss photographer one message, and it's a message I'd like to pass on to Mindy: Doc, you got eyes!

—Andy Merrifield, May 2020

*We are caught in an inescapable network of mutuality, tied in a single garment of destiny. Whatever affects one directly, affects all indirectly.*

—Martin Luther King, Jr.

# Introduction

*And therefore I have sailed the seas and come*
*To the holy city of Byzantium.*
—W. B. Yeats, "Sailing to Byzantium"

IN 1979, I WAS SELECTED by the American Psychiatric Association for a fellowship program that supported minority residents. Dr. Jeanne Spurlock and her team introduced us to a network of accomplished minority psychiatrists, financed our attendance at association meetings, and provided each of us with a stipend that we could use to create projects in our own training programs.

As a black resident in an all-white hospital, this experience was liberating. Much of what I was learning in my residency had to do with the internal world of the patient. I didn't know what to do regarding racism and other forces I knew existed outside the individual's realm. The people I met through the fellowship—Charles Pinderhughes, Ezra Griffith, Bruce Ballard, Carl Bell, Altha Stewart, Joyce Kobayashi, Earline Houston and many others—helped me to articulate the relationship between the internal and the external in people's lives and to manage the dilemma of seeing this complex picture when others in my program did not.

Many of those I met at APA offered useful advice, but one piece stands out. At the time of the 1982 convention in Toronto, I was writing a paper on the meanings of skin color in two short stories by Jessie Redmon Fauset, a major figure in the 1920s Harlem

Renaissance. Fellow resident Ernest Kendrick challenged me. "Doctors don't think fiction is science. To reach a medical audience, you need to connect this literature to medicine. Why not use Engel's biopsychosocial model?"

## How Mr. Glover Was Saved by His Boss and Then Almost Killed by His Doctors

George Engel, a psychiatrist who helped surgeons and internists understand their patients' needs, had just published a paper demonstrating how his "biopsychosocial model" worked in the clinical setting. In contrast to the "biomedical model," which focused on what was going on inside the human body in a circumscribed biomedical sphere, the biopsychosocial model encompassed the sociology of illness.[1]

Engel told the story of Mr. Glover, a man who had had a heart attack. The biomedical way of telling the story would be something like this: This fifty-five-year-old well-nourished, well-developed white man with a previous history of myocardial infarction began experiencing chest pain at 10:00 A.M. and was brought to the emergency room by ambulance at 11:00 A.M. He was hospitalized in the intensive care unit, where he experienced cardiac arrest due to ventricular fibrillation. His heart was successfully restored to its normal rhythm. The rest of his hospital stay was uneventful, and he was discharged to follow up with his internist.

Engel's approach to the story started at the same place, acknowledging that Mr. Glover had had a heart attack, a coronary artery occlusion, which affected the cell and tissue levels of the systems hierarchy, producing the symptom of pain that Mr. Glover experienced.

But then Engel turned his attention to the hour between the onset of the heart attack and Mr. Glover's arrival at the hospital. At first, Mr. Glover hoped that the feelings of unease and pressure inside his chest were signs of indigestion. He avoided talking to anyone in his office. As the pain increased, he realized that, if he were having a

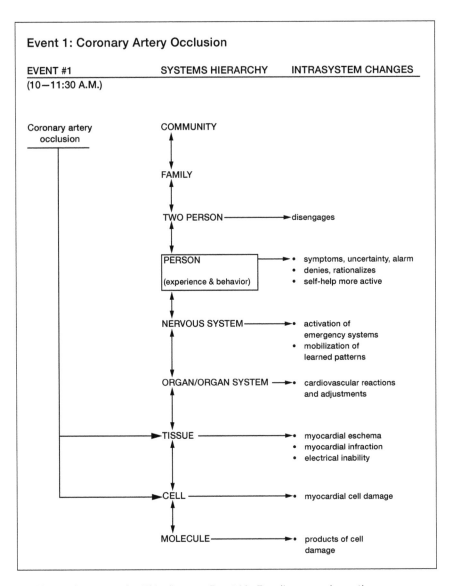

## Event 1: Coronary Artery Occlusion

| EVENT #1 | SYSTEMS HIERARCHY | INTRASYSTEM CHANGES |
|---|---|---|
| (10−11:30 A.M.) | | |

Coronary artery occlusion

COMMUNITY

FAMILY

TWO PERSON ──────────► disengages

PERSON

(experience & behavior)
- • symptoms, uncertainty, alarm
- • denies, rationalizes
- • self-help more active

NERVOUS SYSTEM ──────►•
- activation of emergency systems
- • mobilization of learned patterns

ORGAN/ORGAN SYSTEM ──►•
- cardiovascular reactions and adjustments

TISSUE ──────────►•
- myocardial eschema
- • myocardial infraction
- • electrical inability

CELL ──────────────►•
- myocardial cell damage

MOLECULE ──────────►•
- products of cell damage

Mr. Glover's heart attack. This diagram, Event 1 in Engel's paper, shows the numerous levels of the biopsychosocial model, and indicates what was happening to the person and his internal systems at the opening of the episode of coronary artery occlusion. *From Engel, 1980, used with permission.*

heart attack, he should get his affairs in order. Mr. Glover went off on that track, instead of going to the hospital.

What was it that got him on the right course? Mr. Glover's employer noticed his distress. She complimented him on his sense of responsibility, assured him that she and his coworkers would be able to manage because he'd done such a great job, and emphasized that his most urgent responsibility was to get well so that he could continue to be the fine family man and coworker she knew him to be. In the diagram below, Engel showed that while the processes inside Mr. Glover's body were continuing, important systems outside of his body were being mobilized.

Once he arrived at the hospital, Mr. Glover was admitted to the intensive care unit on a protocol for those with heart conditions. He relaxed and accepted that he had had a second heart attack. The cardiac team wanted to put a catheter in Mr. Glover's artery.

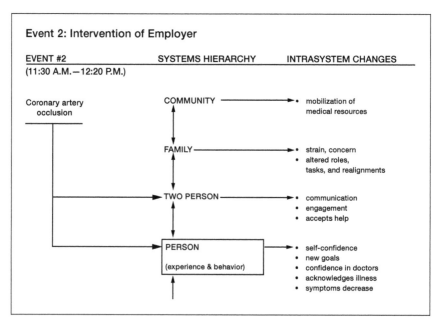

Not just his heart attack.  This is a portion of Engel's Event 2, showing the ways in which the personal problem was affecting larger social systems, specifically the two-person, family, and community systems.
*From Engel, 1980, used with permission.*

The residents in charge of this task were not able to perform it. After several tries, they left to get help.

It was at that point that Mr. Glover had a near-fatal arrhythmia. Dr. Engel, in the diagram for this event, noted that at the person level, Mr. Glover experienced a wide range of emotions, including frustration, pain, anger, self-blame, and giving up, which mobilized responses of the nervous system, including the fight-or-flight reaction. The activated nervous system released a massive load of chemicals into the blood, which, Engel postulated, triggered the arrhythmia and cardiac arrest. Had the doctors taken the time to talk to Mr. Glover and learn the story of his dependence on authority, they wouldn't have left him alone after a failed arterial puncture.

Happily, Mr. Glover was successfully resuscitated. The rest of his recovery was "uneventful," and he was discharged home. In taking us carefully through this assessment of Mr. Glover's experience, Engel made the point that the biomedical model, which considered only the factors that were interior to the person, missed crucial events at higher levels of scale, including the patient's experience of

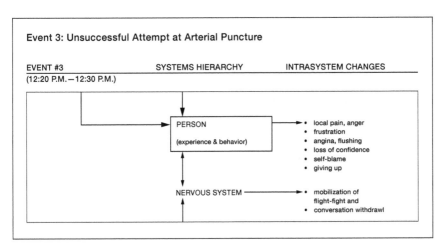

How the doctors caused a setback. This portion of Engel's Event 3 shows the ways in which the actions of the medical residents affected the physiology of the patient. Specifically, the failure to introduce the arterial line caused the patient many emotions, and mobilized the fight-flight.
*From Engel, 1980, used with permission.*

the event and the influence of other actors on the unfolding drama. When we have the full hierarchy of systems in front of us, we have a more accurate view of what is happening and better odds for saving the patient.

## The Psychology of Place

It is this model that helped me link Fauset's fictional coming-of-age stories to the real-world problem of skin color.[2] I applied the model by systematically investigating each of its levels—person, family, community, and world—within the context of a past that was ultimately unknowable due to kidnapping and enslavement. I concluded, "The final integration of color in identity includes the known/unknown, chosen/rejected parts of self and society. In the consolidation of that identification it is the person who must grapple with truth, justice, honesty, and feelings for others. It is the person who at that moment becomes an adult."[3]

Engel's model proved to be a reliable companion as I plunged into the study of epidemics of AIDS, violence, and addiction that were sundering communities before my eyes. To get a handle on what was happening necessitated thinking constantly at many levels of scale.

This required a team of people and a window into the crises. I am reminded of the remarkable story of the documentation of digestion because a trapper named Alexis St. Martin had a gunshot wound that healed improperly, creating an opening to the stomach. Dr. William Beaumont recognized that this created an opportunity to peer into the workings of the stomach. This led to important discoveries about digestion and revolutionized the study of the human body.[4]

For me, the team and the window came together in 1990, when I was recruited to work at the HIV Center of Columbia University, located at the Columbia-Presbyterian Medical Center in New York City. While the Medical Center is a fortresslike building that dominates Washington Heights, the HIV Center arranged for my then husband, Bob Fullilove, and me to have offices at 513 West 166th Street, a large semi-abandoned building in the middle of a neighborhood that was traumatized by crack cocaine and all its related ills. To get to work, we walked down a sidewalk littered with crack vials, so prevalent there because one of the most important dealers in the area lived across the street. In that setting, walking to work was a constant source of inspiration.

We had other assets: We had a suite of offices that included a lounging area, and we had access to two conference rooms and a kitchen. We soon assembled the kind of multidisciplinary team that we needed to tackle the rapid-fire series of epidemics that were swirling around us. Calling ourselves the Community Research Group (CRG), we carried out studies of AIDS, crack addiction, violence, mental illness related to violence, and multidrug-resistant tuberculosis.

All of this was taking place in a context of social disintegration. Rodrick Wallace's 1988 paper, "Synergism of Plagues," had been crucial to directing our work from the minute we received it.[5] We were even more fortunate that Rod worked at the New York State Psychiatric Institute, part of the Medical Center, and was a willing collaborator and mentor. He taught us how a 1970s New York City policy called "planned shrinkage" had destroyed inner-city neighborhoods, dispersing the residents and creating the conditions for the rapid dissemination of the AIDS virus.

One of the first projects we undertook was to ask our intern, David Swerdlick, to take photographs of Harlem and to search in the archive of the Schomburg Center for images of what it used to be like. The contrast he documented was shocking: The structure of the neighborhood had been destroyed and its vitality vitiated. I could not explain in scientific terms how the built environment and social system were connected. Using the biopsychosocial model as my guide, I began to search in geography, environmental psychology, anthropology, sociology, and history to find the answers.

The geographers taught me about "place," bounded areas that have social and psychological meaning, such as one's home. The environmental psychologists explained that there are essential connections between individuals and place, as well as among residents of a given place, and between and among residents of different places. These are connections of attachment, such as those described by John Bowlby and others, the strong and weak social bonds that Mark Granovetter has described, and the powerful influence of behavior settings, established through the work of Roger Barker and his colleagues. Anthropologists and sociologists parsed crucial incidents, looking for clues. Anthony F. C. Wallace examined mazeway disintegration by looking at an attack on an Iroquois village; Alexander Leighton documented community response to upheaval by following how the Japanese managed internment; and Kai Erikson documented the aftermath of the disastrous flood at Buffalo Creek, West Virginia.[6]

From these scholars, I was able to piece together a set of propositions about the psychology of place.[7] I tested my hypotheses by looking at place in the stories of my family, which I shared in my book *House of Joshua: Meditations on Family and Place*. The CRG team—Lesley Green Rennis, Jennifer Stevens Dickson, Lourdes Hernandez-Cordero Rodriguez, Caroline Parsons Moore, Molly Rose Kaufman, Bob, and I—was able to use the psychology of place in tracking epidemics, walking the streets, inventing interventions, and naming the chaos around us so that others might understand. We published over one hundred papers, several dissertations, and my second book on place, *Root Shock: How Tearing Up City Neighborhoods Hurts America and What You Can Do About It*.

Reading history was a major part of that work. The United States, despite arguing that its revolutionary fight was for "freedom," established itself as a slave nation, preserving and protecting the rights of slave owners, and counting enslaved people as only three-fifths of a person. African Americans and their white allies carried out a sustained struggle to abolish slavery and establish freedom and equality. However, gains in the Reconstruction era were largely lost as inclusive democratic institutions were replaced by the Jim Crow system, which was later copied by admirers in Nazi Germany to create fascism and in South Africa to create apartheid. The long civil rights struggle, which we can date from W. E. B. Du Bois and William Trotter's founding of the Niagara Movement in 1905, culminated in marked victories in the mid-1960s, with the signing of the Civil Rights Act, the Voting Act, and the establishment of Medicaid, which desegregated hospitals.

A paradox of the post–civil rights era has been that the problems supposedly "fixed" by the movement have endured and even worsened. What emerged instead of an integrated nirvana was the "urban crisis," a polite way of saying "inner-city black poverty." Conservative politicians promulgated the idea that this was a failure of "personal responsibility," which took hold in the public's imagination but was patently false.[8]

The perspective of the psychology of place helps us track a different story, that of a series of forced displacements that had devastating effects on inner-city communities. Through that lens, we can appreciate the strength of segregated communities that managed to temper the ravages of racism through the Jim Crow era, and build political power and many kinds of wealth. It was the power of these communities that was expressed in the civil rights movement. The example of the Montgomery bus boycott can illuminate this point. Rosa Parks's legendary act of civil disobedience took place on Thursday, December 1, 1955. By Monday morning, December 5, at 6:00 A.M., fifty thousand black people initiated a boycott of the buses. For more than a year, they walked, endured threats and attacks, faced layoffs, organized car pools, fed one another, conducted weekly rallies, and held firm until they won. Only a very well-integrated, powerful community—one with deep spiritual principles—could have accomplished such a feat.[9]

Against the backdrop of those impressive achievements, however, federal, state, and local governments had launched an attack on the collective power and wealth of African American communities, which started with urban renewal, as carried out under the Housing Act of 1949.[10] Known among black people as "Negro removal," the Housing Act authorized cities to clear "blighted land," using the power of eminent domain, and sell the land at reduced cost to developers for "higher uses," like cultural centers, universities, and public housing. During the fourteen years of the urban renewal program, 993 cities participated, carrying out more than 2,500 projects. Of the one million people displaced, 63 percent were African Americans; the areas destroyed included substantial portions of such important black cultural centers as the Hill District in Pittsburgh and the Fillmore in San Francisco.

The Kerner Commission's study of civil disorder in 1967 included urban renewal in the list of factors that triggered the rebellions.[11] The process of urban renewal tore communities apart, destroying their accumulated social, cultural, political, and economic capital, as well as undermining their competitive position vis-à-vis neighborhoods that were not disturbed.[12] This profoundly weakened affected neighborhoods; those harms were repeated in subsequent displacements due to planned shrinkage, mass incarceration, HOPE VI (which was directed at federal housing projects), the foreclosure crisis, and gentrification.[13]

The series of displacements from neighborhoods occurred contemporaneously with deindustrialization, which undermined the economic foundations of older American cities, leaving unskilled workers at a severe disadvantage.[14] This created the massive deindustrialization diaspora to the Sun Belt, destabilizing both sending and receiving cities. In the upheaval caused by serial displacement and deindustrialization, the epidemics of heroin and crack cocaine took off, violence soared, and AIDS became a serious threat to health. Asthma and obesity flourished. Trauma, as a result of these accumulating disasters, became a major source of psychiatric illness and contributor to ill health.

The economic and social dismemberment of African American communities stole their wealth, their power, and their capacity to engage in problem solving. Returning to the biopsychosocial model, we can begin to name the processes that are happening at each level of scale. The vulnerability of the individual stripped of the protection of a known and loved place is greatly increased. The experiences of trauma, grief, and anger, as well as the stress of losing one's embedding community, have effects on the individual. These can lead to psychiatric illness, the use of drugs and other addictions, eating and autoimmune disorders, and infectious diseases.

At the level of the neighborhood, the processes of urban renewal, deindustrialization, and planned shrinkage are centrifugal: They are pulling us apart from one another. In my book *Root Shock*, I described the ways in which the centrifugal processes tear at people's places and their lives. I asked the question, "When the center fails, what will hold?"

The answer in the short term is that people take on the work of place in order to keep their lives together. They band together in groups defined by "strong ties," the ties of family, religion, and tribe.[15] Yet these ties partition society. In the aftermath of urban renewal and planned shrinkage, the reformation of society around strong ties fed antagonism and intergroup hostilities: The solution became part of the problem, triggering a reinforcing, exhausting, and dangerous downward spiral.

At the next level of scale, the effects of neighborhood destruction on the larger embedding society are very serious. This point is often overlooked, because, as I've described here, the neighborhoods that are destroyed are those of poor and minority people. The larger society is thought of as "white" and "middle-class," and therefore comprised of people whose lives and fates are quite different and even insulated from the problems of the disadvantaged. The ecologists who mentored me, Ernest Thompson, Michel Cantal-Dupart, and Rodrick Wallace, taught me about the fallacy in this assumption of separation.

Rodrick Wallace, with his colleague and partner, Deborah Wallace, documented the ways in which the systematic destruction of minority inner-city communities had direct connections to the health of the larger society. They emphasized that concentration of people in ghettos did not mean that the harms inflicted on those communities would be contained within those spaces. *Concentration is not containment*, they emphasized. In fact, they identified what they called the "paradox of Apartheid," the finding that segregation actually tightened connections between communities thought to be divided by race and class.[16]

In light of this serious history, which poses a substantial threat to the whole country, Rod made one of the most important advances in our field of social psychiatry: He described the workings of collective consciousness in our segregated society. Drawing on a large body of literature in many fields of study, Rod articulated the workings of "distributed cognition," the ways in which people think together, across time and space. He built on this work by examining the threats to collective consciousness posed by rigid, Manichean systems of racial segregation. I collaborated with him on a book entitled *Collective Consciousness and Its Discontents*. In that book, we pulled together the fields of distributed cognition and social history. We wrote:

> [A] neighborhood [has the ability] to perceive patterns of threat or
> opportunity, to compare those perceived patterns with an internal,
> shared, picture of the world, and to choose one or a few collective
> actions from a much larger repertory of those possible and to carry
> them out ... This phenomenon is, however, constrained, not just
> by shared culture, but by the path-dependent historic development
> of the community itself. Recent work demonstrates that "planned
> shrinkage," "urban renewal," or other disruptions of weak ties akin
> to ethnic cleansing, can place neighborhoods onto decades-long
> irreversible developmental, perhaps evolutionary, trajectories of social
> disintegration, which short-circuit effective community cognition.
> This is, indeed, a fundamental political purpose of such programs.[17]

## Not Spared History

While CRG was learning history, we were not immune to the

processes we were describing. CRG was not a group that got major grant funds for big, long-term studies. Instead, we survived on small grants and contracts that allowed us to track processes unfolding all around us. The recession dried up our usual sources, and the team had to disperse. Gentrification hit Washington Heights, and we were evicted from our home at 513 in 2008.

This turned our attention to problems of rebuilding: Where were we to go? Like others displaced by gentrification, we had to go somewhere. At first, this seemed like a catastrophe, but we realized it was an opportunity to follow the path other displaced people were taking. Visits to Orange, New Jersey, my hometown, soon led to our joining local leaders to found the free people's University of Orange. Eventually, we reestablished our research group under the name Cities Research Group of the University of Orange. Our experience rebuilding taught us a lot and helped me integrate the many lessons I'd learned through the careful tutelage of the renowned French urbanist Michel Cantal-Dupart, known universally as Cantal. I became deeply aware that rebuilding was about fixing the injuries to place as well as mending the social fractures.

In my book *Urban Alchemy: Restoring Joy in America's Sorted-Out Cities*, I presented nine elements of urban restoration I'd seen Cantal and others use in the rebuilding process: City in mind, Find what you're FOR, Make a mark, Unpuzzle the fractured space, Unslum the neighborhoods, Make meaningful places, Strengthen the region, Show solidarity with all life, and Celebrate your accomplishments. These elements guide us toward the work that needs to be done, slowly and carefully, building on the existing assets of our cities.[18]

## Main Street in the Mix

While working on that book, I went to downtown Englewood, New Jersey, to get some coffee at Starbucks. I was sitting by the picture window, looking at the crowds passing by, and was struck by the liveliness of the scene. I, like most people, thought of Main Street as dead, but that day, I realized our Main Street was not dead at all. I started to think of all the functional Main Streets I knew and loved, civic, commercial and social centers that had been part of my life since childhood. Then I thought, if Main Streets are alive, what role are they playing in making our common life?

I started with the plan that over the coming year I would visit Main Streets in one hundred cities. It took longer and was harder than I thought it would be to discern the contribution of Main Streets to our collective mental health. From visits to Main Streets in 178 cities in fourteen countries, I have learned that these civic and commercial centers are designed and built to provide a centripetal—gathering—force for a community. Our survival is built on people's coming together, and our social nature has evolved to reinforce gathering with pleasure. We have a built-in "Joy of Being In," which explains the powerful "Fear of Missing Out." When we go to Main Street, we take in fashion, culture, and sociability. We shop, mail letters, get library books, and have coffee. Or we loiter, whether on a bench or in a Starbucks window. Sometimes we take our laptops to be in the flow and in the know while ostensibly working. This makes us happy. It is a Machine for Living.

I also learned that this Machine for Living can be adapted to help us solve the horrific problems we face now: climate change, racism, militarism, and concentration of wealth, among them. One of my favorite Main Street spots is the Thomas Edison National Historical Site in West Orange, New Jersey, Edison's "Factory of Invention." It turns out that the great man needed a lot of people to get from idea to patented product. And he needed materials, spaces to experiment, ways to document the process, a library, and a couch for naps. The Factory of Invention is the remarkable space in which these things were meticulously organized as a place of distributed cognition.

Because of his recognition that this was the way people can innovate, Edison received 2,332 patents. While respect for his fertile imagination is universal, few of us know of the system that supported it. At the heart of that system was not a single great man, but, rather, a very large team that could think together, a working group with a massive collective consciousness, informed by science, mechanics, art, and imagination. It should not be a surprise that Edison's Factory of Invention had a movie studio and a chemistry lab. This ability for humans to think in a collective manner is an extraordinary evolutionary advantage humans have over other species. Emphasis on collective: Had Edison not been hobbled by such antisocial character defects as anti-Semitism and belligerence with competitors, he might have died with four thousand patents.

When I first visited the Factory of Invention, I understood immediately that we at CRG had had such a factory at 513, where we could track epidemics and explain their social roots. Our factory, I would say, encompassed the whole neighborhood, which we scoured in our search for comprehension. We also had the luxury of a suite of offices that included places to share, to chat, to do the collective work of comprehension, what Rod would come to call "collective consciousness." We could sit in the lounge or a conference room and pool our knowledge, tossing ideas around until we came to an understanding that fit all the facts.

One of my tasks in the wake of our displacement has been to rebuild CRG's factory of invention. But I've also realized that the challenges and resources of Main Street offer groups large and small their own "factories of invention." In the course of my study of Main Streets I've encountered many of these organizations and I tell some of their stories in this book. I am deeply impressed by what they have accomplished and what they might do next. Main Streets offer a unique combination of assets that can help us name and solve our problems.

But this potential tool is not in good shape. While Main Streets are not dead everywhere, many are. It took me a while to see this. Perceiving what is not there is tricky: It is the task of seeing the black hole. When Main Streets disappear, the center is gone; people are thrown into a centrifugal crisis. When enough of the disparate centers are gone, whole regions are impaired. When enough regions are reeling, the nation becomes paralyzed. When enough nations are paralyzed, the world falls into profound crisis.

And this is the situation in which we find ourselves in 2019: a dark situation with too little connection to make problem solving possible. Mounting crisis may force us to work together, but increasing anxiety may feed anger and hatred faster than solidarity. In our terrified apartness, we could fall into the worst-possible outcomes of the current crises of climate change, species extinction, and international warfare.

Greta Thunberg, a teenage leader in the fight to face climate change, called on us all to shift to "cathedral thinking." As she said to the European Parliament:

> It is still not too late to act. It will take a far-reaching vision, it will take courage, it will take fierce, fierce determination to act now, to lay the foundations where we may not know all the details about how to shape the ceiling. In other words it will take cathedral thinking. I ask you to please wake up and make changes required possible. To do your best is no longer good enough. We must all do the seemingly impossible.[19]

I contend that *cathedral thinking* is another term for Factory of Invention. We can create on Main Street the spaces and sentiments for collective problem solving, embracing the great diversity of our nation to find the way forward. In the following chapters, I will describe how Main Streets work, with a view toward explaining how we might transform these magnificent Machines for Living into the Factories of Invention that can see us through.

# Part One

# Learning Main Street

# 1   Weather Permitting

SOME YEARS INTO the Main Street study, I found myself waiting for my daughter, urbanist Molly Kaufman, at the Cleveland airport. She drove up in a metallic blue Corolla that popped against the gray sky. "Do you mind if we do an errand before we go to the hotel? I need some tights," she explained. "I looked for an American Apparel store in a cool neighborhood and found one seven minutes from where we're staying. It's going to be snowy and cold tomorrow. I brought a dress and I think I should wear it to the conference dinner today, before the weather gets worse."

Our destination was an American Apparel store on Coventry Road in Cleveland Heights. The store was bright and spacious, with excellent sale racks. A young salesman showed Molly all the colors of gray tights and then left us to the hedonism of searching their clothing displays. The need for tights expanded to all the pleasures of possibility: pants, shirts, skirts, dresses in assorted colors, textures, and drapes.

It was satisfying to find useful, beautiful garments that we liked. We left with our purchases, in too much of a hurry to visit the other stores on that two-block Main Street, but we promised ourselves we would to return the next day.

It snowed three inches overnight—in April—but Cleveland's excellent snow-removal system had the streets in pretty good shape. The sidewalks were another matter, poorly cleared and laced with black ice. I walked with trepidation. We started our foray onto Cleveland's Main Streets by stopping in Little Italy, which we'd passed the night before on the way to Coventry. It, too, was a short section—two blocks—with a potpourri of old Italian eateries and new galleries and tchotchkes stores. We drove on to Coventry, and this time surveyed the possibilities. We opened our visit at Big Fun, which Molly had heard was the best toy store in the world.[1] It was packed with action figures, fake mustaches, toy cars, games, playing cards, stuffed animals, Silly Putty, and things I'd never seen before. We picked our way slowly through the aisles, wondering what my grandson Javi might like for presents, and fully aware that it's very convenient to have a child in the wings when you want to shop at a toy store.

Early on in the Main Street study, on Bloomfield Avenue in Glen Ridge, New Jersey, I encountered a small sundries store that offered a great collection of Matchbox cars and trucks. The vehicles—bulldozers, tow trucks, and such—caught my attention, and I bought a few. I started looking for Matchbox toys everywhere I went, but they are not to be found in that many places. Big Fun had several Matchbox cars and trucks, and after some debate with myself, I decided to get a blue Volkswagen Beetle with souped-up wheels. We also got some mustaches for Javi—great fun for the movies he was making—and a very big safety pin that would look as if it were stuck through his nose. We also got a bumper sticker that read CLEVELAND IS MY PARIS. Much to my delight, the clerk gave us a Big Fun sticker. I don't know what it is about stickers, but I love to put them in and on my notebooks.

We passed several beauty parlors and then came to Mac's Backs—Books on Coventry. Bookstores have largely disappeared in New

York—first the independents were pushed out by Barnes & Noble, and then the Barnes & Noble stores began closing, vanquished by Amazon. The few stores left have exactly the same bestsellers, which is really discouraging when you're in search of a good novel or a really interesting nonfiction book. Mac's Backs presented us with gripping titles I hadn't seen. I came across Frederik Backman's *My Grandmother Asked Me to Tell You She's Sorry*, an enchanting book about an eccentric grandmother who leaves the task of making amends to her granddaughter. This was especially touching, as I would be seeing my own granddaughter Lily later that day. Seeing *Spain in Our Hearts*, I was reminded I'd read a great review and wanted to read this new book by Adam Hochschild; his memoir, *Half the Way Home*, had been important to my early studies of the psychology of place. Molly found *The Nest* and *This Is an Uprising*. The latter is a book by a college friend, and she got it in solidarity. "I always buy my friends' books. I have to support them," she explained.

This is the kind of place Mac's Backs is: After I got home, I ordered a book from its website. I got a personal response from Suzanne, who said, "I didn't meet you personally when you were in Cleveland for the conference, but I want to thank you for the scholarship and comprehensive wisdom of your books."

That day in Cleveland Heights, we peeked into the coffee shop next door to see if it were a place for coffee and some reading, but it seemed more like a lunch spot. We decided to leave Coventry and head over to the next destination on our list: West Side Market, in the Ohio City neighborhood, about twenty-five minutes away, on the other side of town.

Parking was tough when we arrived at the very popular market. We drove around and finally found a spot on a side street. Oh, was it scary to navigate the slippery streets and sidewalks! The wind was blowing and I was cold; we pressed on.

Walking over to the market, we passed TownHall, a café that served light fare. By this time, we were in the mood for lunch, so we stopped to eat. Over lunch, Molly shared a conversation she'd had with her nephew, Lily's brother Javi, debating whether God was a man or a woman. "He's black," Javi had insisted. "He was a man who was married and had children. He had his trials. And when he died, he was immortalized and he became God. This was about a thousand years ago."

After lunch, we continued a few more doors down to the market. We passed from the dreary cold streets into a palace of food, with bright tiled walls, high vaulted ceilings, and light streaming in from the clerestory windows. The first area we entered was the fruit and vegetable section, where the produce was piled high, to be touched, smelled, chosen, and enjoyed.

In the larger building, the aisles were lined with food cases filled with meat, cheese, condiments, snacks, and pastries. We were dazzled by pink pork chops, sausage ropes, chocolate-covered biscotti, and many flavors of popcorn. As this last is a favorite of Lil's, Molly did a taste test to find out which of the offerings Lil would like best.

Strolling around, we saw lots of signs: banners hanging from the ceiling with a history of the market, signs above each stall naming the business, and signs in the cases describing the food and its prices. There were also lots of decorations around the stalls. D. A. Russ had a buffalo head over its stall, while Wiencek's Meats had an assemblage that included a whimsical wooden cow, several smaller plastic cows, a plastic train set, and a plastic pig with a big grin.

The throngs of shoppers passing through this emporium had plans and moved with deliberation toward their favorite stands. Some places had long lines for their products. Others seemed nearly neglected, their clerks looking a bit bored as the crowds passed them by. Molly and I were pretty limited in what we could get. Otherwise, we would have wanted some of everything: lamb, tomatoes, cheese, bread. In addition to the popcorn, we got some exceptional wild thistle honey from Walter Jorgensen, whose apiary was in Oberlin.

We left the market to go look around some more. We drove over to see downtown and the warehouse district. Neither drew us out of the car. After driving around for a bit, Molly suggested that a coffee shop would be just the thing. We could warm up, have a nice hot drink, and read our new books. Thanks to the Internet, we found Phoenix Coffee on Lee Road—not far from Coventry—and we headed there. Its big windows and open space were welcoming, and its chairs comfortable for reading. People were there with friends or working at computers, while the baristas turned out a steady supply of fancy drinks.

We eventually headed back to the hotel to meet medical educator Martin Kohn, who was to take us to East 105th Street to see the building that had once served as his grandfather's synagogue. A year before, I had toured this street with a group called Neighborhood Connections. It had been a thriving Main Street serving Cleveland's big East Side African American community, but it had fallen apart in recent years. I had seen a big Jewish Community Center that I'd asked Marty about it. He'd explained that East 105th was a Main Street for the Jewish community before they moved to the Heights and the African American community moved in. "My grandfather's temple was on that street." He related a story of his reconnecting with a place he'd known in childhood, getting to know the Pentecostal minister and going to a service there. "It was fun, except I should have brought earplugs."

Being in this place had brought up a surge of memories for him, and these eventually became a poem. I loved the poem and had asked if I could visit the place with him next time I visited Cleveland. So Marty, Molly, and I set out for East 105th Street and the old temple.

We drove around the neighborhood a bit, taking in the scale of the disinvestment. Many years ago, while working in Harlem, I had invented a "community burn index" to compare the extent of neighborhood destruction to severe burns on the human body.[2] Being old and with paint peeling on the trim and gutters falling apart, and signs of moldering, represented the first level of neighborhood burn; moldering plus scattered loss of buildings, the second level; while moldering plus widespread loss of buildings represented the third, and most severe, level. In Cleveland, as in Harlem, Pittsburgh, Newark, and many other Rust Belt cities, the damaged area covered wide swaths of land, especially in the poor and minority neighborhoods. That was what we saw here. Yet its history as a Jewish community had not been obliterated: Several smaller synagogues, repurposed for new uses, were scattered among the buildings still in use.

We stopped in front of Apostolic Faith Tabernacle and knocked on the door. No one was there. We took photos of the building. Because it was cold, we sat in the car to hear the poem, "Transfiguration."

Let's say it's been 60 years
half of which you've had an itch
or an inkling or a vague sense
that nearby your Jewish soul was born
So you drive north on 105th
past the VA and Cory Methodist
where Moses and Rashi and a host of your prophets
still sit on the shoulders of that fine church

There! See that black brick building
sturdy gritty rectangle
transfigured in '58 from
Kenneseth Israel!?

For what do you hope
as Apostolic Faith Tabernacle opens its doors
and with outstretched arms points to the Stars
of David hovering above the baptismal font—
that watery tent of meeting
for the faithful
who greet you strong handed and voiced with
"Praise the Lord"
until the arm waving swaying of the mini-multitude begins
amid the din of drums and choir

And Baruch Hashem
soon you know
for the holiness remains

just under a different name

And then you watch it flow out the doors and
down the streets of Glenville –
Drexel, Columbia, Yale
St. Clair Avenue
past Moses and Rashi who
turn east with their minyan
from the heights of their lofty place
shouting "justice, justice, you shall pursue"

"Justice, justice you shall pursue," Deuteronomy 16:18, theologians agree, is central to Judaism. And so, on that sad, depleted street, Marty emphasized to us the duty to help. It felt like a very ancient admonition, heard in that place on that day.

We took Marty back to the hotel, and he headed home. Molly and I headed to Oberlin. We walked along Main Street on our way to meet Lily. There was a flurry of snow, and two young men passed by. One was saying the cold and snowy weather was an aberration, as the usual temperature in April was in the fifties. The other rejoined, "I think it's God's fault."

I could almost hear Javi saying, "Why do they always got to blame it on the black guy?"

## Outer Weather

In visiting Coventry and East 105th Street in Cleveland, Molly and I got to see a reality of Main Streets in our nation: that they are not equally endowed with resources. This inequality is, of course, fundamental to our problems as a nation. We are a capitalist nation, which concentrates wealth among the people who own companies and therefore control the means of production. And we are a segregated nation, which stratifies both within the class structure and the neighborhood structure. Black working people make less than white working people, and are forced to live in neighborhoods that are given fewer resources.

# Cleveland Scroll, 2016

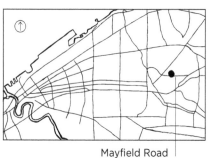

Mayfield Road

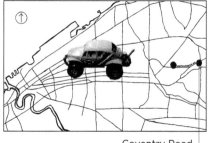

Coventry Road

We started our foray onto Cleveland's Main Streets by stopping in Little Italy, which we'd passed the night before on the way to Coventry. It was a short section—two blocks—with a potpourri of old Italian eateries and new galleries and tchotchkes stores.

We drove on to Coventry, and this time surveyed the possibilities. We opened our visit at Big Fun, which Molly had heard was the best toy store in the world. It was packed with action figures, fake mustaches, toy cars, games, playing cards, stuffed animals, Silly Putty, and things I'd never seen before.

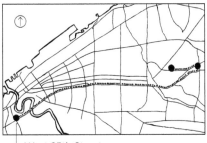

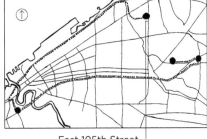

West 25th Street

East 105th Street

There were also lots of decorations around the stalls. D. A. Russ had a buffalo head over its stall, while Wiencek's Meats had an assemblage that included a whimsical wooden cow, several smaller plastic cows, a plastic train set, and a plastic pig with a big grin.

The neighborhood's history as a Jewish community had not been obliterated: Several smaller synagogues, repurposed for new uses, were scattered among the buildings still in use. We stopped in front of Apostolic Faith Tabernacle and knocked on the door. No one was there. We took photos of the building. Because it was cold, we sat in the car to hear Marty's poem.

These arrangements represent hundreds of years of very conscious thought and effort on the part of the ruling class, which understood and used the divisions of racism to their advantage. As I will discuss in chapter 8, the early roots of Euro-American colonialism involved usurpation of the land of the Native people and the creation of slavery for people stolen from Africa. Historians have been able to reconstruct the thinking that powered these processes and the ways in which a philosophy of dehumanization evolved to justify heinous acts.

These foundational processes did not miraculously go away with the American Revolution, but, rather, were written into the Constitution and other founding documents. As Octavia Driscoll, a student in my 400 Years of Inequality class, noted, when the Constitution was finalized, women could vote only in New Jersey, which took away that right in 1807. It would take 113 years for women to be fully enfranchised by the Nineteenth Amendment. In the meantime, they were unable to speak and act on their own behalf in many facets of society. We are still mired in debates about women's rights, and the emergence of murderous misogyny has given a new and terrifying face to these issues.[3]

In visiting Main Streets, we are outdoors in a space created by our society's processes for distributing crucial resources. This creates a social climate that has implications for the weathering of our bodies: the deprivation that we can see on Main Street is indicative of the other kinds of deprivation that cause people to age more rapidly than those with greater access to resources do.[4] We are also outside in the weather, which is shaped by the larger and more long-term processes of climate. "*En plein air,*" the French say, to describe eating or painting outdoors. It means literally "in full air," but closer to the sense of the expression is "fully in the air." Main Street is very much "*en plein air.*"

There's lots of weather on Main Streets. One hot summer day when I was about five, my best friend, Sally, convinced me that we should go to Main Street and get Hostess cupcakes, which she declared were the greatest treat of all time. And, she said, we could go barefoot, because she had tough feet—I didn't get the irony at the time. My feet were burning on the pavement, a feeling I have never forgotten.

And I will never forget walking in the rain in Kyoto in March 2015. I went to Japan to visit my son Bobby, who was then doing well in his fight against multiple myeloma. His wife, Haruko, and her parents asked if I would like to see a bit of Japan during my stay, and we decided to go to Kyoto, the historic city of temples. They indulged my fascination with shrines by taking me to the temples that ringed the city. We visited Kiyumizu Temple, which has a famous balcony, overlooking a steep hill. We saw a lot of people jumping and taking pictures. Haruko explained there is a famous saying, "to take a leap from the balcony at Kiyumizu," which means to make a big decision. I wanted to participate, so Haruko demonstrated a leap on the balcony, which made us all laugh.

As we left the temple, rain started, at first a happy sprinkle but then a more serious pelter. My hardy hosts turned up their collars, but I wanted an umbrella. My solicitous daughter-in-law immediately took me to a convenience store that sold white plastic umbrellas, which made me feel immensely better. As it turned out, a block past the convenience store, the street upgraded to an arcade, which sheltered us from the rain, but the wind and cold were picking up. I was longing for a tea shop, but we needed to meet my colleague Hirofumi Minami, who just happened to be in Kyoto that day.

We went into a department store to wait, and I was thawing out, thinking about tea and never going outside again until summer. Hiro arrived, bringing with him a rush of excitement. "Come see!" he exclaimed.

To calm my obvious dread, he promised that what he had to show us was just nearby and I had to see it. Out into the rain and cold we went, a short walk to a Main Street celebrating its four hundredth anniversary. My "What am I doing out here?" feeling vanished and I was caught up in the utter thrill of walking such a street. It was well lit and covered with a multi-colored glass roof. The booths on either

# Kyoto Scroll, 2015

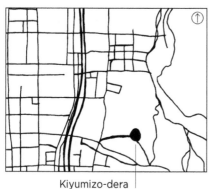

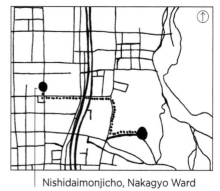

| Kiyumizo-dera | Nishidaimonjicho, Nakagyo Ward |

Haruko explained there is a famous saying, "to take a leap from the balcony at Kiyumizu," which means to make a big decision. I wanted to participate, so Haruko demonstrated a leap on the balcony, which made us all laugh.

To calm my obvious dread, Hiro promised that what he had to show us was just nearby and I had to see it. Out into the rain and cold we went, a short walk to a Main Street celebrating its four hundreth anniversary. I followed Haruko.

Nishidaimonjicho, Nakagyo Ward

Nishidaimonjicho, Nakagyo Ward

Hiro and I paused in the middle of the market for a photo. Notice the bright glass roof.

And, as Haruko had shown me, I got a stamp for my shrine book. At that shrine, they had one already prepared, so I inserted the loose leaf into my book, a memento of all the places at which I had prayed.
*Stamp reprinted with permission.*

side of the central aisle were small and offered things neighborhood people needed for cooking and living, like lots and lots of pickles, flowers, teapots, and tea. The crowds of people swirled by on their daily rounds. I stared in awe at this place Hiro had revealed.

At the end of the street was Nishiki Tenmangu Shrine.[5] Hiro led me through motions that were becoming familiar: washing my hands, bending in humility, and then ringing the bell to get the attention of the gods so that they might hear and answer my prayers. My prayers during that trip were always the same: Help Bobby in his fight against cancer; keep his family safe. Thank you for the kindness with which they shower him.

And, as Haruko had shown me, I got a stamp for my shrine book. At that shrine, they had one already prepared, so I inserted the loose leaf into my book, a memento of all the places at which I had prayed. Before I went to Japan, I had been thinking that I should do the pilgrimage to Compostela. Yet it turned out that I could do a pilgrimage on Main Streets. Somehow, the Japanese knew that we needed time to pause while on Main Streets, maybe especially when March had roared in like lion and was pelting us with rain.

It is pilgrimage plus weather that makes Main Street what it is. Open to the weather, Main Street is also open to panhandlers, parades, pop-up art projects, electioneering, block parties, demonstrations, murder, and blooming trees. We could become confused by all that, but centuries of development have yielded a form with a place for everything, and everything, more or less, in its place.

## Inner Weather

Just as Coventry Road delighted me, East 105th Street enlightened me, and the Nishiki Tenmangu Shrine centered me, all of our Main Street moments contribute to our inner weather, the thoughts and feelings that empower us to act in the world. When Mariano Rivera was to be installed in the Baseball Hall of Fame, the *New York Times* "Sports" section featured a photograph of Main Street in Cooperstown, New York, on a brilliantly sunny day. The three baseball fans in the photo were carrying their gloves, and sporting jerseys that riffed on the Abbott and Costello routine, "Who's on first?" They were walking down a street lined by brick buildings of modest size, past planters blooming with flowers and under a marquee that read ENTER SANDMAN 100% UNANIMOUS. For those fans, it must have been the dream of lifetime.[6]

The time Molly and I spent venturing around Cleveland was not like that. We had to contend with the weather and with the city's inequality. The warm places, filled with people, and dazzling arrays of the strange and wonderful, lifted us up. The Main Street which had been devastated by disinvestment—East 105th Street—was a completely different experience. It is hard to see a neighborhood that has suffered, that is suffering, without feeling some of the pain of the place. It is also hard for me, as a physician, and for Molly, as an urbanist, because we know that the people there are weathering faster than those who live in more privileged places. In that moment, in that city, we were helpless to change the situation. Such moments are so uncomfortable that those who can avoid them do, and those who cannot leave suffer the full range of emotions—from grief to rage—that accompany abandonment.

Over the past fifty years in the United States, despite our progress on civil rights and inclusion, a growing divide has separated the haves and the have-nots, compounded by processes of "sorting out" our cities by race and class, and then making invisible and inaccessible the places where the poor and deprived are sequestered.

My early training was as a family therapist, and I draw on my many experiences of dysfunctional families in thinking about these issues. In family therapy, we would call the disconnection of family members from one another a "cutoff." It is a trauma that resonates over generations and must be fixed. The concept of cutoff is useful to our thinking about cities—for example, the abandonment of the neighborhood around East 105th Street. The parallels, however, are inexact. Most of the families that I was called to treat expressed real, albeit frustrated, love that could temper their anger and pain.

In U.S. society, intergroup hatred has been allowed to fester, impairing empathy to the point that killing the "other" becomes conscionable. The Trail of Tears, the long history of lynching now made evident in the Equal Justice Initiative's museum, and the current spate of mass murders are all evidence of this sorry part of our history. These obvious murders are, of course, the tip of the iceberg. Harder to see are the myriad ways in which people are crippled and die prematurely because of these festering processes. And hardest to see are the ways in which these processes entrain the whole society. White people are not conveniently excused from early death because of their skin color.

The profound divisions of our society affect every aspect of our common life, including our ability to meld our individual thinking into a functional collective consciousness. Human beings have an extraordinary capacity for cooperation. It has enabled us to reach the moon and plumb the depths of the ocean. But our collective action and our collective thinking are only as strong as our ability to unite. In a deeply divided society, that is what we cannot do. When our division has become so toxic that we start to kill one another, we have destroyed the very strength that made our species king of the world.

Our collective "inner weather" reflects a terrible dilemma. We need to work together to solve problems, such as climate change, that are larger than any we've faced before, but we are divided so profoundly that we cannot collaborate. What are we to do?

I think we can learn from Main Streets.

I didn't leave Cleveland in despair. I didn't leave Kyoto weaker. Both places offered me new strengths. In Cleveland, I learned a deep spiritual principle. In Kyoto, I was offered succor, which helped me face my son's illness and eventual death. Our Main Streets are an amalgam of social, spiritual, and economic tools that provide what we need to get through the daunting future. In fact, Main Streets were invented for just such a moment. As in the adventure films where the solution lies in getting an old rusty machine to work again—

think Humphrey Bogart and Katharine Hepburn getting the boat to work in *The African Queen*—we can escape our current troubles by turning to the old machine for living that's right there, in the center of the neighborhood, or in the middle of the town.

In the following chapters, I want to explain how I think the Main Street machine works. People get strange ideas about how to fix Main Street, mostly having to do with stirring up commerce. I got into a fight with an investment banker who had heard about a Main Street in his wealthy neighborhood that had many shuttered stores. Somewhere in the conversation, he got the idea that food trucks would solve the problem. I tried to say, "No, that's not how you fix an amalgam."

He said, "Okay, but it will do for now."

Maybe.

But if you really want to get this old machine back on its feet, you'll do better if you take the time to learn how it works—what I call the what I call the "box-circle-line-tangle over time" model of Main Street.[7]

# 2  Synmorphy

*Walking by an old abandoned building*
*that once housed a penny candy store,*
*I envisioned all the wide-eyed children*
*As they gazed at the display of candy galore.*
　　　　　　　　—Joseph T. Renaldi, "A Penny Candy Store"


I'VE GONE TO MAIN STREETS all my life, starting back in the day when
my mother let me spend my weekly allowance at Bill's Candy Store,
a small sundries shop on Central Avenue in Orange, New Jersey. It
was next to Lee's Laundry, owned and operated by the family of one
of my classmates, and three doors over from the Harmony Bar, which
is still there. I've visited 178 Main Streets in fourteen countries, and
fabulous photos of them line the walls of my study. There is a very
real "on Main Street" thing: buying penny candy in Orange, having
breakfast at Sunday Coffee on Dogenzaka Street in Tokyo, strolling
the Boardwalk at Asbury Park, or following the names of the great
up the Canyon of Heroes in New York City.

The enumeration of magical moments is the first layer of
understanding Main Street, but it can be incomplete, leaving out the
shuttered stores, the floods, the homeless people, the weary citizens.
Main Street, as I've come to know and respect it, is a complicated
public space, where teens ogle the sneakers in store windows, libraries

hawk their wares, the destitute beg for change, and politicians run for election.

It's Roger Barker's theory of ecological psychology that gives us a start on organizing this complexity.

## Barker's Theory

Psychologist Roger Barker started off studying behaviors in the usual way, which is to say, one at a time. Soon he realized that behaviors occurred in a stream, one after another, adding up to thousands and thousands of behaviors each and every day. As he watched this stream, he noticed that behaviors followed the dictates of setting. People had ways they acted in school, around the playground, at the dinner table, and while watching TV. In some settings—on the playground or watching TV—shouting out was quite appropriate and part of the scene. In others—in school or at the dinner table—shouting was largely frowned upon.

| Behavior of the Same Children in Different Behavior Settings | | | |
|---|---|---|---|
| Setting | Second-Grade Academic Class | Playground | Second-Grade Music Class |
| Behavior Pattern | Organized activity; little change in position; slow tempo; serious mood; limited variety of behavior, with sitting, reading, writing, and reciting predominant. | Unorganized or partly organized; fast tempo, exuberant mood; large variety of behavior, with games predominant. | Organized activity; variation in tempo; medium cheerfulness; little variety of behavior, singing predominant. |

In one set of observations, Barker and his team watched as second graders moved from class to playground and back to class. As we can see in the table[1], the team noticed that in the academic class the children sat and read in a serious mood. On the playground, they moved as they liked, quickly and exuberantly. In music class, they sang and participated in organized activities.

From many observations such as these, Barker theorized that people's behaviors are tailored to fit the situation. The situation was defined by the place and the operating rules of that location. He called these "behavior settings," which were defined as "stable, extra-individual units with great coercive power over the behavior that occurs within them."[2] Behavior settings have a place, a time, a purpose, and rules of behavior.

Barker's team carried out extensive fieldwork in a small midwestern city. Some of the behavior settings they found were:

- Elementary School Third-Grade Academic Subjects
- Burgee Beauty Shop
- Elementary Lower School Lunchroom
- Chaco Garage and Service Station
- Blanchard Hardware Store
- High School: A Team Football Game
- Presbyterian Church Worship Service
- Keith Barber Shop
- Rotary Club Meeting
- Presbyterian Church Funeral
- Halloween Dance
- Methodist Church Kindergarten Sunday School Class.[3]

In each of these behavior settings the team found "standing patterns of behavior," defined as "a bounded pattern of behavior of persons, en masse." As most of us have seen a football game, it is a good one to consider. The standing pattern of behavior was composed of the behaviors of the two opposing teams, the referees, the cheerleaders, the coaches, and the spectators. Everyone coming to a football game would know the part they were supposed to play. The Presbyterian funeral, by contrast, would incorporate quite different standing patterns of behavior, but they, in turn, would be well known to attendees, who would do their part to carry out the appropriate actions.

In addition to the standing patterns of behavior, these settings also had a well-defined physical aspect, which Barker and his colleagues called "standing patterns of behavior-and-milieu." The football game, for example, would require a football field, a football, uniforms, including protective gear, and cleats. Football also requires a time and place a game will be held, and the specific teams playing.

The milieu, they noted, encompassed the behavior and fit with it. We play football on a football field, baseball on a baseball field, and basketball on a basketball court. The setting is designed to fit and support the action, a "synmorphy," which is part of the very power of the behavior setting.

Main Streets are a 24/7 behavioral setting. It was to understand how this particular setting worked that I set out on my study.

## The Method of Study

I used observational methods for this study. Starting in January 2008, I set out to visit Main Streets in 100 cities, with a loose plan to take a friend and have lunch. I posted semi-regularly in a blog, kept field notes, and took thousands of photographs. The method evolved over time. The first part of the study, which involved the first fifty cities, followed my initial proposition and resulted in the proposal of the box-circle-line model. The second part of the study, carried out with Jacob ("Jake") Izenberg in 2012, was a detailed examination of the box-circle-line in Essex County. That, and additional observations using my initial method, took the project to about 75 cities. The third part of the study, launched in 2012, on the heels of the work with Jake, involved learning from Hirofumi Minami, an environmental psychologist from Japan, about the "psychoanalysis of cities." His method involved what he called the "stroll and scroll," which meant walking the city, then reflecting on what we had seen through the lens of a wide array of materials. David Chapin, an architect and professor of environmental psychology at the CUNY Graduate Center, was the third member of our team, bringing his encyclopedic knowledge of buildings and urban form to our voyages.

To apply the psychoanalysis of cites to Main Streets, we decided to walk Broadway. It runs the length of Manhattan, which we learned is 13.4 miles long. It was an Indian trail and then, when the colonists arrived, became the Boston Post Road. We planned five walks: northern tip, southern tip, Times Square, Upper West Side, and Dyckman Farmhouse.

Hiro was only in New York City for a few months, so we had no choice but to start in winter if we were to get this done. On December 17, we made our first Broadway foray, taking the train up to 231st Street in the Bronx, so that we could walk down Broadway through Marble Hill, a bit of Manhattan that is north of Spuyten Duyvil.

On New Year's Day, 2013, we met at the National Museum of the American Indian, at the base of the Canyon of Heroes, where

Portrait of Hiro.
Photo by David Chapin, used with permission.

New York City holds its ticker-tape parades. This made a natural arc for our walk and we followed this route. It took us past the famous Wall Street Bull, past Zuccotti Park, site of the Occupy Wall Street encampment, past St. Paul's Chapel of Trinity Church, the oldest church in Manhattan, and, behind it, the new World Trade Center, rising, so to speak, from the ashes, until we reached City Hall.

We walked Times Square on January 17. Times Square was turbocharged by throngs of people who filled the sidewalks. There was a flight of stairs by the TKTS Booth, where one could buy half-price tickets for Broadway shows. People could climb the stairs and see themselves on a massive TV screen just across the street. This was really a car commercial and the people were all in the car, driving away at the end. For some reason, this little story made people wave wildly, with great delight.

# Broadway Scroll

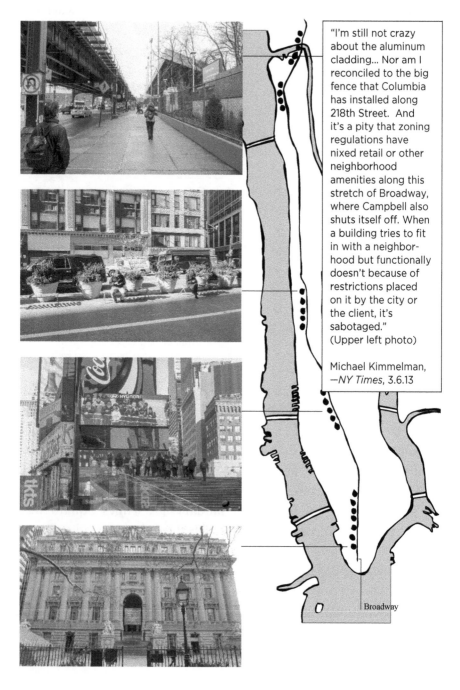

"I'm still not crazy about the aluminum cladding... Nor am I reconciled to the big fence that Columbia has installed along 218th Street. And it's a pity that zoning regulations have nixed retail or other neighborhood amenities along this stretch of Broadway, where Campbell also shuts itself off. When a building tries to fit in with a neighborhood but functionally doesn't because of restrictions placed on it by the city or the client, it's sabotaged."
(Upper left photo)

Michael Kimmelman,
—*NY Times*, 3.6.13

Broadway

The stroll-and-scroll is an iterative process. On the left of this scroll are photos from our walks on Broadway. Some of the many events and writings we associated with Broadway. A review of a building we saw (upper left), *Here is New York*, David's plan for our walks, segregation of creatures in Times Square, and Brave Girl facing the Bull on Wall Street.

Its name comes from the wall built here by the Dutch against the Native Americans.

Walking Broadway for our fourth foray, on March 2, 2013, took us to the Upper West Side. We decided to rendezvous at Zabar's, which declares on its website, "Zabar's is New York... New York is Zabar's!" We walked north, through the heart of the West Side neighborhood.

Our fifth walk, on March 5, 2013, took us to Dyckman Farmhouse at 207th Street, a Dutch colonial farmhouse built about 1784.[4] It sits on a small hill, just above Broadway, surrounded by stone retaining walls topped with an iron fence. Following our visit there, we walked over to Dyckman Street and had lunch at Chacapas y Mas.

This was a lot of information. How were we to digest it? We had a "scroll session" in March, after the five walks. Hiro arrived with a pile of books, and he explained how we might take ideas and reflections from many sources and link them to what we had seen. He started with the simplest and most dramatic: Miroslav Sasek's children's book, *This is New York*. Hiro opened the book to the page about Wall Street, which noted that a wall was built there "against the Indians." We reflected on the irony that the Museum of the American Indian is now behind the place where the wall used to be. We were able to bring newspaper articles, conversations, art, and other materials into the process of reflection and association. This was what created the "scroll."

While I understood the principle, I came to a deeper appreciation of "scroll" at a 2019 lecture on Japanese perspectives on landscape, given by Dr. Ryuzo Ohno.[5] He analyzed the way the Japanese design a garden, emphasizing that each point is meant to provide a new perspective in an unfolding landscape. He linked this to the art form of the scroll, which depicts a series of images that tell an unfolding story revealed with each turn of the rollers.

Oh, scroll! I thought, much surprised. When I shared my insight with Hiro, he happily sent David and me explanations and examples of scrolls. He connected us to a thirteenth-century scroll on the Kyushu University Library's website.[6] He explained that we should look at it from right to left. He was deciphering the hard-to-understand medieval writing, which told the story of a brave man who was pleading with the emperor to send troops to resist a Mongolian invasion. This has relevance for Main Streets, which, like Japanese gardens, are not taken in at a glance. One must walk the street, appreciating the contents as they unfold, but also adding to that one's own musings, drawn from many sources.

The stroll and scroll is necessarily iterative. As I visited more cities in the third part of the study, I added to the ideas I'd refined in the first two parts. I came to understand the "tangle" and I realized how important it was to think about changes over time. I came to have more associations to each aspect of a new Main Street.

Here are some of the behaviors I've observed on Main Street:

| | |
|---|---|
| Walking | Gossiping |
| Flirting | Asking directions |
| Telephoning | Texting |
| Kissing | Mailing a letter |
| Checking email | Sitting on a bench |
| Waiting for a bus | Handing out leaflets |
| Discussing business | Eating ice cream |
| Walking a dog | Doing homework |
| Pushing a stroller | Leading children |
| Running for a bus | Driving |
| Maintaining | Decorating |
| Carrying things | Parking |
| Painting | Photographing |
| Waiting in line | Making deliveries |
| Skating | Playing |
| Picketing | Cleaning |
| Planting | Fighting |
| Parading | Shoveling snow |
| Befriending | Advertising |
| Rendez-vous-ing | Reading signs |
| Sleeping | Campaigning |
| Panhandling | Having a parade |
| Sightseeing | Eating a meal |
| Repairing | Patrolling |
| Sleeping on the street | |
| Celebrating a victory | |
| Looking at store windows | |
| Lounging against a building | |
| Vending food or goods | |

## The Standing Patterns of Behavior on Main Street

In Barker's model, behaviors and the places in which they occur are closely related to one another. What we do on Main Street will be consistent with what we think Main Street is. There are many acts in the public consciousness that are appropriate for

# Table of Main Streets

**Austria**
Salzburg

**Canada**
Vancouver

**France**
Bordeaux
Borget
Boulogne-Billancourt
Collioliure
Enghien-les-Bains
Epinay-sur-Seine
Gennevilliers
Gonesse
Ivry-sur-Seine
Louvres
Marseille
Montauban
Nantes
Palaiseau
Paris
Pantin
Perpignan
Rion des Landes
Saugnac
Sellis
St. Sever
Vieux Pays de
 Goussainville
Versailles

**Germany**
Berlin

**England**
Cambridge
London

**Italy**
Bellagio

**Ireland**
Dublin
Howth

**Japan**
Hiroshima
Kyoto
Tokyo

**North Macedonia**
Ohrid

**Norway**
Oslo

**Romania**
Bucharest

**South Africa**
Capetown
Johannesburg

**Spain**
Barcelona

**Turkey**
Istanbul

**United States**
*Alabama*
Birmingham
*Arkansas*
Little Rock
*California*
Carpenteria
Los Olivos
Monterey
Oakland
Riverside
Santa Barbara
Santa Monica
Venice Beach
West Hollywood
*Colorado*
Denver
*Georgia*
Atlanta
*Illinois*
Champaign
Chicago
Urbana
*Indiana*
Indianapolis
*Louisiana*
New Orleans
*Massachusetts*
Amherst
Boston
Cambridge

Northhampton
Somerville
*Maryland*
Baltimore
Ellicott City
Havre de Grace
*Michigan*
Detroit
*Minnesota*
Minneapolis
St. Paul
Sauk Centre
*Missouri*
St. Louis
Kansas City
*North Carolina*
Asheville
Charlotte
Durham
Raleigh
*New Jersey*
Alpine
Asbury Park
Bayonne
Belleville
Bergenfield
Bloomfield
Bogota
Burlington
Caldwell
Camden
Cedar Grove
Cliffside
East Orange
Englewood
Essex Fells
Fairview
Fort Lee
Glen Ridge
Hackensack
Hillsdale
Hoboken
Irvington
Jersey City
Leonia
Maplewood
Milburn
Montclair

Newark
North Caldwell
Nutley
Orange
Paterson
Philipsburg
Princeton
Roseland
Secaucus
South Orange
Teaneck
Tenafly
Verona
Weehawken
West Caldwell
West Orange
*New Mexico*
Albuquerque
Santa Fe
*New York*
Albany
Avon
Binghamton
Buffalo
Dansville
Fort Ann
Geneseo
Hudson
Johnstown

Lewistown
Lima
Mount Morris
New York City
Niagara Falls
Nunda
Nyack
Pawling
Piermont
Rochester
Saratoga Springs
Syracuse
Warwick
Whitney Point
*Ohio*
Cleveland
Oberlin
*Oregon*
Portland
Seaside
Tillamook
*Pennsylvania*
Allentown
Bethlehem
Bellefonte
Easton
Erie
Philadelphia
Pittsburgh

*South Carolina*
Columbia
*Tennessee*
Memphis
Nashville
*Virginia*
Charlottesville
Roanoke
*Vermont*
Bennington
Brattleboro
Ludlow
Manchester
Middlebury
Newfane
North Bennington
Putney
Ripton
Rutland
South Londonderry
Williamsville
Woodstock
*Washington*
Seattle
*Wisconsin*
Milwaukee
*Washington, DC*

---

Main Streets. People dress for Main Street. People moderate their noise to fit in with the scene. People expect to be entertained. People hold themselves with dignity, befitting the milieu. People come prepared to do a Main Street thing, and then they leave. In the box, I've listed many of the activities that I've seen on Main Streets, from lounging to parading, from kissing to running for a bus. Examining the list helps us to understand the behavior setting, its standing patterns of behavior, and its standing patterns of behavior-and-milieu.

We can compare Main Street behaviors to mall behaviors. Malls, useful as they are for shopping, flirting, and eating ice cream, do not permit protests, panhandling, or lounging against a building.

# Chartres Scroll, 2016

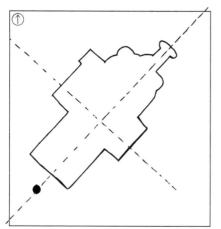

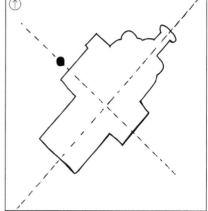

Cantal and I had entered the cathedral district from the west, and we knew that wasn't Main Street.

When we got to the great north door, Cantal pointed. The absence of stores and people demonstrated that that sleepy direction had not become Main Street.

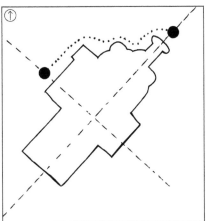

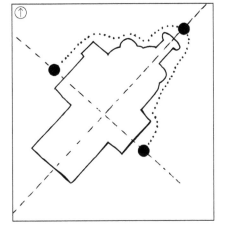

We continued, passing through the gardens at the eastern end, Jardins de L'Évêché, verdant, calm, and filled with people enjoying the sun, but not Main Street.

To the South, the pace quickened. Looking down the street from the Cathedral, we could see the vegetable market. At Porte des Changes we found the concentrated commerce, people, energy and signs of Main Street.

Malls are not public spaces, and people and activities that are not acceptable can be excluded. Main Streets are civic spaces, belonging to "we the people": We are reasonably free to express ourselves in the spaces we own. Conversely, when our Main Street behaviors are suppressed, we are shocked.

In Barker's theory, the milieu can be closely tailored to support the behaviors that will take place there. Form fits function. Given the broad array of uses of Main Street, what is the form that works?

## Milieu: The Setting of Main Street

I didn't come to the study of cities directly. I trained in psychiatry and, after completing my studies, worked in community mental health. In 1986, I had an opportunity to join an AIDS research project, with the specific assignment to investigate the high rates of AIDS among African Americans and Hispanics in the United States. This work led to an understanding that poor management of cities had caused this horrific problem. I wanted to know more about cities. I was lucky to make the acquaintance of a renowned French urbanist, Michel Cantal-Dupart, and he agreed to be my teacher. My studies took place in France, where I regularly traveled for my lessons.

During my visit in 2016, Cantal and I traveled to Chartres, where he was working on a project to install a museum under the square in front of the great cathedral's main doors. During a quiet break in the afternoon, he said, "I'd like to contribute to your study of Main Streets."

He pulled out some sheets of paper and began to describe the Roman system of city planning, which was organized based on two roads, the north-south cardo, and the east-west decumanus, which cross each other in the center of town. Although all Roman towns start with these two roads, one or another portion, he averred, would evolve into a "Main Street." In Chartres, the cathedral was at the intersection of the cardo and decumanus. In the Middle Ages, the cathedral housed various commercial activities, any one of which might have been the seed for Main Street.

Textiles were sold around the north transept, while meat, vegetable and fuel sellers congregated around the south porch. Money-changers (an essential service at a time when each town or region had its own currency) had their benches, or banques, near the west portals and also in the nave itself. Wine sellers plied their trade in the nave, although occasional 13th-century ordinances survive which record their being temporarily banished to the crypt to minimize disturbances.[7]

"So where is Main Street?" Cantal asked after we considered the possibilities. "Let's go see."

Cantal and I emerged into the bright sun of a March day. We had entered the cathedral district from the west, and we knew that wasn't Main Street. We walked up the very quiet street that ran along the cathedral's north wall. When we got to the great north door, Cantal pointed. The absence of stores and people demonstrated that that sleepy direction had not become Main Street. We continued, passing through the gardens at the eastern end, Jardins de l'Évêché, verdant, calm, and filled with people enjoying the sun, but not Main Street. To the south, the pace quickened, and at Porte des Changes we found the concentrated commerce, people, energy, and signs of Main Street.

Chartres's covered fruit and vegetable market was located there, south of the cathedral, as had been the meat, vegetable, and fuel sellers of old. An array of modern commerce had flourished all around that area. Such markets, historians explain, were the nidus for the evolution of the city. In its historic form, the market was held in the open air, with merchants bringing their goods to display. One author noted:

> As most people lived in the country, grew their own food, and made their own clothes, they needed places close enough to herd the animals and carry their wares to the market and then return home in the same day. Crossroads and river bridges were popular locations, especially if a church was nearby. Crafts people found it advantageous to build their workshops close to the market places. This helped villages and towns to form and grow.[8]

As markets grew, they differentiated, with separate markets for vegetables, meat, clothes, and tools. As cities grew, markets evolved, gradually becoming first covered and then stores. As stores differentiated, Main Streets emerged.

As Main Streets emerged, they found a form that worked. Main Street came to signify that blossoming of civic life, that section of road where you could exchange your book, cash a check, buy shoes and candy—or a bedroom suite, if you needed one. And as it came to be "a thing," architects elaborated styles so that it hugged the street with panache. David Chapin, riffing on the metaphor of blossoming, taught me, "Just as blossoms were a strategy to replace gymnosperms, so, too, is this evolution about conflict and jostling and contention."

Men controlled Main Streets by having command of the money to build, but women's adoption of them made it possible for the streets to survive. Ladies' Mile in Manhattan emerged as a major shopping center encompassing 5th and 6th avenues, between 50th and 24th streets. It was a stage in the liberation of women, as it was safe and women could shop without male companions.[9]

Children liked Main Street, too. They could bring their allowance to spend on candy or plan a major purchase, like a bottle of perfume for mom on Mother's Day. They could go to the movies, and in my day, everyone did, spending long afternoons as the pictures played over and over, watching the films to one's heart's content.

Main Street is, thus, a complex space that embodies cultural norms developed over millennia. The physical aspects of this space—the milieu, to use Barker's term—can be understood in the following four dimensions: box, circle, line, and tangle, all of which evolve and change over time.

## The Box

I started my Main Street New Jersey study in Englewood. Its six-block commercial center has the drama of arriving by a small descent into a tree-lined and leisurely business and civic section that ends at a statue, known locally as "the Monument." This Main Street is long enough to feel big, and short enough to be a pleasant stroll from one end to the other. It has the advantage of a modest downtown area surrounding the street, with nooks and crannies that people have packed with an ever-changing array of stores, restaurants, and services. Having lived in Englewood awhile, I was likely to run into someone I knew, and this was especially true in Starbucks.

The distinct beginning and end, and the well-defined street "walls" made by the buildings on either side, gave it the feel of a box. I think this feature of Main Streets is the heart of what Americans call to mind when we think of Main Street. These boxes come in all sizes and shapes and all kinds of conditions.

The "box" of Main Street is formed by buildings, street, and sky. The buildings on either side create the "walls," while the sidewalks and street create the "bottom" and the sky creates the "top." The feeling of the box—the sense of enclosure—is fundamental to what a Main Street is. That is what puts the "there" there. Some Main Streets, like the Canyon of Heroes along lower Broadway in Manhattan, are famous for the enclosure that has been created.

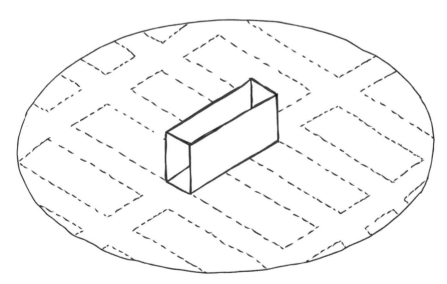

Box, Circle, Line. This diagram depicts the "box" of Main Street with its enclosing walls, the "circle" of the embedding neighborhood, and the "line" of the street passing through.

Inside the box, we expect to find an amalgam of useful places like the post office, candy store, shoe store, grocery market, movie theater, and bank. In my early field notes, I called this a "good collection of main things," and I think that about sums it up.

### The Circle

Englewood, I came to appreciate, also benefited from reasonably strong connections with the surrounding residential areas. There were lots of people living within a half-mile radius, and there were no awkwardly large streets to impede their strolling over for some milk or a lottery ticket.

Englewood's neighbor Tenafly, by contrast, had a charming Main Street disconnected from its surroundings. The Main Street was a short two blocks, anchored by an old train station turned coffee shop. That section was supported by the commercial activity arrayed along the perpendicular Washington Street, which ended at the post office. The little downtown had charm and really useful stuff: a bookstore, bakery, pharmacy, diner, movie theater, coffee shop, kitchenware store, and more.

But it was not inviting to walk any distance from that area. To the north, for example, crossing Riveredge Road, the town had scooped out buildings to create parking lots, obviously one of those ill-considered efforts to compete with the malls. This meant that after the confined shopping area, one encountered parking lots in all directions, as well as wide streets given over to cars, speeding as they do when there is no competition from bicycles or pedestrians. As in other well-to-do areas of the United States, the cars had morphed into large SUVs, most bearing prestigious labels like Mercedes or Lexus. There are few things more frightening than a late-model luxury truck bearing down on you as you are trying to cross the street, although high-speed delivery bikes on the sidewalks of New York are giving Mercedes and Lexus a run for their money in the fear department.

Tenafly taught me to look at the integrity and interconnectedness of the area around the Main Street. I came to think of this as the "circle." The ways in which Main Streets are embedded in the city are important to their functioning. A Main Street with very strong interpenetration between it and the surrounding neighborhood is much more likely to flourish.

Washington Street | West Railroad Avenue

The Circle in Tenafly. This diagram depicts the many parking lots, shown in black, that had been inserted into the Main Street circle in Tenafly.

## The Line

Because I frequently drove on Palisades Avenue to get to work in New York City, I gradually realized that Main Streets were streets entering and leaving the commercial center. There is a sharp contrast between the areas that are and those that aren't the commercial center. When Englewoodians say, "I'm going down Palisades Ave," they don't mean a random location on the street; they mean they're going downtown, the part of the street where the action is. But this preeminence of the shopping area is only one part of the story of Palisades Avenue. Going east, Palisades Avenue goes all the way to the Palisades, the magnificent cliffs along the Hudson River. The road continues down to a beautiful park along the river, where there is a boat basin, a picnic area, and a Snack Shack, a small Main Street in its own right. Going west, Palisades Avenue runs through a residential area of Englewood and ends at Tryon Avenue.

That "Main Street" is a section of a street is an important part of its charm and function. Lots of roads run for long distances and are dotted with commercial areas. These prosper from many people going to and fro. Bus lines, subways, easy walking from home to shops enticingly set on a busy road—these are the factors that make a Main Street successful.

Descent into Englewood. This photo of Palisades Avenue entering the center of Englewood is an example of the line of Main Street.

*Tangle*

In the course of Jake's work examining the Main Streets of Essex County, New Jersey, he created a series of maps of the county that showed the welter of roads and a rather precise geography of high-functioning Main Streets. It was the lines of the roads—the underlying thicket of streets—that stayed with me as an unnamed entity and always came to mind while driving around southern Vermont. Eventually we named this "the tangle."

Tangle in Essex County. Jacob Izenberg made this version of the tangle to show the dense networks of streets and highways in Essex County and the surrounding area. Map data from Mapbox and OpenStreetMap and their data sources. http://www. openstreetmap.org/copyright.

## Time

As I have mentioned, at the outset of this work, I thought I would look at Main Streets for a year or eighteen months, and then be done with it. This didn't happen. I had only begun to guess at what was going on in that period of time; I kept looking. As time went on, I began to notice changes: Stores turned over, cities underwent urban renewal, gentrification set in, storms blew through. Just as in the story of Main Street in Salt Lake City I recount below, things changed with time. Eventually I realized that time was a crucial fifth dimension of what I was seeing. The full model is, therefore, box-circle-line-tangle over time.

This model—box-circle-line-tangle over time—helps us understand how Main Street fulfills crucial functions. It lays the groundwork for imagining how this "neural" system can become our Factory of Invention. And it suggests the ways in which an inclusive system of Main Streets, by offering us the democratic spaces we so desperately need, will correct the tribal tendencies of social media and reinforce our path toward problem solving. I have capitalized "Main Street" throughout the book to indicate that I am referring, not to a street bearing the name "Main," but rather to this complex system.

Time. The layers of signs on this building tell us much about the passage of time.

## Standing Pattern of Behavior-and-Milieu

Having described behavior and milieu, I want to illustrate how the standing pattern of behavior fits in the milieu by examining a strange case, that of Main Street in Salt Lake City, Utah. I got interested in this story in 2009, when I read about a protest because two men got arrested for kissing on the easement.[10] I called the Reverend Tom Goldsmith of the First Unitarian Church. He told me the story actually started much earlier, when the easement was first put in place.

In 1999, the city sold a block of Main Street to the Church of Jesus Christ of Latter-day Saints, a powerful entity in the city and in the state of Utah, which had major buildings on either side of the street. To ease movement between their buildings, they replaced the street with a private park, governed by the Mormon Church. The *New York Times* reporter Michael Janofsky opened a 2001 article by saying, "Until recently, Main Street here was all its name implied, an uninterrupted public thoroughfare passing through the heart of downtown."

The collective thoroughfare had been interrupted, and a new way of organizing behavior was inserted. The Mormon Church created a plaza, with colorful gardens and waterfalls. In addition to changing the space, they changed the rules for the space, insisting that people dress and behave as determined by the Mormon Church while in that space. For example, women wearing halter tops would be told their appearance was inappropriate. Smoking was prohibited. So were political demonstrations and the distribution of literature by other groups. A man and woman could hold hands while strolling through the gardens, but two men could not. "In essence," the Reverend Goldsmith was quoted by Janofsky as saying, "the plaza has become a bully pulpit for the Mormon Church, a space given to one religion and moral viewpoint to the exclusion of all others."[11]

The LDS spokesperson had a different take. "We want the plaza to be an inviting place of beauty and serenity that everyone can enjoy," the *Times* article quoted Dale Bills as saying. "Regarding behavior on the plaza, we will be courteous, patient, and respectful of others, and we hope they will be respectful of us."

The Reverend Goldsmith recalled that the city's sale of the block had been a shock to him and others and had met with immediate opposition. In fact, when he read about it in the paper, he knew that his congregation and others would be very concerned. He invited key leaders to speak at the church that Sunday. It was clear to them that the sale meant that the space had been privatized. The public's behaviors were censored; those of the Church remained free.

The official easement given to the LDS Church by the city noted:

> 2.2. Right to Prevent Uses Other Than Pedestrian Passage. Nothing in the reservation or use of this easement shall be deemed to create or constitute a public forum, limited or otherwise, on the Property. Nothing in this easement is intended to permit any of the following enumerated or similar activities on the Property: loitering, assembling, partying, demonstrating, picketing, distributing literature, soliciting, begging, littering, consuming alcoholic beverages or using tobacco products, sunbathing, carrying firearms (except for police personnel), erecting signs or displays, using loudspeakers or other devices to project music, sound or spoken messages, engaging in any illegal, offensive, indecent, obscene, vulgar, lewd or disorderly speech, dress or conduct, or otherwise disturbing the peace. Grantee shall have the right to deny access to the Property to persons who are disorderly or intoxicated or engaging in any of the activities identified above. The provisions of this section are intended to apply only to Grantor and other users of the easement and are not intended to limit or restrict Grantee's use of the Property as owner thereof, including, without limitation, the distribution of literature, the erection of signs and displays by Grantee, and the projection of music and spoken messages by Grantee.[12]

This was a collision waiting to happen. A young man was arrested for wearing a T-shirt deemed over the line. The shirt proposed "3.2% tithing and 10% beer," which was a joke about the 3.2 percent alcohol limit on beer and the Mormon tradition of tithing

10 percent of income to the Church. The American Civil Liberties Union was ready to bring suit. The First Unitarian Church agreed to be the plaintiff. "I asked everyone to vote on this, because this was a major confrontation for us to take on. The vote was unanimous," the Reverend Goldsmith told me.

The suit was difficult. First Unitarian was lambasted for attacking the Mormon Church. The Reverend Goldsmith explained over and over that it was not a case of one church attacking another, but, rather, of the protection of First Amendment rights, which belonged on Main Street. "I got over a hundred nasty emails and phone calls," he said.

The case wound slowly through the courts, and was won on appeal. A public easement was granted that allowed free speech as Main Street passed through the plaza. No sooner was that settled than the mayor agreed to swap the new easement for land to build a much-needed community center in one of the poor areas of the city. A second suit was brought, but later it was dropped. Generally, people were willing to trade free speech on Main Street for civic support of the poor.

But the contradiction between our expectations of Main Street and the reality of privatization did not go away. In 2009, Matthew Aune and Derek Jones were strolling through Main Street Plaza.[13] Aune gave Jones a kiss on the cheek, and they were immediately stopped by security guards, thrown to the ground, handcuffed, and arrested. While

Prohibited behaviors:

loitering,
assembling,
partying,
demonstrating,
picketing,
distributing literature,
soliciting,
begging,
littering,
consuming alcoholic beverages,
using tobacco products,
sunbathing,
carrying firearms (except for police personnel),
erecting signs or displays,
using loudspeakers or other devices to project music, sound or spoken messages,
engaging in any illegal, offensive, indecent, obscene, vulgar, lewd or disorderly speech, dress or conduct,
or otherwise disturbing the peace.

Main Street is a fine place to show a little affection, Aune's kiss was over the line when it came to the behaviors allowed in the plaza. Protests followed, and the LGBTQ community of Salt Lake City supported Aune and Jones by holding a "kiss-in."

This is where the story takes a turn for the better. Perhaps because the security guards were so discourteous on Main Street, the protests opened the door to private talks between leaders of the LDS Church and the LBGTQ community. The talks gradually led to increased understanding and paved the way for a historic breakthrough and protections for gay rights in Salt Lake City.

This is the "synmorphy" that Barker and his colleagues studied so extensively. Within the spaces of Main Street—the shops and civic buildings, the thoroughfare, the sidewalks—are embedded a wide array of behaviors that are "Main Street" in their character. This is a case where the sum is greater than the parts. A fully assembled Main Street, viewed in all the dimensions we have described, acts—to use my medical metaphor—as a ganglion transmitting information in many directions. Each Main Street is an essential component of a national communication network, foundational to our collective thinking and collective action.

# Part Two

## Box - Circle - Line - Tangle
## Over Time

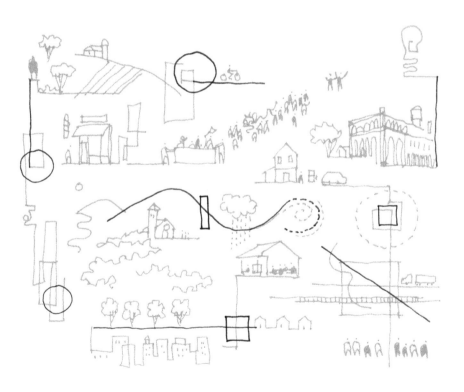

# 3  Box

                              —Joyce Kilmer, "Main Street"


WHILE I COULD DESCRIBE many streets that entice me to stroll, rue
de Bretagne, my favorite street in Paris, stands out. After my return
from the 2016 trip to Chartres with Cantal, I had a few hours free. I
set out from my hotel and headed over to rue de Bretagne. The first
block of that street had little commerce, but at the intersection with
rue Debelleyme there was an understated restaurant and bakery that
offered organic bread. I passed it a few times before I recognized the
communal table of Pain Quotidien, a favorite Main Street place. It
heralded the beginning of a Main Street filled with cafés, sidewalk
vendors, and shops of many kinds. Throngs of people were out
to enjoy the spring weather; the crowds were densest around the
entrance to a market, the Marché des Enfants Rouges.

The market is in the interior of the block. One gets there by

# Rue de Bretagne Scroll, 2016

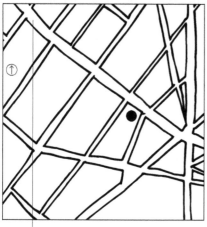

Rue De Bretagne

Rue De Bretagne

I passed an understated restaurant and bakery that offered organic bread a few times before I recognized the communal table of Pain Quotidien, a favorite Main Street place. It heralded the beginning of a Main Street filled with cafés, sidewalk vendors, and shops of many kinds.

Throngs of people were out to enjoy the spring weather; the crowds were densest around the entrance to a market, the Marché des Enfants Rouges.

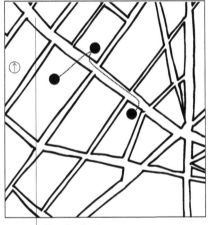

Rue De Bretagne

Rue De Bretagne

The market is in the interior of the block. One gets there by passing under an archway and down an alley lined with small shops. The market sparkles with the bright colors of food and flowers. I looked up to see the covering, and it took my breath away to see the style of glass used to cover the Nishiki Market in Kyoto.

While buying another bag, I saw deNeuville Chocolates, full of eggs and bunnies for Easter. It was packed with shoppers, admiring the display. We smiled at each other as we waited to be served. I left, singing to myself, "Oh my friends and family, here I come with spring cheer!"

passing under an archway and down an alley lined with small shops. The market sparkles with the bright colors of food and flowers. I looked up to see the covering, and it took my breath away to see the style of glass used to cover the Nishiki Market in Kyoto. The layout was different, but the beauty of the merchandise, the tight energy of the place, and the diffuse light were the same. I strolled around, having a moment of Paris envy as I realized that shopping in this spot was a daily activity for some people. It turns out that the Marché des Enfants Rouges is the oldest covered market in Paris, built in the 1600s,[1] about the same time as the Nishiki Market. As Westerners were in contact with Japan from 1543 to 1614, it is possible that they traded tips on market architecture, or maybe they did that later, achieving this remarkable similarity.

Leaving the market through the passageway to the street, I stopped at a store that sold old postcards. I spent way too much money—and I already had so many books, boxes of tea, and presents for those at home that I needed an extra bag. While buying that bag from a street vendor, I saw Chocolats deNeuville, full of chocolate eggs and bunnies for Easter. It was packed with shoppers admiring the display. We smiled at one another as we waited to be served. I left, singing to myself, "Oh my friends and family, here I come with spring cheer!"

At its peak, the box of Main Street feels like that. It is the realization of the Petula Clark song that advises lonely people to go downtown, where all the lights are bright. People can feel alone in a crowd, and everyone has at one time or another. But the point of the crowd—and why the great American urbanist Jane Jacobs insisted people like to go where other people are—is that it has the ability to disrupt our mood. So much is happening that we wouldn't want to miss, the odds are that something will shake us out of sorrow or lethargy. Seeing the Easter bunnies on rue de Bretagne was such a moment: I was enjoying myself, but the opportunity to get Easter chocolate for my grandchildren elevated my spirits to singing.

To follow Roger Barker's point about synmorphy, we need to explore the features in the built environment that create our sense

The photo on the left shows the "box" on a high hospitality Main Street, in the historic district near the waterfront. The street walls are close and the trees add to the friendliness. The stores have many openings for people to go in and out, keeping "eyes on the street," as Jane Jacobs recommended. The photo on the right shows a box that is broken, and has lost its power to convey enclosure.

of the box. St. Louis was one of the first cities I visited in the Main Street project. Two of its streets demonstrate the contrast between a box with a strong enclosure and one without. In the city's historic area, just off the Mississippi River, I found a charming street with brick buildings on either side of a tree-lined street.

Slightly away from downtown, I found many streets that lacked trees and seemed too wide. The continuity of the street wall had been undermined by the loss of buildings. These features created a sharp contrast in the feeling of "box."

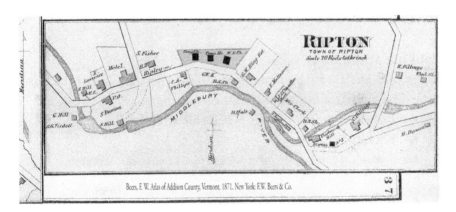

This map shows the village of Ripton, taken from Beers Atlas of Addison County, Vermont, published in 1871.
*Courtesy of Charles Billings.*

The architecture of box—cleverly revealed in this 1871 map of Ripton, Vermont—is created by three elements. First, there is a concentrated grouping of buildings; second, buildings face one another; and, third, this happens on the two sides of a public thoroughfare. These elements give Main Street the box structure that we recognize, even when it has lost some of its parts. Ripton today lacks many of the buildings on this old map, but we can tell that we are on "Main Street" as we pull up to the Country Store.[2]

The box can evolve with an interior architecture, a well-known fact that my granddaughter Lily Johnson investigated for her 2009 science fair project, "The Other Side: Eastside, Westside, Are the Prices the Same?" Lily, with the help of her classmates, went to every store on Palisades Avenue in Englewood, asking what were their highest- and lowest-priced items. She used the railroad tracks that run through the town as the dividing line. On the east side of the tracks, nearer to the wealthy neighborhoods, the prices went as high as $220,000 for a watch at Time Collection. On the west side of the tracks, the highest price was $300, at the Helen Hirsch lingerie store. I note that even that was inflated, due to the incursion of the "Towne Centre, " which had wiped out modest businesses like Jack's Hardware Store. Lily concluded, "This project gives people a little more insight into the city of Englewood and shows us an aspect of it that not many people notice."[3]

## Looking at the Box

When Jake and I were hammering out our understanding of the box-circle-line model, we listed these aspects of the box:

- Coherent, human-scale, permeable street wall
- Enclosure
- Seating, pedestrian safety features, pedestrian signage
- Road width
- Building scale
- Business mix

These features were easily assessed on the Main Streets of Essex County, New Jersey. In Newark's Ironbound District, Ferry Street was an example par excellence of the enclosure formed by the road, sidewalk, and walls of the buildings. Cars were restricted to one lane in either direction, with parking on both sides. Because of its popularity, the street was congested and cars moved very slowly, paying attention to the multitude of pedestrians. A variety of buildings hugged the sidewalk. Most had storefronts at ground level, with large windows, welcoming passersby. This made the street wall highly permeable, both visually and physically.

Orange, New Jersey, another one of the busiest Main Streets in the state, had a similarly strong box, with a clear enclosure, an attractive and permeable street wall, excellent signage, and attention to pedestrians, who had the protection of wide sidewalks. Buildings of various sizes stood shoulder to shoulder and contributed to the street wall. Most, as on Ferry Street, had active storefronts with large windows, creating permeability.

By contrast to these Main Streets, there were others whose box was not coherent or strong, undermining the capacity of the Main Street to do its job of creating hospitality. East Orange's once-strong Main Street had been undermined by disinvestment, followed by inconsiderate, car-oriented redevelopment. For example, a drive-through Wendy's broke the enclosure, disrupted pedestrian flow, and reoriented signage away from pedestrians to cars.

Livingston, New Jersey, built a mall that was important in its era, and did not build a real Main Street. The set of shops at the intersection of Livingston Avenue and Northfield Road is about as close as the town gets to "Main Street." But there was no sense of enclosure, no awareness of pedestrians, and no one walking about.

The box matters because its concentration of buildings offers a set of opportunities that serves the purpose of efficiency: I can get many errands done in a small space. Efficiency is complimented by sociability: I can get things done *and* see friends, acquaintances, and passersby.

What I call "the collection of main things" varies widely. It can include City Hall, the post office, the library, a monument, a movie theater, a toy store, a grocery store, a sundries store, a bookstore, a restaurant, a house of worship, an ice-cream store, and a coffee shop. Variations on these are infinite, which allows Main Streets to become very long, with many varieties of food, things to buy, and civic services. A Main Street with a strong collection of main things is a great joy.

The point of all of these attributes of the box is that they create the feeling that we are inside something that is safe, interesting, and rewarding. I'm not sure that the womb was interesting—maybe it was at the time—but I do imagine that we are all born with a memory of being enclosed. Within that enclosure, we can stroll around, look, and consider.

We can also get a message. Carl Jung, among others, taught us that art is full of archetypal symbols, images that we use to understand the world. What, I wanted to know, are all the signs on Main Street *saying*?

## What About Jane?

I call her Jane, because she reminds me of the Jane in the Dick and Jane readers we had back in grammar school. She arrived on Main Street in Orange in 2015, a character in a mural on the wall of the old YWCA, where I swam throughout high school. Jane is depicted running along in a bucolic scene, looking to the side, at us. I find it a leering glance, a side eye some would call it, which is why I think of her as "Evil Jane." The mural also has a very large squirrel eating an equally large tomato, letting us know all is not as it seems. I encountered her in my usual walks around Orange, but I had to stop to take in this thing that had arrived on the scene.

I was really stunned by it—hated it, to be blunt.

I started to show the photo of the mural to people. Braddock artist LaToya Ruby Frazier looked at the photo and then looked me. Her look suggested I was slightly out of my mind. "That's not a black woman," she said flatly. "It's a white woman painted brown.

And that's not art. It's just a comic. There are no black people in that mural—just white people painted brown. They should have gotten Emma Amos: that's art, that's black people."[4] I showed it to architect Liz Ogbu, whose work is focused on creating equity in cities. She looked at the photo in shock. "I can't believe they did that," she said, the hurt evident in her voice.

I showed it to my cousin Geanine Thompson. She looked at the ponytail streaming behind the jogging woman and said, "Hair doesn't do that."

I asked random people who lived in or around Orange; it turned out most of them had not even noticed the mural.

I begged Molly's class in youth urbanism at the New School to look at Evil Jane during a visit to Orange. And while they were at it, I hoped they'd also look at the Revolutionary War statue, the Dispatch Rider, just across the way, nicknamed "Paul" by me. Molly and fellow teacher Robert Sember were very supportive of this exercise. Together, the class and the professors sought the meaning, exploring the site of each and the many symbols that were involved. Molly was particularly pleased to take her class to Orange, as she was leading the University of Orange, a free people's university located there. The UofO considered the whole city its campus; Main Street was part of Molly's domain. At UofO we like to say that everything you want to learn about the American city, you can learn in the 2.2 square miles of Orange, New Jersey. Molly is a master of such a tour, and started by showing the students the Stickler Memorial Library, designed by Stanford White and built in honor of a doctor who died too soon.

After that, they walked over to Main Street and Robert and Molly, aided by their students, plunged into the exploration of the meanings of Paul and Jane and the conversation they were having on Main Street. Paul, the Dispatch Rider, Robert pointed out, stood above one of the major intersections in town, making an announcement about the kind of place Orange was. The statue denoted a seriousness of purpose and a commitment to high ideals, albeit embodied in a Disney prince. Jane, at street level, required a great deal of dissection to get all the parts: the buildings floating in the air, the *déjeuner sur l'herbe*, the giant squirrel eating a tomato.

One of the students made the prescient observation, "It's like a cartoon of the renderings they make to advertise new condos in the city."

Robert commented, "We have this experience where you can go from city to city now and walk down the Main Street and they're identical. They've unpacked this plan in some central place that says you're going to have Applebee's, and you're going to have Starbucks, and you're going to have McDonald's, and so basically Main Streets are produced so that you're in the same place no matter where you are. This is opposed to the idea that Main Street tells you the story of a unique place, and that it grows out of the story of that place, and brings together everything that's happening around it. The aesthetics of this mural—where nothing is anchored, just seems to float— underscores that it doesn't feel like the story comes from a place or is the story of a place. It's one of these operations of a kind of Main Street where every Main Street is going to have a picture that actually is kind of meaningless, just decoration."

Another student reflected, "It reminds me of the kind of random art I see in cities in Trinidad. I know they did it to try to beautify, make it more, like, welcoming, but it just seems so, like, out of place."

Robert then said, "I'm now imagining—imagine if this mural were going to be replaced and the beginning was, 'Can we create something that truly is in conversation with the Dispatch Rider?' What might that look like? What might a conversation be between that condition of history—the Revolutionary War, the young white guy, the heroic figure, all of that sort of stuff—and then something that says, 'This is our city today, and our city arises out of a history, and that history includes ups and downs, contestations, new ideas, old ideas'?"

Molly added, "If you think about that question, and then you think about the near neighbors, you have Rossi Paint Store, which has been in the same family for three generations. You have the Rosa

Parks School, which is predominantly kids who are first-generation immigrants—it has the biggest Haitian population—and all the classes are in different languages, and Aubrey and I love every kid there; it's such an interesting, fun school. You have the Y. You have the post office across the street, and who knows what's going to happen to the post office. There's this massive construction project that's at the Orange train station. Mindy's church is right around the corner. So how would you create a conversation that acknowledges everything? How dynamic is it that all of those different institutions and people are all right around us?"

This was followed by a profound silence, during which we all considered the implications of what Robert and Molly had proposed: What if Main Street reflected its own story? What if Main Street had its own icons?

Instead, Jane and Paul are rooted in highly racialized art. When I was twelve, I got interested in sculpture. My mother got me a how-to-sculpt book by Malvina Hoffman, famous for creating the "Races of Mankind" collection at the Field Museum.[5] In the book, she described the work of creating an object that resembled a person. She went from the armature to layers of clay, carefully built to resemble muscle and skin, and then molded it to give the features of the person. It was very complicated. I couldn't imagine learning how to do all that.

The sculptures she made for the Field Museum exhibit were organized to show the progression of races from savage to barbaric to civilized, a concept I was taught in world history in high school. Not surprisingly, it was the Europeans who were civilized, and therefore at the top of the heap. It was an exhibit that demonstrated the "truth" of scientific racism. I don't remember if the book told the whole story of scientific racism, but I do remember that it made me uncomfortable. I didn't like the idea of depicting the races of man. I gave the book away decades ago, but the distaste for that work has lingered.

# Class visit to Orange

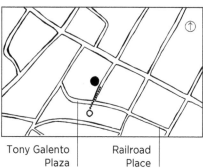

Tony Galento
Plaza

Railroad
Place

Molly was particularly pleased to take her class to Orange, as she was director of the University of Orange, a free people's university located there. The UofO considered the whole city its campus; Main Street was part of Molly's domain. We like to say that "everything you want to know about the American city, you can learn in Orange, New Jersey." Molly started the tour of Orange at the library, a beautiful building designed by Stanford White and built as a memorial to a young doctor.

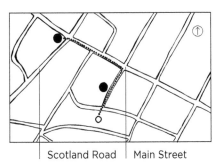

Scotland Road | Main Street

Main Street

The Dispatch Rider, Robert pointed out, stood above one of the major intersections in town, making an announcement about the kind of place Orange was. The statue denoted a seriousness of purpose and a commitment to high ideals, albeit embodied in a Disney prince.

One of the students made the prescient observation, "It's like a cartoon of the renderings they make to advertise new condos in the city."

More than fifty years after I'd read her book, I was intrigued to learn that Hoffman's sculptures were on display at the museum that had originally commissioned the exhibit. While in the 1930s the exhibit was explaining the differences among the races, the 2015 exhibit, "Looking at Ourselves: Rethinking the Sculptures of Malvina Hoffman," was designed to show that science had discredited those ideas.[6] The sculptures were being brought back in order to look at the ways racism had caused problems in society. And they were being brought back because they are actually compelling depictions of people. The sculptures, viewed in terms of the resonance of the evil intent that triggered their creation, come to life in a new way. Although the idea was to model a "racial type," Hoffman was, in the end, committed to sculpting the individual. Her great skill did bring the people alive, not as subjects of a strange classification system, but as themselves.

Power is inherent in this shift. People of all ethnicities have asserted their humanity, and this has pushed back against the belief in racism. That racism is still highly active in determining people's fate is not to be denied, and indeed the exhibit acknowledged that fact. But there was another power involved, and that was the power of money. It was one of the granddaughters of Field—the department store magnate who founded the museum—who funded the exhibit, wanting the sculptures to be displayed together again. She had the power to re-collect the statues which had been disassembled and scattered since 1969, and thereby recollect their story.

This brings me to Paul and Jane, denizens of Main Street in Orange, New Jersey, at the same time Hoffman's work was on display. Jane was not in Hoffman's schema, which makes sense, because, as my friends and family insisted, nobody looks like that. But Paul is there, the heroic Nordic type—which she claimed was the highest expression of civilization. That Nordic type was the model for the Revolutionary War hero—tall, majestic, with a flowing cape, he towers over the street from a corner of the city's colonial-era graveyard. I don't know about Revolutionary-era dispatch riders, but

I once read a great book about the Pony Express, whose riders were youths who raced across the country delivering the mail in the brief era between the opening of the American West and the installation of the telegraph. Those youths were small, wiry daredevils, prepared to outrun annoyed Native Americans and get the mail to its destination. I have the sense that the real dispatch rider looked more like those skinny, brazen kids.

## 719 Statues to Interpret

At the height of my "I hate Jane" period—March 2016—was my visit to Chartres with Cantal. When I first arrived at his office, he grinned with pride and demonstrated the long section of his bookcase filled with books about cathedrals. I started reading my way through them, starting with a massive illustrated volume. After I'd finished that book and a lovely history of the building of the cathedral, I asked for his advice on what to read next. "This is not bad," he said, pulling an old paperback off the shelf. "It's written by a priest."

It turns out "this" was a historic volume written in 1858 as a guidebook to the cathedral.[7] Monsieur l'abbé Bulteau spent years studying every statue—daring the heights and touching each one so that he would really understand it. His task, in the book, was to help people interpret the art that decorated the cathedral. His approach was to take the viewer around the cathedral, examining each of the statues in turn—there are 719 on one porch alone. His slow deliberation of each statue got me thinking about this whole undertaking. The cathedral was built nearly one thousand years ago—that is, before electricity or bulldozers or steam shovels, or any of the power tools we take for granted in erecting the great edifices of our times. It was built with money collected from the faithful, some of them rich, many of them poor. And it was constructed during an era of cathedral building that swept France in a concentrated period of time. The cathedral at Chartres was not the first to be constructed, but it was built quite rapidly: Begun in 1194, it was completed twenty-six years later. The cathedral was consecrated in 1260. I'd always thought of cathedrals as taking hundreds of years to build, perhaps because New York's Cathedral of Saint John the Divine is still unfinished after 127 years (as of 2019). Yet Chartres was completed in just over a quarter of a century, and they had no electricity!

According to Father Bulteau, the statues were designed to tell stories from the Bible, with a focus on the birth, ministry, and ascension of Jesus. He explained that his book was very brief so that it might serve as a guide. Therefore, it did not present the arguments underlying his assertions. He lamented, "...today the symbolic traditions and legends of Christianity are so completely lost that to unearth their meaning requires archeological dissertations, like the Rosetta Stone and the Denderah Zodiac..."[8]

I read bit by bit, but every once in a while, Father Bulteau would stop to provide the big picture. While describing the porch, he paused to tell the reader:

> Before getting to know these [719] statues, it is good for the reader to remember that all the iconography of churches of the Middle Ages was a book of doctrine and morals; the point was the instruction of people and the edification of the faithful; and we see another thing that Christian theology in summarizing the facts of the ancient and new Testament, is mistaken, and fails to understand the art of our fathers. The windows, the paintings, the sculptures, everything in the gothic cathedral represents the Bible, the Gospel, the life of Saints with their mysterious dogmas, their divine teachings; but offered with a method, a profound knowledge ... Oh are they wrong, those writers who only saw whims of the imagination installed with neither taste nor logic, products of ignorance and barbarism in this admirable statuary that peoples the exterior of our Catholic cathedrals![9]

Without the knowledge of the complex iconography of the Middle Ages, I would have no way of knowing that any particular grouping was meant to depict a specific subject. I was intrigued by a story Father Bulteau told about one statue, which had been subject to mutilation during the French Revolution. "For an inexplicable reason, most Chartrains see, in the Massacre of the Innocents, a scene of adultery: the three people that they point out to strangers are in reality a poor mother who is holding her baby that a soldier just cut in two with his sword. We don't even know how to tell you all the stupid jokes and disgusting obscenities that we've heard with regard to this evangelical scene: there are people to whom it seems very titillating to be able to show an adultery among the sculptures of the Cathedral."[10]

As another example of the challenge of decoding the statues, there is a series of statues depicting the labors associated with each month of the year. Examining that for December, I was perfectly willing to accept that this was what was being depicted, but it could easily have been any other scene that involved a man at a table.

Over dinner with Cantal, his son, Xavier Cantal-Dupart, and a number of their friends, I raised the challenge of decoding symbols. I showed them Evil Jane and related the story of the (mis)interpretation of the Massacre of the Innocents. Xavier, a filmmaker of growing renown, shared a story of a recent visit to an early church. "What was fascinating," he said, "was that many of the symbols were pagan symbols that were being used by the church."

This is evident at Chartres as well, as intertwined with the months are the signs of the zodiac, which date back to the Babylonians around 1000 B.C. "Your Jane mural," added Xavier, "is a very pagan picture. The squirrel eating the tomato is the heart of the matter."

The next day, Xavier came to see me off at the train station. As he kissed me on my cheeks, he said, "Our conversation about symbols gave me much to think about."

I was glad—Main Streets are full of signs and symbols, and I needed help. One of the people I turned to on a regular basis was the poet Michael Lally.

## Blue Sky

From time to time, Michael met with me to discuss my work on Main Street. We met at restaurants on Maplewood Avenue, the Main Street of Maplewood, New Jersey. It was the quintessential Main Street, with a movie theater, supermarket, fish store, bookstore, toy store, three classes of pizza, a take-out Chinese place, a Thai restaurant, a hamburger place, an ice-cream parlor, a jewelry store, a post office, and two banks. You can get a lot done in a short amount of time.

One of the dynamics of Main Street playing out during the course of this study was the addition of "Towne Centres"—I'd seen one built in Englewood—to other Main Streets. Maplewood was one site of this evolution. The post office, which had been centrally located and created the crossroads of the street, was moved in 2015 to a smaller location at the end of the commercial core. That opened up the central site for redevelopment and a contest for what would be built and how.

Sitting in a coffee shop next to the site, I asked Michael what he thought about this. He was sad. Prices were going up for housing in Maplewood, and that meant that the kind of people who'd been able to move there ten or twenty years before would be shut out. The newcomers would be people in finance, with a great deal of money at their disposal. "The building will be tall and we won't be able to see the blue sky from where we are sitting."

Consider that sentence: "The building will be tall and we won't be able to see the blue sky from where we are sitting."

I looked up and was convinced of the truth of that point.

But that is not what Michael the poet was saying to me.

He was helping me to see that the reorganization of Main Street would shift the form of the street, shift the flow of the street, shift the symbols on the street, shift the kind of people on the street. At some point in the inconsiderate rush for money, the needs of people would be lost, needs like blue sky that can be seen from the coffee shop window.

But what is blue sky? People talk about "blue-skying" and they mean that they are thinking big, or maybe thinking impractically. What flashes into my mind is that by the train station near my house, someone had spray-painted "They would charge for air if they could." Michael didn't separate the shift in who might live in

Maplewood from our access to the sky, to the freedom to be an artist because the housing prices were within reach, to concern about the life of the mind and the soul, to a desire for the city to be a size that was happy and free for children of all ages.

When I first imagined talking to a poet about Main Street, I thought he would give me a guidebook so that I could decode all the signs. Basically, I imagined a Rosetta stone, kind of like Father Bulteau's book on Chartres. I wanted him to walk down the street with me and say something like "See, when they put up a SALE! sign, it really means [whatever he would say]." Or he would look at the accumulation of statutes and explain the stories that selection was telling me.

Instead, we talked about simple things. We first met at the Laurel, owned by someone who was family. "I think of it as gourmet comfort food," he said. And it was. Simple but so complete. I took my family there and they loved it. We would just get in the mood for the Laurel's "gourmet comfort food," and there it would be, until a death in the family caused it to close. But you see, when the poet is the food critic, you get the perfect description of the restaurant as your guide. In these simple conversations, therefore, what I got was not the "this equals that" I was imagining would help me understand Main Streets, but instead these exquisite offerings from his life and work, from being inside the world in all its complexity. That shifted my gaze.

That is how I came to understand it wasn't the SALE! sign that was to be decoded; it was the whole dance of all of us, coming and going and looking at all the signs under the blue sky, that I needed to wrap my head around.

That is the point of the box.

# 4    Circle

*The steps from the hill lead down into Harlem,*
*through a park, then I cross St. Nicholas,*
*Eighth Avenue, Seventh, and I come to the Y,*
*the Harlem Branch Y, where I take the elevator*
*up to my room, sit down, and write this page...*
—Langston Hughes, "Theme for English B"


THE PARKING LOTS in Tenafly had first made me conscious of the area around Main Street, but it was Cantal who had taught me to look at the "fullness" of a place. He took me to Labastide-d'Armagnac and to Bagnolet, which were starkly different places. Armagnac was dense and vital, whereas Bagnolet was sundered by highways, which had undermined its functioning.[1]

Jake and I defined these features of the circle for our study:

- Walkable neighborhood scale
- Frequent local connections with clear paths
- Viable (i.e., populated, maintained, intact) neighborhoods
- Fewer barriers separating Main Street from adjacent communities

In Livingston, we noted that the surrounding neighborhoods lacked sidewalks and the routes were unclear, with intervening parking lots. It was not safe or interesting to walk in the area. Main

Street in East Orange was also challenged by parking lots, as well as by vacant space and major impasses due to the rail line and the interstate highway.

By contrast, around Ferry Street in Newark, the adjoining neighborhoods had streets with sidewalks, no major impediments to getting to Ferry Street, and lots and lots of habitable buildings, which were filled with people. It was a very delightful neighborhood.

## Slicing the Circle

In May 2016, I got to visit Sauk Centre, Minnesota, Sinclair Lewis's hometown and the model for his novel *Main Street*—a book that is the wellspring of our thinking about these streets and to which I'll return in chapter 9. I wanted to see the origin site, which is located two hours northwest of the Twin Cities. The drive up was blissful. Spring had illuminated the Minnesota countryside with greens of trees and shrubs and purples of huge lilacs. My eyes drank in the gentleness: the slight roll of the hills, the silver of the silos, the soft movements of the cows, the dark brown of newly tilled soil, and the bright green of freshly sprouted crops.

The town was clearly marked on the highway, and I had the growing anticipation of seeing the miles go by—thirty-two, then twenty-four, then ten, and finally one. Driving through the town, seeing the Main Street marquee on the movie theater, pulling up to the curb, I entered legend. I was unprepared for it to look so beleaguered. The core of Main Street was one block of one- or two-story buildings, with most of the stores for lease, buildings for sale, nearly all closed. The florist stood out for its good cheer and beauty, the theater for signs of actual life. Not that anyone was going in or out of the theater, but the shows were current and there was a signboard out front welcoming people. I walked four blocks down Sinclair Lewis Boulevard and arrived at a field.

On my way back to Main Street I stopped to study a mural of the town's history, going back to the Native People, and ending with Sinclair Lewis. The next-to-last panel showed a World War

I doughboy writing home from the trenches in France, with Main Street in the background, alive and surrounded by verdant fields, the Main Street that is in our heads. The mural has an important lesson about what was wrong: The form of Main Street had been destroyed. While in a dense city the "circle" might extend a few blocks, in this rural area the Main Street served a much larger unit of farms extending out for miles in all directions. The town is, to this day, a small nucleus of buildings in the midst of a much larger farming community. The small nucleus was not what had sustained Main Street, but the larger area all around.

This form has been destroyed by the highway and the speedy cars that make the trip to St. Cloud or other larger centers an easy one. The highway also shifted the center of gravity to itself—it's not Main Street qua street that's the focus of the cars, but the highway, making it easy to move from one center of population to another. The

Doughboy writing home. This painting from the Main Street mural in Sauk Centre depicts the larger area that sustained Main Street. It is an example of the circle, intact and supporting the core civic and commercial center.

# Sauk Centre Scroll, 2016

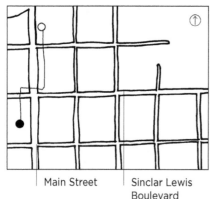

| Main Street | Sinclar Lewis Boulevard |
|---|---|

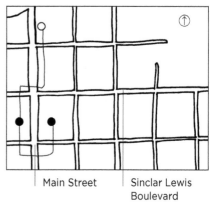

| Main Street | Sinclar Lewis Boulevard |
|---|---|

The core of Main Street was one block of one or two story buildings, with most of the stores for lease, buildings for sale, nearly all closed. The florist stood out for the good cheer and beauty, the theater for signs of actual life.

One of the stores that was going out of business.

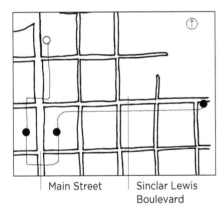 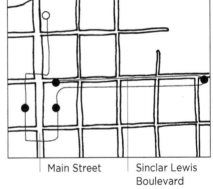

| Main Street | Sinclar Lewis Boulevard |
| Main Street | Sinclar Lewis Boulevard |

I walked four blocks down Sinclair Lewis Boulevard and arrived at a field. The small nucleus was not what had sustained Main Street, but the larger area all around.

It would have been utterly disheartening had not there been a mural of the town's history, going back to the Indians, and ending with Sinclair Lewis.

highway is now the main roadway, draining Main Street of vitality.

Architect Bill Morrish once told me, "I was studying small towns in the Midwest and I got to know all the signs of a dying Main Street. You'd get to a town and there would be a gas station with a Coke machine and that would be the whole Main Street. But when even the gas station and the Coke machine were gone, I said, 'Well, this town's finished.'"

His words echoed in my head. It wasn't that there was no investment going on in Sauk Centre, but, rather, that it had abandoned Main Street and moved along the highway. The inevitable Walmart had raised its banners there, as had a string of gas stations and fast-food joints.

My hometown, Orange, New Jersey, was sliced by a highway that ripped out the middle of the city, and sent African American and Italian families, organizations, and businesses scrambling for space. As with most such projects, a few managed to stay, while many others left town. Deindustrialization followed, undermining the economy on every front: taxes for the city, income for working people, political strength to fight for justice and equality.

Orange fifty years later is an entirely different place. There are few whites. The majority now is black, which could mean African American, African, Jamaican, or Haitian. Hispanics are a growing part of the population, and they, too, hail from a long list of places, including Colombia and Peru. The Catholic parishes and the mainline Protestant churches have lost the place they once held in the community. Lots of new evangelical churches have sprung up. Main Street lost its movie theater, the palace of childhood when I was growing up. The city has gained a series of ethnic markets that draw people from a very wide area, searching for plantains, okra, mangoes, sugarcane, and massive bags of rice. The annual Hispanic Festival is unofficially a pupusa throwdown. The Haitian patties are a party favorite—you can get four dozen for under forty dollars.

The economy, too, has shifted. Though a few small ironworks remain, industry and the local hospital have gone. People commute to service and retail jobs in other cities. Orange is lucky to have exceptional bus connections in all directions, which makes this possible. But people don't earn much and rents are climbing out of reach for those with constrained and often irregular wages. Young adults get caught in the ever-widening trap of trying to go to college, amassing more debt than course credits, and kept from finishing by a very long list of obstacles presented by precarious living. Yet still they rise—a hip-hop event is sure to turn out young women and men dressed in their finest, supporting their heroes and enjoying a moment of relaxation. It is not the nightclubs of the bygone era, but it is the same joy of Saturday night.

In the chaos of churning employment, unstable housing with frequent evictions, and global displacement from war, unemployment, drought, and oppression, a small city becomes a crossroads of the world and we are called to understand our neighbors, to make a new "us." That is where Main Street steps in. Orange's Main Street serves its working-class, multi-ethnic majority, offering things they like—what some call "urban" goods—such as sneakers, jewelry, ethnic food, electronics, hair supplies, and fast food. There is also the library, post office, bank, elementary school, and a park. Most important, there are people out and about, doing their chores, waiting for a bus, or just hanging out. The people can see one another. As the children grow up and go to school together, they make nets across the differences and say, "Hi, how you doing?" on Main Street.

But the more well-to-do, who live in the south end of town, on the other side of the highway, don't like the working-class vibe. They don't need trendy Adidas sneakers or want big gold earrings. Cantal visited Orange in 2009 to help the University of Orange write a plan for the "Heart of Orange," the area from Main Street south to Central Avenue. He commented that the middle class saw the area as a dead end, rather than as the center of the city, its throbbing heart. Once we saw it as the center of the city, we would ask, "What should be going on in the center?" We would think of transit connections, gathering, and residences near transit, without barriers.

Instead, these more privileged residents turn toward wealthy South Orange, seeing themselves as part of the Starbucks crowd. This is not entirely their fault—when the highway ripped the city in two, it created a no-go zone in the middle, the dead end, as Cantal noted. The north and south lost track of each other. Main Street lost half of its circle. Main Street can only do so much. Then we have to step in.

Winston Churchill famously said, "We shape our buildings, and afterwards our buildings shape us."[2] The same is true of our cities. A divided city makes a divided citizenry. Happily, we never lose our ability to remake the building—or the city—and by so doing, remake ourselves. We can mend broken connections. One of the most accessible tools is "the occasion," a concept we learned from Phil Pappas of Pittsburgh. He taught us that to make an occasion, you have to set "the table." It has to feel joyous and welcoming—like a party, not like a lecture.

A block party on Main Street offered an occasion to reflect on the injuries created by Route 280. I shared with my UofO colleagues that I wanted to have a booth that would say "The doctor is IN," as Lucy has in the *Peanuts* cartoons. Jamy Lasalle, a carpenter and Orange enthusiast, designed a portable booth that we could take to the block party. Molly, Mike Malborough, and others decided to invent a game, Alternate Orange, in which people imagined what Orange would have been like if the highway had not been built. They bought crazy glasses, invented a treasure hunt, swore people in as secret agents of Alternate Orange, and created a password: "The Chasm Is Real."

All kinds of people became secret agents of Alternate Orange that day, enjoying the silliness, as did the inventors. But there is profound seriousness underlying the joke, as perhaps there is with all jokes. In this case, we do want Orange to be something other than a fractured city; we want it to embrace its complexity and find a way to keep it, against the odds of gentrification in the New York City region. The game planted the suggestion that we could critique the "what is" and invent a new future. However implausible these futures might be, we

The chasm is real.   The University of Orange invented "Alternate Orange," a game imagining what might have happened had no highway cut through the center of the city.  These young women had played the game and succeeded in becoming agents of Alternate Orange.
*Photo by Molly Kaufman, used with permission.*

have a right, and even a duty, to find a direction.  Then we can make the city that will make us as we wish to be.

## Mapping Assets

The congregation I belonged to—First Unitarian Universalist Church of Essex County—became part of this mending process when we were falling apart and some said it was time to quit.  Rehanna Azimi and Monique Baena-Tan, students in the Parsons Design and Urban Ecologies program, in which I was an adjunct faculty member, did a thesis on anchor institutions, and showed us that, were we to stay, our congregation had a role to play. They wrote:

> *Planning to Stay*, a community report written by Catherine Brown and William Morrish for a small town in Minnesota, defines anchoring institutions as "the places where the cultural, educational, and social activities of our community are focused." Anchoring institutions literally anchor people in a community, staying when other institutions go, and helping people situate themselves in a constantly changing environment. We recognize these as vital stabilizing points for a constantly changing population.[3]

It was impressive to members of our little congregation to think that we were an "anchor institution," vital to the city of Orange. As an anchor, we had special work to do, such as stabilize the city. But to do those tasks, we had to plan to stay. We hadn't expected to learn that that we had a social obligation to keep going, but we took the report and its implications seriously.

We did not know what we were supposed to do next, but a visiting clergyman, the Reverend John Gilmore, explained that our greatest asset was that we owned our buildings. This was quite a shock. Our little congregation was largely supported by renting our space to nonprofits and other congregations. We had the world's least attractive ramp leading up to our front door, the plaster in our sanctuary was cracked, yellowed and falling, and the building's shingles were shrinking in on themselves. One member said she felt like a slumlord. The church board spent years debating what to do about these problems, without coming to any resolution. We thought of the buildings as an albatross, not an asset.

"Because you own your buildings, you can invite others to use your space," the Reverend Gilmore said. "Turn outward and you will grow again."

He explained his logic with a simple drawing, which said that church was the center of community—not just the church community but also the surrounding area. It was supposed to be of service as a place for our congregation to gather but also for lots of other groups that needed a place to meet. Some of the people meeting in our space would share our worldview, and some would join our congregation. All of the people would benefit from the use of the space, and such spaces are a precious commodity in urban areas.

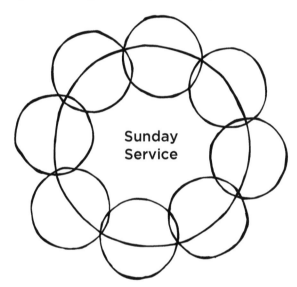

Reverend Gilmore's diagram of the way in which opening church to the community would lead to intersections. He noted, "Many kinds of groups use the space. Some people also come for Sunday service. It's not necessary for everyone who's coming here [pointing to the outer circles] to come here [pointing to Sunday service]."

Many of us had just been through an eviction from a space we did not own: the eviction of the youth arts program, ORNG Ink, from a building called "Ironworks," which had originally been renovated for the use of those involved in the program. The building had become the home of an architecture firm that had no connection to Orange but could pay a handsome rent. This lesson in loss helped the Reverend Gilmore's words to sink in.

What's more, it sounded exciting. We decided that we would turn outward by using our buildings to make a community center we would call the HUUB, with two U's, in honor of our denomination. So far, so good. The next question was, "How do we turn outward?"

The Reverend Alison Cornish, a minister who'd heard of our

dilemma, sent an article entitled "Death and Resurrection of an Urban Church."[4] It described how Broadway Methodist Church in Indianapolis had closed its food pantry, tutoring program, and youth activities, and instead turned to asset-based community development (ABCD), a method pioneered by John McKnight in the 1990s. The ABCD method taught that we should stop looking for community deficits and look instead for community gifts. This was a radical departure, yet it was the Reverend Gilmore's assertion that we had an asset—our buildings—that had given us energy to reinvent our ministry.

One of the stories Broadway Methodist's minister, the Reverend Michael Mather, told was about Adele, a woman who came to the church seeking help. Instead of asking her to fill out a form stating she was poor, the Reverend Mather asked her what her gifts were. "I'm a great cook," she said.

He asked her to prove it by cooking for his team and him. They loved the food, and started to support her by paying her to cook for meetings at the church. When the Chamber of Commerce asked to hold a meeting there, the Reverend Mather suggested they ask Adele to cater. "Then we made our only investment—twenty dollars to get Adele one thousand business cards." They gave out the cards to the Chamber of Commerce, and Adele's business grew. Eventually, she opened her own restaurant, Adelita's. The Reverend Mather concluded, "If I'd asked her how poor she was, nothing would have gotten better and we would have missed a lot of great eating."

We decided to give Broadway Methodist's approach a try and soon found ourselves on the phone with the Reverend Mather and his close associate, DeAmon Harges. We learned from them about their basic approach, starting with asking people about their gifts, and then finding ways to support those gifts. They also connected us with a nearby ABCD trainer, Bob Francis, who was able to do a workshop with us to orient us to this new way of thinking.

Sixteen people came to the training in September 2016, including several of our future listening fellows. Bob Francis, who'd met John McKnight twenty years earlier and was on the national faculty of

ABCD, opened with a story/joke that got us laughing. He then plunged into the ABCD view of community as a place of care, not services. He explained that community assets consist of five parts: the gifts of individuals; the citizen associations, which were possibly the most untapped resource; the institutions, which could be fortresses or treasure chests; the public space; and the community economy, including the new economy that was growing.

Mapping these assets was the beginning of the work. Once we knew the lay of the land, we could begin to sort out the functions of each of these groups. What functions, for example, could people perform for themselves? What functions could the neighborhood achieve with some help? What functions must the institutions perform? Sorting in this manner would give us a much more detailed understanding of the work ahead.

We shared the situation in Orange. At that time, young artists had lost the fight to keep Ironworks as the home for their organization, ORNG Ink. Khemani Gibson, one of the founders of ORNG Ink, commented that the various powerful organizations fighting for control of the space had undermined youth power. "It's frustrating," he said.

His feelings were echoed by Patricia Rogers, who noted the conflict between people who care and people who want to provide services. "ORNG Ink cares, and we're in conflict with the organizations with the money."

Becky Doggett said that reminded her of her young days in Orange when she and other youth felt they were not given a place at the table. "It's not a new problem. Perhaps we can identify how to do it differently."

| HAND | HEAD |
|------|------|
| Bake | Write |
| Sew/quilting | Tell stories |
| | Promote health |
| HEART | HOME |
| Justice | Friends and family |
| Being of service | |

Mindy's 4-H Table. All the participants made a box with four parts, and listed their personal assets.

Bob listened carefully to our problems, then got us working. We made personal inventories, listing our own assets in the domains of Hand, Head, Heart, and Home. We all noted assets, and they weren't all the same. It reminded us of the breadth of skills in our group.

From personal assets, we turned to citizens' associations, which Bob pointed out were likely to be overlooked in any effort to build community. At that time, I belonged to six organizations and was on the board of three of those. I knew of thirteen; others knew of even more than I did.

Then we worked on identifying the local institutions, ranking them from "treasure chests" to "fortresses." This was a lively exercise, as saying an organization was a fortress was a form of shade. We were yelling out to the person making the chart, "No, no, all the way to left!" or "No, no, all the way to the right!"

That energizing exercise was followed by another list about the local economy. Bob asked us to list where the money was, which was also funny, largely because it wasn't with anyone in the room. Our answers ranged from the state of New Jersey to the Berkeley Tennis Association, a private club with clay courts in the wealthy Seven Oaks section of Orange. Our next list answered the question, "Who do you know who can get things done?" There were a lot of people who could get things done, depending on what you needed.

At the end of making all these lists, Bob asked us to consider what we had. Then he asked, "How are you feeling?"

Patricia Rogers replied, "You've helped us look at our city again."

Bob nodded vigorously. "You spent fifteen minutes being negative, and five hours and forty-five minutes being positive and not so negative. There are real problems. Assets solve problems. Work with the assets, you'll have small successes, and you will get empowered to take on bigger issues. Remember that you are enough: the sixteen people in this room can influence an exponential number. I got labeled 'the asset man' because I never shut up about assets."

It is one thing to make a list and another to put it into action. Bob had even told us a story about the city of Yonkers, New York, which mapped the assets of 80,000 of its 100,000 people, but nothing happened because city leadership fell apart. Our own next steps were not exactly like the initial image we'd had of roving listeners finding all the gifted people on Cleveland Street, but we undertook major shifts. One of the most visible early changes was in the state of the First UU's campus. The creaky, disintegrating ramp was replaced by a beautiful walkway with two big planters that flanked the stairs up to the main door. Various parts of the roof were mended, the boiler replaced, the sanctuary replastered and repainted, and the aging shingles addressed.

The HUUB was open for welcoming people, and that put us in the space of partnering, something that had been beyond the capacity of the congregation. The most important partner was the University of Orange. We were a church without a congregation; they were a university without a campus. These fit well together, we found. Other partners followed, including HANDS, the local community-development corporation, and Fueling Main, an organization with a new strategy for promoting local investment.

The young listening fellows started small projects related to their own talents. Holly, for example, decided that a monthly potluck supper would be a great activity. It turned out she was an amazing baker. She set the expectation that people would share delicious homemade eats.

Cesar, who was a budding musician, decided to hold a series of concerts featuring young artists. This provided a platform for many young people to share their music, including him. These concerts shifted as new musicians were drawn to the HUUB for performance and listening. By the third year, we were able to suggest that the fellows program be named in honor of Joe Thomasberger, a local minister and youth advocate. His friends and family approved that plan, which helped secure a base of donors going forward.

Our efforts with ABCD shifted us to a dialectical approach. On the one hand, we could see more and more of the existing materials for building stronger communities. We could imagine many versions of Adele's trajectory from "good cook" to "restaurant owner," and along with that, the animation of the whole city. On the other hand, we were keenly aware of the anti-community forces that were at work, tearing at the fabric of Orange. We knew that gentrification was pushing rents out of reach and was going to affect Orange in a profound way. Dominic Moulden, our partner in research, told us that the city would replace all the historic buildings on Main Street with high-rises, to fill out the "transit-oriented" development plan. I didn't believe him, but his community, the Shaw neighborhood in Washington, D.C., had already been through the wringer of gentrification, so he had a longer perspective than I did.

## Mapping Deficits

Orange, like other U.S. cities, has mapped what it liked and what it didn't for a long time. In the 1930s, Essex County was mapped by the federal Government's Homeowner Loan Corporation (HOLC) as part of its infamous "redlining" maps. Those maps rated parts of cities on the basis of the age of homes and the race/ethnicity/immigration status of people who lived there. Rather than concluding that the areas with the poorest people and oldest homes needed government support to prosper, those areas were rated "D" and marked in red on the maps to signal to banks and insurers that they were "high-risk." The Orange redlining map shows the underlying segregation of the city, which was the basis for school segregation maps, which I discuss in chapter 9.

In 2018, the city of Orange continued this decades-old practice, commissioning an "area in need" study, led by the Nishuane Group, which was also leading the master plan effort. Both of these efforts were endorsed by Mayor Dwayne Warren and carried out under the leadership of the business administrator, Chris Hartwyck. The plans demonstrated a vision of Orange as a prosperous middle-class community. The fly in the ointment was that the proposals to realize that transformation were designed to push the poor out and bring in new people with money.

The draft Main Street "area in need" study had a cover that revealed the true intent. It had the title "Area in Need of Redevelopment Study with Condemnation."[5] The "Condemnation" in the title was the key word, as that word meant that the city government could condemn "blighted" properties, demolish them, and give the land to developers for new projects. The underlying concept was to clear space for new five- to ten-story, market-rate apartment buildings, following the model of other nearby towns, like Maplewood, South Orange, and Montclair, which had built "luxury apartments" in their centers, especially in areas close to the train. Such buildings change the character of the area, both as an architectural environment and as a people place. There were to be no poor people in any of those buildings. Even those with some "affordable" units were not serving the very poor, a group of people that was being left out and pushed out, all around the nation.

Reading the report was, for me, an experience of déjà vu. My Root Shock project had studied 1950s and 1960s urban renewal, and these were exactly the tools that had been used then to clear land in 2,500 projects, carried out in 993 American cities.[6] James Baldwin coined the famous phrase "Urban renewal is Negro removal," which my father amended to "people removal," because it was directed at poor white, black, and brown people throughout the nation. Urban renewal caused great harm in those cities by destroying people's wealth, shattering their social networks, and replacing functional communities with projects that offered much less, if any, life to the urban ecosystem.

It was especially shocking to read in the Main Street study the superficial descriptions of the buildings and the casual list of reasons that they were no good anymore. It is important to note that every parcel automatically met criteria for "redevelopment" because the city's sewer system was more than fifty years old, Main Street was an Urban Enterprise Zone, and the proximity to transportation meant that it was a "smart growth" area.

The report's list of parcel-by-parcel accounts opened with

a discussion of the historic First Presbyterian Church, which is surrounded by a colonial-era graveyard. The report noted that the spire was in need of work and that the site could use renovation or redevelopment. What the report didn't say was that the First Presbyterian Church had been founded in 1719 and had held services in Orange until 2010, when it was closed by the Newark Presbytery, at which time the building was put on the market. It was sold to First Shiloh Baptist Church, a rapidly growing Haitian congregation. The new congregation maintained the church and the historic graveyard, which has tombstones going back to the 1740s. One student of mine, while helping with a planning investigation, found a tombstone of an ancestor there.

The report, in casually dismissing the history of the city, and discussing only the problems of facades, created an entirely wrong idea of Main Street. This study was not an effort to strengthen what was there; rather, it was an effort to get rid of it. Having interviewed

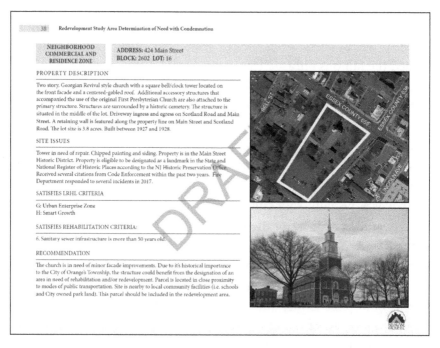

First Presbyterian Church in the city plan.

many people who had had their homes seized by eminent domain, I found an exchange between the planner who wrote the report, Shauna Eubanks, and a woman who lived in the area, Lorraine Jones, to be particularly egregious.

Ms. Jones's home was situated at 27 Prince Street, a small street at the eastern end of Orange, in an area with some of the city's oldest homes. The only critique of the home was that the front porch roof was in need of repair. Nothing was said of the historic value of this 1881 home. Ms. Jones spoke at the hearing, saying, "The house on Prince Street that I live in is certainly more than fifty years old, because my family has owned it since 1948. Now, because it's fifty years old, we've been trying to keep it up, and certainly it's livable to a family. Do we just say it can be taken by eminent domain because it's fifty years old? I mean, it's Prince Street, it's not even on Main Street, so, you know, and I moved here from out of Orange—I was born and raised here—but I moved out for a while and it's my senior

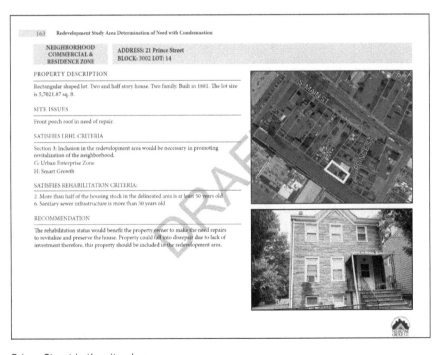

Prince Street in the city plan.

home and my assisted living place and all of that and things we're trying to do to it. We don't want to do all of that, and then you come and tell us it's gone. What are your suggestions?"

These are serious worries when a redevelopment plan is imposed. Such plans can freeze investment and undermine the stability of functioning urban areas. In the Gainsboro section of Roanoke, Virginia, an urban renewal designation, followed by no action, contributed to the steady decline of the neighborhood, until it lay in ruins.[7]

Ms. Eubanks's answer was, "You will be notified at every step of the process."

Of course, that is distinctly different from, "No, the city won't seize your home."

And that is because the intent of the study was to authorize eminent domain. Chris Hartwyck spoke directly to that point. "There are a variety of reasons why you want to approve a redevelopment district that includes eminent domain—it gives the city power. Some owners want condemnation because it gives them tax breaks. There are a lot of benefits to the power of eminent domain."

There are also a lot of negatives and sound reasons not to give a city the power of eminent domain, but those facts were not disclosed, either in the report or in the hearing.

## Place-based ABCD

We knew that we needed to articulate the ABCD approach. We didn't know many people who were engaged in asset-based community development, other than Bob Francis, who'd come to give us our original training. That shifted when he and others convened the "northeast network of asset-based community development" in April 2019. Charlie and Aubrey Murdock, lead designer of the University of Orange, attended that meeting. They came back with expansive new ideas.

At the same time, two other projects were contributing to our thinking. Aubrey and Molly were working with colleagues at the Design Studio for Social Intervention on a project to define "horizontal development," the idea that benefiting people should be at the center of our development plans.

We were also part of a research project called "Making the Just City," led by Derek Hyra of American University, Dominic Moulden of ONE DC, and me. Our study compared the early signs of gentrification in Orange to the full-blown experience of the process in the Shaw neighborhood of Washington, D.C., where Dominic Moulden was working. From the comparison of the two and from rapidly emerging data from all around the nation, we were able to ascertain that the early signs pointed to a very real threat of displacement for the poor people of Orange.

We found a powerful confluence of the ABCD work, the horizontal development project, and the gentrification study. The Reverend Mather, DeAmon Harges, and Bob Francis had taught us that if we asked our neighbors about their gifts, our church would be in a better position to help. The horizontal development study had taught us that we had to think horizontally in order to do development, rather than vertically. And the gentrification study had demonstrated that people wanted to love Orange but were afraid because they could see the handwriting on the wall.

Let's call this new theory "place-based ABCD." Applying this theory to one church—First UU—we had become convinced that by turning outward, we could share our gifts and help the city. Applying this theory to Main Street, we knew that the outward activation of our congregation supported the street by the comings and goings of people, by our showing them Main Street, by our partnership with anchor institutions and other associations throughout the area, and our frequenting the street and its businesses.

From our experiences doing this, we had become aware of the sixteen churches in the Main Street circle. We had celebrated Rosa Parks at Ebenezer Baptist Church, attended the HANDS Leadership Awards at Church of the Epiphany and Christ Church, learned the story of the now-demolished North Orange Baptist at the Joe

Thomasberger Street naming, and discussed possible future uses of the Sunday school building with First Shiloh.

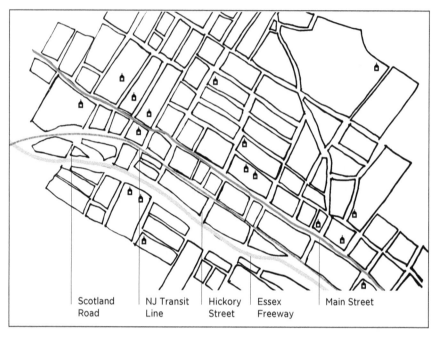

| Scotland Road | NJ Transit Line | Hickory Street | Essex Freeway | Main Street |

The churches that ring Main Street, Orange. There are 16 churches that surround Main Street in Orange, an asset for strengthening the civic and commercial center.

Each of these churches was contributing to the strength of Main Street in more or less the same set of ways that we were. But what if the city's "Main Street Plan" were specifically developed with all of the churches participating, according to the ideas and ideals of horizontal development? This would offer a dramatically new opportunity to build on the real assets of the city. Bill Morrish said to us, "Main Street is not a set of facades and streetscapes! Like a river, its health is based upon the reach of its shed, the rich territory lying behind the facade. The many organizations, like churches, that exist in that territory are key background support, as well as intermediary space through which people flow among the many worlds of life!"

That is the point of the circle.

# 5 Line

"An uninterrupted public thoroughfare passing through the heart of downtown" is an excellent definition of what I mean by the "line."[1] To define this, Jake and I selected these criteria:

- Physical and social connections to the region
- Transit and road connections to the region
- Way-finding support for outsiders and strangers
- Perceived welcome
- Perceived access

I brought to the concept of line the experience of studying two long streets, Bloomfield Avenue and Springfield Avenue, in an earlier project, the Transect Study, which Rod Wallace, Cynthia Golembeski, and I had carried out in 2004, examining the effects of displacement in Essex County, New Jersey.[2] Close examination of those avenues documented a gradient of disinvestment that reached a nadir at the outskirts of Newark and then rose slowly as the avenues approached the wealthy suburbs. We also examined the movement of African

Americans out of Newark from 1970 to 2000. From this data, Rod was able to create a model that showed a slow but inexorable process of displacement and disinvestment, a glacier of destruction creeping across the county. While the affluent populations might perceive their cities and investments as safe, Rod commented, "Ultimately... an advancing glacier grinds down all high ground."[3]

The line that runs through Orange Main Street—the "Orange Line"—is known as Orange Street at its beginning in Newark. Orange Street changes its name first to Martin Luther King Boulevard and then to Main Street as it rolls through Newark, East Orange, Orange, and West Orange. This transect demonstrates more or less the same gradient of disinvestment that we saw in the Transect Study: new investment near Broad Street, followed by hollowing out by deindustrialization and highway building, with pockets of stressed neighborhoods gradually giving way to stronger neighborhoods in West Orange, just as the road goes up First Mountain to areas that were developed in the 1950s as suburban tract housing.

The Orange Line is home to an extraordinarily beautiful set of churches, beginning with the new Church of Latter-day Saints and followed by the historic St. Rose of Lima, the elegant Grace Episcopal Church, the famous Brick Church, the sweetly situated Church of the Epiphany, First Presbyterian (now Shiloh Baptist) with its colonial-era graveyard, St. Marks, and Our Lady of Lourdes.

The Orange Line is not the industrial center it once was. Some shells of former factories remain; others have been torn down or converted to new uses. But there are all kinds of small manufacturing and small businesses, some very old and some brand-new. A craft brewery in Orange, which opened in August 2019, was the latest addition at the time of this writing.

The key issue of the line is that, when thinking of Main Streets, we focus on the civic and commercial center—that is, the box, usually defined as being contained within a city. But the street that passes through that commercial center must flow if the center is to prosper. Therefore, the vitality of the line is fundamental to the vitality of the box. In the case of the Orange Line, there were multiple problems. Cantal's comments about the Heart of Orange being treated as the "end of the line" when it's really center city come to mind. The Orange Line is treated as disconnected pieces of street, defined by the breaks made by trains and highway and city limits, rather than as the major artery running westward from the center of Newark that it really is. This is a major loss to the cities all along the line, similar to what happens to the feet when the arteries of the leg get clogged.

## Lines of Fear

The lines of Main Street can take on many emotions. In July 2016, it was summery hot in the New York City area. My email was down to a trickle and there were no students needing my help. It should have been a time of relaxation and regrouping for the rigors of the next academic year. But that July was, instead, a time of fear and trembling. The *New York Times* columnist Charles Blow called one week of that month "the week from hell."[4] That was because two black men were killed by police; then five policemen were killed by a black man. That was perhaps particularly horrifying because the policemen were killed while monitoring a Black Lives Matter demonstration on Main Street in Dallas.

A protest is a very "Main Street" activity. We go to Main Street because it is the thoroughfare through the heart of downtown and therefore the place to parade. The Black Lives Matter movement was taking to the streets to protest the terrible series of murders that had punctuated the spring and the first part of the summer of 2016. One hundred and thirty-four black men had been killed by police by July 5, when Alton Sterling died in Baton Rouge. The next day, Philando Castile became the 136th.[5] The protests had sprung up all around the United States, focusing on the need to address the issue of police shootings.

Thus, the Dallas protest on July 8, which started at 7:00 P.M., after some of the summer heat had died down, drew hundreds of people, who were chanting the slogans that had become such a part

# The Orange Line, 2019

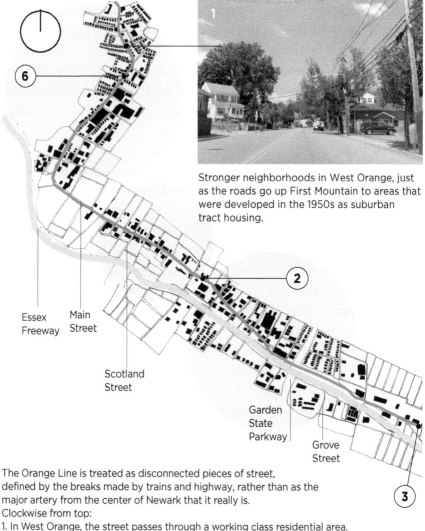

Stronger neighborhoods in West Orange, just as the roads go up First Mountain to areas that were developed in the 1950s as suburban tract housing.

Essex Freeway

Main Street

Scotland Street

Garden State Parkway

Grove Street

The Orange Line is treated as disconnected pieces of street, defined by the breaks made by trains and highway, rather than as the major artery from the center of Newark that it really is.
Clockwise from top:
1. In West Orange, the street passes through a working class residential area.
2. The Orange line passes through sections of dense, functional box.
3. More box
4. In East Orange, the Orange Line passes under railroad bridges and over highways, a desolate and empty stretch separating that city from Newark. It was remarkable to see how people were walking along this part of the road.
5. In Newark the Orange Line passes through former industrial areas that were vacant.
6. In West Orange, a mural depicted Thomas Edison admiring a lightbulb.
The Thomas Edison National Historical site is nearby.

Passaic River

Orange Street

W Market Street

Essex Freeway

of the Black Lives Matter movement. In a few seconds of gunfire, the confident forward strides of the marchers turned into a melee. People ran in all directions, seeking cover from the unseen assailant: a black man with a long rifle and deadly aim, who killed five police officers and planned to kill many more.[6] These murders chilled the nation, defining the "week from hell."

Part of the shock was the horror at cold-blooded murder.

Part of the shock was at the massacre of police officers.

Part of the shock was that it was murder on top of murder.

And part of the shock was that it occurred on Main Street.

## Lines of Connection

The murders in Dallas represent the profound breaks in our world, and raise the questions, "How are we to heal after violence and murder? Can Main Street play a role?"

In my Main Street collection is a photograph of Pierre Perron's contribution to the celebration of the millennium. It was my teacher, Cantal, who introduced me to Pierre, an artist in Nantes. For the millennium, he invented *Le cortège de l'an 2000*, an allée of dancing ancestors going back many generations, so that we might stroll within the continuity of their lives just as the clock stood at 11:59:59. The world had talked so much of that second that I held my breath, a little shocked when it sailed unhesitatingly past and we could all yell "Happy New Year!" just as we always did. I saw Perron's ancestors that summer and let go of the last remnants of my fear. Seeing the gesture and the spaciousness of the allée helped me pull some pieces together that had made no sense.

It helped me appreciate the contributions to healing made by photographer Wing Young Huie. I met Wing in 2016. We were both part of events on diversity and equity offered by the St. Paul Riverfront Corporation Placemaking. The first of these was a panel. Wing shared his story of growing up in Duluth, a port city in northern Minnesota, where his immigrant parents owned and operated a Chinese restaurant, Joe Huie's Café. For most of his public school

Pierre's allée. Pierre Perron created this allée to place the millennium in context of many generations of people.
*Photo by Pierre Perron. Used with permission.*

education, Wing was the only Asian student in his class.

After orienting us to his story, he showed a series of his photographs, which he had placed along avenues in Minneapolis and St. Paul. Whatever I thought those cities looked like crumbled in face of what he was showing. I knew I was in the presence of a true master. I was privileged to have tea with him between engagements that day. I wanted to know more. Particularly, what was it like for the cities when those photos went up?

I got back to Minneapolis later that year. Wing picked me up at the airport and took me to the Third Place, his gallery and event space. His building, he explained, had been empty for forty-seven years. A new owner refurbished and rented it to him. In addition to the open first floor, it had a basement with a karaoke machine, which got used after Friday- and Saturday-night events were over. His corner at Thirty-eighth and Chicago had been considered scary.

There had, in fact, been a murder in front of his building, and an altar was set up there by the teenagers who knew the young man who died. Wing had invited the mourners in, and they had asked him to take their pictures. Since then, upscaling had taken place. The coffee shop he pointed to on the corner was the latest hipster operation to open in the neighborhood, part of the gentrification that was taking place.

We drove to Lake Street, where the first major exhibit had taken place. Wing had trained as a journalist, but he turned his attention to photography early on. He took a one-week course with the great street photographer Garry Winogrand, and that was the beginning of his work taking photos of people on the street. He talked a lot about going up to people and asking them if he might take their picture. "The first person I went up to said, 'Sure. Let me get my gun.'"

Writing about this visit in my field notes, I said, "Wing is retiring, but so gracious, I think anyone would agree to do what he asked." By "retiring," I think I meant nonintrusive, connecting from within his own space, like a gentle knock at the door. As part of that stance, he didn't take or choose photographs that made an obvious statement about the person in the photograph. I think he would not impose an "image" on another person.

Which is also his larger take on the "what happened" of the exhibit. When I asked about the impact of the Lake Street exhibit, he asserted politely but firmly, "That's not my role. I'm an artist; I am showing photographs."

By contrast, he was perfectly willing to speak of the task of preparing an exhibit that occupied the walls and windows of 150 businesses along the six miles of Lake Street. He took photographs for four years, wandering the shed of inner-city neighborhoods that lined Lake Street to take pictures of the area's residents. He rented an apartment in the area, and he said he seldom went outside without his Minolta.

From the thousands of photos he had taken, he selected the 675 photos that were to be shown, some outdoors on the walls of buildings and some in shop windows. He worked with a business

Wing Young Huie from the Lake Street Exhibition. *Used with permission.*
Above: Boy going home, a photo in the exhibit.

Below: Two boys, looking at the photos posted on Lake Street.

called Photos Inc., which had a projector on a railroad track that could move back and forth to print the giant photos.

Recruiting the businesses was a massive job, and he had the support of a project manager and a small army of volunteers to approach the three hundred shops along the street. Some were enthusiastic supporters, like the owner of Ingebretsen's, a Scandinavian gift shop and deli at the corner of Sixteenth and Lake, which had been in business since 1921. Others, especially those in the high-rent district at the northern end of Lake Street, wanted nothing to do with his photos, though they were to change their minds when the exhibit went up and was hugely popular.

I think it is very telling of his stance in life that there was no announcement of the exhibit or what it was. The photos just started to go up. There was no key for people to find themselves; they had to search. Walking up and down the six miles with family and friends was part of the experience. He tried to put people's photos near where they lived, though in one case, a person had requested that the photo be far away.

His book, *Lake Street, USA*, has five hundred of the photos.[7] I've spent many hours examining photo archives of poor neighborhoods. Wing's photos are unlike those of, say, Charles "Teenie" Harris, who, as a newspaper photographer, had an eye for the drama of the Hill District. Nor are they like the photos by Esther Bubley and Richard Saunders, who worked with the Pittsburgh Photographic Project in the 1950s and captured "moments."[8]

Concomitant to studying Wing's Lake Street book, I was watching a television show called *The Kindness Diaries*, which showed the adventures of Leon Logothetis, who was traveling the world on the kindness of strangers. The show depicted Leon asking people for help—he needed gas, food, lodging, occasionally clothes or a plan ride, but he wouldn't accept money. The strangers he approached had a variety of reactions. Some withdrew. Others embraced Leon and his improbable project; their kindness helped him circumnavigate the globe. The faces of those people reminded me, in their openness and generosity, of the people in Wing's photographs. Wing had made as improbable a request as Leon had, and some people embraced it. You can see it in their body language: They had agreed to be photographed by Wing.

The impact—to return to my wish to understand what happened as a result of the show—can only be described by what my colleague, psychiatrist Kelli Harding, calls the "rabbit effect," the ripples of change that come from being kind.[9] Wing told me he had taken photographs of youth in rival gangs. They looked at one another's photos and commented, "Hey, they're just like us."

And, for many people, the person they were seeing was themselves. Wing did a second version of the long show, held on University Avenue in St. Paul, supported by Public Art Saint Paul, an arts organization that took the burden of funding the work off Wing's shoulders. He was able to achieve his more expansive vision, including photo exhibitions accompanied by events at which the photos were projected outdoors. It was one of those slide shows that caught the attention of a young passerby. He remembered that Wing had taken his photo. Just at that moment, his image flashed on the wall. "Hey, that's me!" he exclaimed. How startling and wonderful suddenly to be part of the show!

"My goal," Wing said, "was to have enough photographs that anyone, no matter who you are, would find some connection, that you're represented in some way, no matter what cultural group you identify. A person approached me saying that they loved seeing all of my photographs along Lake Street because it gave them a chance to stare. That walking or driving down the corridor there is always something or somebody that catches your eye but you don't want to stare. 'Staring can lead to familiarity and understanding,' that person said. 'There is a person in one of your photographs that I see all the time but have never talked to. I finally went up to this person and said, "Hey, I saw your photograph in a window on Lake Street!" Seeing the photograph gave me an opportunity to finally meet and get to know this person.'"

That comment gave me the thought that Wing had broken the fourth wall of Main Street. In theater, the fourth wall is the imaginary wall that exists between the front of the stage and the audience. The fourth wall is largely respected, and when broken, it is a highly conscious act. The film *Ferris Bueller's Day Off* used the technique to great effect. Wing, by making the walls and windows of Lake Street a photo gallery, had broken open the imaginaries of everyone involved: the rich stores which did not want images of poor people of color in their windows, the people on the bus who wanted to stare at that which interested them—and finally could—and, of course, people who were themselves suddenly larger than life.

In 2019, I was in Minneapolis again and took my colleagues Irene Yen and Dominic Moulden to the Third Place for an event celebrating Wing's new book *Chinese-ness*.[10] The event was organized as a "gallery walk" and "circle talk." The photographs were concerned with exploring what "Chinese-ness" meant, a topic he'd investigated by changing clothes with Chinese men who lived other lives, lives he might have led had circumstances been different. After we'd strolled around looking at the photographs on our own, Wing gathered us together and asked us to select photographs that interested us. Then he would say something about these photographs.

It was, in its own way, an invitation to stare, to ask questions that we couldn't normally ask, to wonder about things. One of the photographs was of Walter, a black man who had studied twelve forms of martial arts and felt much closer to Chinese people than to black people. Wing had taken his photo for the Lake Street exhibit. Walter dropped by the studio twenty years after first meeting Wing. His experience of "Chinese-ness" made him part of this new project.

How could that be? Was that cultural appropriation? one woman asked, a definite edge to her voice. "Is it okay for Walter to feel Chinese?" she asked, meaning, of course, it wasn't.

Wing drew a line there. He talked about not judging the truth of other people's stories, instead remaining open to the variety of perspectives that exist in the world. His effort to connect with many versions of "Chinese-ness" had enriched his understanding of his own story, with its unique twists and turns. In fact, that Walter could feel Chinese was part of the joy of the exhibit, the book, and the experience. We were liberated from the rigid stereotypes imposed on us or on others.

Wing has posted on his site some reactions to his work. Porscha Kensey wrote, "Dear Wing, Walking in the studio was really different for me. It was nice walking into a place on the same block where a lot of violence happens and it was good to go into a place where there it was peace. I thought the photos weren't just photos they were meanings and lots of messages."[11]

Wing has said that he didn't want to take commercial photos that blast a single powerful message. Rather, he prefers ambiguity. But if Leon is right, what Wing is pulling for is kindness, which makes the world go round and the line run on to the horizon.

## Lines of Possibility

Which brings me to the last reflection on the line, trying to answer the question, "What *did* they see in Paree?" which is triggered by the question in the World War I song, "How you gonna keep 'em down on the farm after they've seen Paree?"

When I started posing this question to people, one response was a link to *Paris Noir*, by Tyler Stovall, about African Americans in the armed forces.[12] Professor Stovall studied European history and has written extensively on France, with a strong focus on the World War I era. Stovall set the stage for understanding the experience of France by describing the racism African Americans had to endure at that time: living in peonage, not far removed from slavery; denied rights, especially the right to vote; subjected to an unending campaign of terror; and given markedly inferior access to resources like education. At the time of World War I, denied other opportunities, African Americans found that they could vote with their feet and migrate to the cities, where industrial jobs and a less heavy burden of racism created opportunity.

Many African Americans believed that proving themselves in war would undermine racism. They volunteered in large numbers but were often turned away as "unqualified." When the increasing demands of the war made it necessary to accept blacks, the army segregated them, gave them inferior resources, and confined them to unskilled labor. Yet the 400,000 black men who went to France to fight opened a new door. Stovall notes:

> ... they were the first black Americans to go to France in large numbers, introducing the French to the distinctive culture of their people. Many would discover in their dealings with the French people that discrimination and oppression did not have to characterize relations across the color line... In contrast to the poor opinions the army leadership expressed about their abilities, black laborers in France often performed impressive physical feats, especially black longshoremen... In one instance, African American longshoremen unloaded five thousand tons of material in one day, when French officials had estimated that six thousand could only be moved over an entire month. During the month of September 1918, black stevedores set a record by unloading an incredible twenty-five thousand tons of cargo per day for several weeks.

The black soldiers were abused, overworked, and denied the kinds of leave and recreation that were common to white soldiers. In spite of that, the vast majority worked to win the war against Germany and the war against racism. Stovall wrote, "This determination [to prove their skill and value to the American war effort] also characterized the black American soldiers who fought in France. At one point, several African Americans stationed in Ohio while waiting to be sent overseas were asked if they were going to France. 'No, sir, I am not going to France,' replied one of them. 'I am going to Berlin and I may stop in France for a short time on the way.'"

The black GIs and the French people developed tight bonds. Music was a core part of the bonding that took place between African Americans and the French. Stovall wrote:

Right from the beginning of its history in New York, the 368th Infantry Regiment included an excellent forty-four-piece jazz band, led by two of Harlem's finest musicians, the bandmaster James Reese Europe and the drum major Noble Sissle. The people of France first heard Europe's band when the 368th Regiment landed at Brest. As an American reporter noted, "The first thing that Jim Europe's outfit did when it got ashore wasn't to eat. It wanted France to know that it was present, so it blew some plain ordinary jazz over the town. Twenty minutes before the 369th disembarked, Brest wasn't at all la-la, so to speak; but as soon as Europe had got to work, that part of France could see that hope wasn't entirely dead."

Experiences like these—working and sharing music—laid the basis for celebration when the war was over, and the African American soldiers got to see Paris. Stovall noted they went all around Paris, visiting the tombs of Lafayette and Napoléon, the chapel of the Invalides, and Père Lachaise Cemetery, where many notables were buried. At the end of the day, they might take a boat ride, "where, somehow, one came in more intimate touch with historical Paris."

Imagine for yourself. Many of these men were themselves heroes, having been decorated by the French for acts of courage on front lines, or decorated by nobody but themselves for having performed outstanding work. To stand at the tomb of a fellow hero—Napoléon or Lafayette—and to identify with the way each fought for a vision of different future. To take a boat ride on the Seine and to experience Paris from its origins on the banks of the river, with natural access to the Louvre, the Eiffel Tower, and Notre Dame. To spend the evening in sidewalk cafés and music clubs, and therefore walking freely from place to place, participating in the feeling of Paris, that certain something that city has above all others, which is the result of the cumulative genius of the people who make and tend the dense urban fabric of the City of Light.

The line, by giving us freedom to move, offers us all those emotions: peace, fear, reconciliation, and hope.

# 6  Tangle

*Keep tangling and interweaving and taking*
*more in,*
*a thicket and bramble wilderness to the*
*outside but to us*
*interconnected with rabbit runs and*
*burrows and lairs.*
                    —Marge Piercy, "The Seven of Pentacles"

THEORETICALLY, I UNDERSTAND interconnection. In practice, it was not easy for me to see that there was a sum of Main Streets that was greater than its parts. When Molly and I visited Cleveland in 2016, I wrote about what we'd seen. It was only on rereading my description of our trip that I noticed the extent to which I had written about the places where we found something (if you go back to chapter 1, you'll see what I mean). We found goods and services in some places, history in others. But I didn't describe the long, nearly empty stretches we drove through in going from one side of town to the other. The fluid interconnections of the mature city had been lost; Molly and I were hopscotching from one bit of intact fabric to another. My understanding of the day elided the empty spaces.

In this diagram of the tangle, Jake indicated the hospitality rating of each Main Street. Our awareness of the tangle is submerged and our eyes are drawn to the high hospitality Main Streets, organized in a line at the foot of the mountain. We see these Main Streets clearly and they are all thriving, even Orange Main Street, which serves poor people and therefore might be expected to be foundering.

The not-seeing of the "empty stretches" and low-hospitality areas is exactly the kind of repression that Hiro asks us to acknowledge in our work in the psychoanalysis of cities. To bring connectedness into consciousness I had to overcome the ways in which American Jim Crow capitalism had trained me to see and not see. It was the poet Michael Lally who enabled this.

The variable hospitality of Main Streets. This diagram, by Jacob Izenberg, shows the tangle of Essex County, with its great variation in the hospitality of the Main Streets.

## The Poetics of the Tangle

It was Michael's poems that helped me at first. His first book of poetry, *The South Orange Sonnets*, is a small collection of poems. I am haunted by the voice of the poems, a white working-class Irish New Jersey voice I had not heard since I finished high school in 1967.[1] It was very specifically the voice of Greg, one of my classmates in grammar school, a big white kid, who shifted between tough and tender. His insights, at twelve and thirteen, were often profound, and I admired him greatly. This gave me the sense that I knew him, but I had never been to his house, did not know who his people were or how they lived.

When I read *The South Orange Sonnets*, I felt that I had gotten to know him for the first time, despite the fact that we had been in school together all those years. Greg and I were separated by race and social group. My mixed-race family was privileged by education and travel; his was ethnic working-class—his father probably worked in a factory in the neighborhood or in construction. I'd never known him before I read this sonnet:

In books it was The Lackawanna Valley,
The Lackawanna Railroad ran through it
separating those on the hill from us.
Lackawanna Place was the toughest block
In the neighborhood until 1952 when
the temptations and reputation moved
to Church Street where THE PINK DEVILS
had roses tattooed between their thumbs
and forefingers, wore delicate gold
crucifixes on chains around their
brown Italian necks, and carried porno
playing cards from Newark, the city
where parades got lost and statues
died. Newark, where we all had lived.[2]

Greg lived in the valley in Orange, and Michael lived in the valley in South Orange, a continuity of culture and ethics and sound, of inflection. I never thought a poem could reveal my life for me in that way, take me to my childhood and open up the meaning behind the words of my classmates. It revealed what had been impenetrable. And it goes a step further, connecting Orange to Newark "where parades got lost and statues died."

"November Sonnet," about the assassination of President John F. Kennedy, starts with standard observations of grief but suddenly twists, as "South Orange Sonnet 1" did, and we find ourselves in the barracks of Fort Monmouth, observing the tragedy from a new perspective:

> On a perfectly clear Fall day, heading back to
> Fort Monmouth, I watched as other cars on
> The Garden State Parkway veered onto the
> shoulder and stopped, the drivers not getting
> out, just sitting there. At the toll booth the man
> said The president's been shot. As I drove on,
> more cars pulled off the road. I could see their
> drivers weeping. Back in the barracks we stayed
> in the rec room watching the black and white
> TV, tension in the room like static. When they
> named Lee Harvey Oswald, I watched the
> black guys hold their breath, hoping that meant
> redneck, not spade, and every muscle in their
> faces relax when he turned out to be white.[3]

We get hints in "November Sonnet" that Michael's empathy takes him inside the lives of other people. In his poem "My Life 2," Michael is quite explicit about how he enters the diversity of the world. He describes thinking that he was Irish, then black, then gay, then a film star, holding these beliefs in spite of evidence to the contrary.[4] It was in those periods that he was inside those identities, assuaging his burning curiosity about the world as seen through the eyes of others.

In 2016 I asked Michael to do a Leap Day reading for the University of Orange from his 2015 book, *Swing Theory*. I was happy that the reading could be at Luna Stage, the small theater on Valley Road, the main street near my house.

During the reading, Michael told stories. One of them was about living in a radical lesbian feminist commune in Washington, D.C. "I just want to read another little section of 'So And' because I think it's kind of interesting. I was talking about the artist Wei Wei, who liked Andy Warhol, who I often criticize, and then I said Warhol got shot by Valerie Solanas. When she got out of the psych hospital they put her in, after her prison time, someone dropped her on the steps of my commune. The women in the commune, who 'til then had been big admirers, became afraid after she moved in. She'd pace, smoking, and mumbling to herself in the communal living room.

"This was, by the way—I should make it clear—this was a lesbian feminist commune. It started out as a revolutionary commune, in D.C., fighting racism, protesting the Vietnam war, all that kind of stuff. And it slowly became lesbian feminist, and I finally moved out. This was before I did. Like the time I came home to find the upstairs toilet plugged because Valerie had ripped up the house copy of her SCUM manifesto, put it in the toilet, then left it, as they all did, for me to plunge.

"For you young people that don't know what that was, it was this: She created it herself, she created this group, but it was just her, called the Society to Cut Up Men. And it got published by a big paperback publishing company. And that's actually why she, one of the reasons she shot Andy. She shot Andy because she wrote scripts for his movies and he didn't pay her and took advantage of people, and she was like, 'He's not gonna get away with that.'

"When I went away for a reading in Boston with some friends, the women in this radical lesbian feminist commune told Valerie I didn't want her there, so she moved out. After I got back and they told me, I was dismayed. I got along fine with her. I kind of enjoyed the way she made all the visitors so nervous with her smoke-filled pacing and muttering in our communal living room. I liked a lot of her ideas, too. She was the first person I knew to explain the difference between men and women by the nerve endings in their genitals and taste buds on their tongues and olfactory absorbers and their sense of smell and color recognition facets of their eyes.

"'Men are simpler,' she'd explain. 'They have so much less of all that, they just miss a lot.' Actually, science caught up with her. She was that crackpot genius who turns out to be right."

It may seem like a leap from my imagining Michael plunging the toilet in the lesbian feminist commune to my seeing the tangle of Main Streets with all its complexity, but that is what happened. When I could hold the whole of the punctured and frayed urban fabric of Essex County in my mind, I began to see parallels with the contraction of urbanism in Southern Vermont. Two disasters allowed me to reflect on the implications of the weakening tangle for our collective lives.

## The Hazards of a Fractured Tangle
### Southern Vermont

I got to know Southern Vermont during annual visits to my medical school classmate, Martha Stitelman. The large cities of Vermont anchor its urbanism, each surrounded by towns, which, in turn, are surrounded by villages. The small villages with a simple general store are the outer edges of this system of organization; it is this outer edge that has wilted as the family farms have disappeared and populations have centralized in the larger towns and cities. I started thinking about the contraction of the small village when we visited Williamsville, a town that had prospered because of its access to water power. Martha pointed out the various parts of what had been center of the village. It struck me, as we stood looking around, that the small village, as a point in the tangle, was dissolving before our eyes.

In the course of our travels, we visited Podunk, which I was surprised to learn was one of four actual places so named. There we saw a marker in the middle of a forest attesting that Daniel Webster spoke to a crowd of fifteen thousand people in that spot. It was difficult for me to imagine where the fifteen thousand people came from. Martha said that she often came across signs of farmhouses as she hiked the second-growth forest. "Remember, all of the forest was cut down and this was all farms."

While Podunk had shrunk more than many of the rural towns of Vermont, this loss of rural population was an on-going process. One of the signs of this was the loss of the general stores, which anchored those small villages. Bill McKibben, a professor at Middlebury College, spoke of the crucial role of the general store in Ripton:

> If towns could write personal ads, this one would be taking pen in hand for the first time in 42 years—making a pitch for companionship, a pitch aimed at finding someone who might be willing to take a chance on something a little out of the Twittery Trumpy twitchy mainstream.
>
> We're a small place—600 or so souls—on the spine of the Green Mountains in the center of the state, not far from Middlebury College. And we're about to lose the heart and soul of our community, the husband and wife who have run our general store since 1976.
>
> Dick and Sue Collitt are retiring, and we need someone to buy them out and take their place. Because if you don't have a store, you can't really have a town.[5]

One day, Martha and I stopped for lunch at the West River General Store. It was operated by the West River Community Center, which raised money to keep it going. We heard about a couple that had come in, sad because they couldn't find their dog. The store clerk happened to know that a dog had been found and was able to reunite dog and family. The story illuminated what McKibben was talking about.

This importance of the disappearance of the general store as the anchor of the small village was not lost on Vermonters. One of the most important signs of this was the annual Strolling of the Heifers on

# Vermont Scroll, 2012–2015

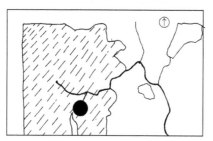

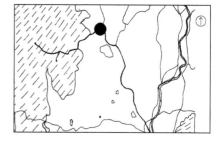

In the course of travels in Vermont, we visited Podunk, where there was a marker in the middle of what is now forest for a meeting with Daniel Webster, attended by 15,000 people. It was difficult for me to imagine where the 15,000 people came from.

While on an annual visit to small towns in Southern Vermont, my medical school classmate, Martha Stitelman, and I stopped for lunch at the West River General Store.

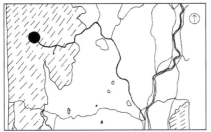

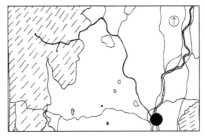

While touring Vermont, Martha pointed out roads and bridges that had been rebuilt, as well as the wash of stones in creeks and rivers that were lasting reminders of the storm damage.

This disappearance of the general store as the anchor of the small village was not lost on Vermonters. One of the most important signs of this is the annual Strolling of the Heifers on Main Streets in Brattleboro, an effort in solidarity with dairy farming, an industry on the decline in Vermont.

Main Street in Brattleboro, an effort started in 2002 to demonstrate solidarity with local farmers, as farming was on the decline in Vermont. In fact, seeing Bernie Sanders stroll down Main Street in Brattleboro in 2015, just as he was launching his first campaign for president, has been one of the highlights of the Main Street study.

It is against this background of a weakening tangle in 2011 that Tropical Storm Irene, predicted to hit the Northeast coast, instead veered inland and dropped eleven inches of rain on Vermont in twenty-four hours. The whole state was affected by the heavy rains and massive flooding, which tore up roads, washed away bridges, felled trees, and battered the sides of creeks and rivers. Residents pulled together in a remarkable commitment to immediate disaster relief. For example, Route 4 near Killington was washed out. People found a half-mile trail through the woods that could connect around the lost roadway. It quickly became a woodlands highway, allowing children to get to school, adults to get to work, and travelers to get from one airport to another. By the time the *New York Times* reporter Michael Winerup got there to investigate for his September 11 article on the trail, the path had acquired porta potties at each end, NO PARKING signs, and volunteers who handed out snacks and water to the walkers.[6]

Winerup talked to the young children who were traversing the woods to get to school. They found the woods a little unsettling. One second grader said, "My hands shaked a little."

> But as Sophia Hussack, another second grader said, "Since Vermont got hit by the storm, people think we couldn't, but we do." And what townspeople do and have done is a thing to behold: they have taken that quiet trail and in two weeks' time turned it into the I-95 of wooded paths. More than a thousand people a day now walk it to get to their jobs and go food shopping on the other side. So many cars line Helvi Hill, the dirt road leading to the path on this side, that handwritten no parking signs have been posted to make sure the road stays passable.[7]

The collaborative spirit did not end with the immediate post-disaster period. The state mounted a thorough disaster-relief intervention and rebuilt the roads, bridges, and other damaged structures. In October 2018, Vermont marked the start of its last Irene recovery project.[8] While touring Vermont, Martha pointed out roads and bridges that had been rebuilt, as well as the wash of stones in creeks and rivers that were lasting reminders of the storm's power.

The state of Vermont was able to deploy effectively resources provided by the Federal Emergency Management Administration to repair damage from Tropical Storm Irene. However, the subsequent effort to get local municipalities to develop disaster mitigation plans was quite slow. A 2016 follow-up noted:

> But [state leaders] also say that only a quarter of the state's municipalities have adopted updated river corridor and or floodplain standards, and a third of municipalities haven't yet adopted a local hazard mitigation plan. Businesses are still shuttering, finding that five years after Irene they weren't able to fully recover.[9]

I would argue that the slowness of that project was a measure of the state of the tangle. I would also argue that a sensitive marker of the state of the tangle is in the stagnation of Vermont's economy. While Vermont ranks high on many markers—it is the safest state in the United States—it is ranked forty-second by *Forbes* magazine as a site for business.[10] *Forbes* predicted stagnation for the foreseeable future. Vermont's major industries are all challenged. Family farming is ill-suited to compete with agribusiness, and climate change will affect its ski, forestry, and maple sugar industries. In such a situation, as with the railways in Essex County, the real test of resilience is the ability to solve a challenging problem. Here Main Streets in general and general stores in particular are an essential but depleted resource.

### Essex County
In Essex County, the tangle, as we have shown in the earlier diagram, was pockmarked with "low hospitality" Main Streets, due either to

disinvestment or to disdain for the older city forms. These breaks have a major effect on the flow of traffic. People don't go where their kind of people don't go. This created a lack of connection throughout the county, and prevented the creation of compassion and empathy that person-to-person connection promotes.

Occasional spots broke the mold. Bragman's Deli in Newark famed for its pastrami and other sandwiches, was a holdover from an earlier time, when the area was a center of Jewish life and culture. A visit to the deli permitted one to cross paths with a wide array of interesting characters, to see the distress of the buildings in the area (and to imagine their potential), and to view efforts at investment, such as a beautiful mural installed across the street. All of these experiences tempered the idea of Newark as a wasteland, and replaced it with a nuanced reality of problems, possibilities, and occasional startling treats.

In general, however, the low-hospitality streets attracted very few outsiders, so these potential experiences were lost. The weak areas were made invisible, which mitigated against the kind of cooperation among cities and neighborhoods, the intergroup solidarity of the people that gets results from politicians. This turned out to be problematic for the larger system of resilience. Superstorm Sandy revealed that the actual harms of low resilience were far-reaching, affecting the well-to-do as well as the poor.

Superstorm Sandy hit New Jersey in October 2012 and caused billions of dollars of damage. Essex County sits on Raritan Bay, and it was hit by a fourteen-foot-high storm surge. As many critical pieces of infrastructure are located along the bay, this was highly disruptive for the whole county.

One of the pieces of infrastructure that was hit hard was the train system, as tracks lie just a few feet above the water and train cars were stored in the wetlands during the storm. New Jersey Transit, the state's bus and rail system, suffered many losses and struggled to recover. The storm damage also uncovered underlying weaknesses in the transit system, which was suffering from years of disinvestment during the administration of Governor Chris Christie. Essex County is served by the Morris-Essex and Montclair-Boonton lines. Train service was badly disrupted in the immediate aftermath of the storm and did not fully recover for months. The underlying problems of inadequate investment and lack of staff were systematically ignored by the state government.

Despite the failure to invest in the railroad system, the state was vigorously pursuing a policy of "transit-oriented" development. This "smart growth" strategy involved densifying housing in the areas around the train stations, from which residents could take the train to work in New York City. This strategy reached Orange, a principal site of the Main Street study. As I have noted in chapter 4, in 2018 the city proposed to adopt an urban renewal plan that would allow it to condemn its historic and thriving Main Street and replace the buildings with transit-oriented new construction for wealthier residents and chain stores.

At the same, New Jersey Transit, burdened by the disinvestment and storm damage, was falling deeper and deeper into trouble. The burden of the collapse of this essential mode of travel was falling on cities and towns all along the rail line, including very poor cities like Newark and very wealthy cities like Millburn and Short Hills.

The problem underlying poor rail service, I contend, was a problem of resilience caused by the extremely poor condition of the tangle in Essex County. That the very wealthy areas were entrained in the process of abandonment of the inner city was predicted by our earlier analysis of Essex County, noted in chapter 5, and confirmed by watching the rail problems intensify.[11] The consequence of the grinding down of neighborhoods is social disintegration, which impedes all efforts at collective thinking and care, among them the debilitating effects of dysfunction on the rails, on the one hand, while pushing rail-oriented development, on the other.

Bragman's Deli.   A deli that stayed in Newark, long after most of the Jewish community had left. It found new fans for its fabulous food.

## Living in the Tangle

From my reflections on Vermont and Essex County, I came to think of the tangle as analogous to the human nervous system, which is organized in a net of nerves and ganglia that relays messages throughout the organism. Doctors have used the study of pathological conditions to learn what happens when a component of the nervous system ceases to function. In a stroke, for example, an area of brain tissue is killed due to lack of oxygen. It might be the part that oversees speech, in which case the patient may not be able to talk anymore, or the part that moves the arms and legs, in which case the patient will be paralyzed. The point is that when one part of the nervous system is not working, this has consequences for the functioning of the whole human being.

To draw out the analogy to the nervous system, when parts of a region have collapsed, this has consequences for the region as a whole. Because it is painful or frightening or taboo to recognize the truth of this, we repress the recognition and act as if everything were fine, as if the pockets of prosperity carried the whole story. We overlook the interdependence of all the parts. We ignore the reality that the prosperous parts also suffer when segments of the city are allowed to fester. There are useful parallels to what happens to people in the aftermath of stroke, when they might ignore the affected part, acting as if it were not there.

This failure to see is lodged deep in the collective consciousness of our country. Miles Orvell, in his excellent book, *The Death and Life of Main Street*, described how this appeared in the seminal work of Helen and Robert Lynd. The Lynds conducted a study of the city of Muncie, Indiana, but only looked at the "white" community, leaving out Jews and blacks who lived in the city.[12] This has been considered one of the most important studies of an American *city*, yet it is obviously not a study of the city. In science, the extension of findings from a group to a whole is a subject of much discussion, as, if not done correctly, such leaps introduce error. This is the scientific error that the Lynds made by their sampling scheme.

Derek Paul argued that medical education makes similar errors because the collective of doctors is not able to take in accurate information about all groups of people. Aptly titled "Ghosts of Our Collective Subconscious," his essay in the *New England Journal of Medicine* marshals a series of experiences to make the point that accurate treatment depends on accurate information, but doctors are not capable of taking in the information they need.[13]

The frayed tangle of Main Streets undermines our functioning; our inability to see and attend to the problem is perhaps even more serious. [14] The tangle, the net of nodes and connectors, is only as strong as we make it. And we are only as strong as the tangles in which we find ourselves. We need to see the tangle so that we can tend it. Per the poet Marge Piercy, we must keep tangling.

# 7   Time

*Look back on time with kindly eyes,*
*He doubtless did his best...*
—Emily Dickinson, poem 8 from
*Time and Eternity*

OVER MILLENNIA, THE Colorado River has run through stone, slowly etching the Grand Canyon. It took the relentless motion of time and water to make nature's masterpiece, one of the seven wonders of the natural world. François Leydet used the phrase "time and the river flowing" to title his gripping book about the Grand Canyon. The canyons of Main Street are similarly shaped by the flow of time and city life. Cantal commented on this: "The urbanist makes decisions that affect our way of life but is not a master of space, which is perpetually remodeled by the individuals who inhabit it."[1]

I didn't know about this incessant process when I started this study of Main Street. In the beginning, I was going to visit two cities a week and be done in a year. Because of competing demands, I had to give up that pace. Then, as I pondered what I was seeing on Main Streets, I found I had more questions than answers. The process slowed so that I could have time. As they say, "Time takes time."

Slowly, I learned to see. My earliest field note described a February 2008 visit to Maplewood, New Jersey, where I had gone for lunch with my sister-in-law, Patty Fullilove. I noted that it was a busy, short, three-block Main Street, not for business, but for middle-class loitering. Mothers or babysitters were out with preschoolers in their strollers. I was impressed by the amount of communication that was going on: It was Election Day and there were Obama posters plastered all over, even in the post office, as well as a message board and signs in many store windows. Although we didn't see the store that Patty used to frequent to get her sons' Scout uniforms, we did see a "good collection of main things": post office, Kings supermarket, movie theater, old-fashioned corner store, and Bill & Harry's Chinese takeout. I was annoyed by a small park across from the train station, which I deemed useless. It was a cold winter day, so no one was on the benches. I couldn't imagine anyone using them at any time. "Not an eddy pool," I declared.

When I moved to West Orange in 2010, I learned that Maplewood's Main Street, with its good collection of main things, was very useful. For example, there was the ice-cream store. In the winter, people go in singly, but in summer, baseball teams, kids attending birthday parties, and Scout troops all show up. There is Words, a bookstore that I frequent, and an outstanding pizza restaurant, which is so good that I can hardly ever get in. I have friends who live in the area, like Michael Lally, and so I run into them while strolling on the street. One day, I ran into Michael in the bookstore, where he was buying Christmas presents in January. "I have a hard time choosing presents," he confided, "but my family is coming over today." We were going in opposite directions, as I had to go to the bank and he had other errands. But I stopped in the bakery a bit later, and there he was, having a bite of lunch. I sat with him and caught up on gossip.

That is the kind of day a Main Street with main things offers to a person with a bit of time and money, but it's a huge shift from the rather stern judgment I felt entitled to make on my first visit to Maplewood's Main Street. I was right about the park and its benches. I have not seen anyone sit on them. There is an annual

Christmas display of little houses—something to do with Charles Dickens—that seems to be a holdover from earlier times, not part of the hip "If Brooklyn were a suburb" place Maplewood has become during these years of my fieldwork.[2] But that is the only use of that park—not an eddy pool, as I declared so forcefully on my first visit.

I see differently when I've had time to visit a place over and over again, but I also see differently even if I'm going to a place for the first time. I have come to see each Main Street as a pastiche of all the Main Streets I've visited and revisited over time. I am aware of the box/circle/line/tangle, I assess the collection of main things, and examine the communications of all kinds, from message boards to garbage cans. I am attuned to appreciate what people are doing, how they are holding on, the ways in which their aspirations are manifesting. I know that a sad, one-store Main Street holds history I can never imagine. I am not so easily dismissive, deeming something useless after a single glance, even if I might be right.

That said, not only do I see differently but also many things are different. Cantal and I were talking about the slow unfolding of change in the French city of Perpignan. He said, "You've seen a lot over these nine years. You've seen projects that took off, and projects that went bust. Projects that should have worked and didn't, and projects that had no reason to work and did. How do you put it all together? Why does it matter?"

## How Main Streets Changed

There are four New Jersey Main Streets that I designated as places I would return to often: Palisades Avenue, Englewood; Main Street, Orange; the Boardwalk at Asbury Park; and Newark Avenue, Jersey City. Watching a street over eleven years allows one to see the unfolding of change, which is the work of time and the river of life. New Jersey, one of the richest states in the nation, went into recession in 2008, along with the rest of the nation. Governor Chris Christie's policies delayed full recovery for a decade, but the explosion of a Manhattan-based upper middle class employed in the finance/insurance/real estate (FIRE) industries spilled over into northern New Jersey. The impact may have been augmented by the lagging economy on our side of the Hudson which made the cost of living seem like a bargain to New Yorkers.

Just before this study started, Englewood's Palisades Avenue ruptured its other-side-of-the-tracks system of segregation with urban renewal that replaced a motley set of older homes and businesses with a "Towne Centre," a nondescript apartment building that occupied a full city block and had large storefronts facing the Avenue, as locals call it. Englewood had undertaken urban renewal before, taking out a chunk of downtown to the north of Palisades Avenue to make way for a Shoprite and its parking lot, and another chunk to the south to put in garden apartments. This was the third chunk of functional downtown to be replaced. In scale and function, the Towne Centre was different from the buildings that replaced it.

It is useful here to turn to the wisdom of the great American urbanist Jane Jacobs, who emphasized the benefits of a mix of buildings with slightly different setbacks from the street, and lots of entrances to promote flow and maintain the stream of eyes on the street. In each instance of urban renewal in Englewood, the complexity of the city was diminished, its entrances minimized, and its flow undermined. The civic presence on Palisades Avenue is small: a modest City Hall that does very little for the street.

The street has struggled to be stable. In fall 2019, Lily Johnson returned to Palisades Avenue to revisit her 2009 evaluation of the difference between businesses on the east side of the tracks and those on the west side. She found the ninety-five stores she'd originally identified were all physically the same, and were serving the same array of commercial uses. On the pricier east side of the tracks, 43 percent of the stores were the same; there were three vacancies, 9 percent of the total. On the more humble west side, 59 percent of the stores were the same; three stores sat empty, 5 percent of the total. The vacancies included one large store on the east side, a former appliance store, and a string of large stores on the west side that occupied nearly a block.

As in Englewood, Main Street, Orange, had ground-floor stores that served the same set of commercial purposes throughout the period. Largely occupied despite some turnover, its businesses were busy serving the people of the neighborhood. I served on the board of HANDS, the local community development corporation, and paid particular attention to the series of stores that operated out of the storefront in the organization's historic headquarters building. There were several restaurants, a natural cosmetics store, a teen center, and a skateboard shop over that period. It was the skateboard shop that managed to take hold, but that was only after a new set of apartment buildings improved the flow past us on South Essex Street. A third apartment building, a nondescript structure opposite the train station, added to new residents around Main Street, but a lack of urbanism meant that the space was not fully integrated and enhanced to make it a workable whole in the way that nearby Montclair and South Orange had managed to do.

I typically visit the Boardwalk at Asbury Park only in the summers, and the pleasure of being there makes it a favorite of mine. We have had that great Jersey pleasure of spending a few days or even a week "down the shore." Besides swimming and barbecuing, such times include the search for the ultimate ice cream. There are always two or three major ice-cream spots on the Boardwalk. The Boardwalk, the beach, and related buildings were damaged by Hurricane Sandy, and walking there with disaster experts was a painful and important experience. It was good to see the Boardwalk rebuilt after the disaster. It has been more challenging to see the arrival of substantial investment, bringing fancy apartments and wealthier people to what was a low-key, working-class town with a beach.

But it's the downtown section of Newark Avenue in Jersey City that has been most thoroughly remade by change in this period of observation. From one end to the other, Newark Avenue is just over a mile long. In the spirit of a long urban street, it passes through a number of different sections. One of my early formal visits to Newark Avenue was with David Chapin in 2010, even before we walked Broadway with Hirofumi Minami. I met David at Journal Square and we drove around for a bit to see some of Jersey City before parking near the Justice Brennan Courthouse and starting our tour. I told him how, when I first started visiting Jersey City twenty years earlier, I had been put off by the motley aspect, that no two houses seemed to be alike. By 2010, I'd come to enjoy it and was very happy during the year I spent living there.

The area around the courthouse was an excellent example of the motley quality I was talking about. The buildings, which were older, housed a variety of shops and law offices. Molly, a longtime Jersey City resident, had commended Moloney's Butcher Shop to me. It was an old-style butcher shop, with sawdust on the floor and meats of every description hanging on hooks. The staff was friendly and welcoming. After Moloney's, we passed some rather forlorn places, such as a thrift shop with a cute monkey and old gel rollers in the window. Lots of the businesses had been taken over by immigrants to serve their communities, giving new vitality to the old. Some of the new businesses were famous, Molly said, like the Phillipine Bread House.

One block west from the courthouse block was Five Corners, with a great display of the variety Jersey City has to offer. We saw a modernist library, a 1920s bank building and office building, and a 1950s pseudocolonial drive-through banking center. As we crossed Summit Avenue and headed down the hill, we passed Monteleone's Bakery, another historic establishment. Across the street, there was a modernist apartment building, which was disconnected from the street, breaking the strong street wall that we'd experienced up to that point.

We crossed Kennedy Boulevard and headed into Little India, the densest and most active part of Newark Avenue. The venerable Singh's Department Store, with a variety of statues in the window, clearly dated back to the 1950s, which indicated that for a long period of time this had been a section of town where Indians gathered. I showed a photo of the store's window to my friend and colleague Nupur Chaudhury, who explained what we had seen. "When I look at this picture, I think about celebration. The colorful sticks are *dandiya*, sticks that are used for a regional Gujarati dance, *Raas Garba*. As Gujarati, we often had evenings of *Garba* during times of celebration, like a wedding. I think about peace. In the window, there are depictions of Ganesh, Krishna, Shiva, Natraj. These are all gods that I grew up worshipping. They provide a sense of peace and comfort when I see them.

"And seeing them all together, I think of home. In this country, there are very few *mandhirs* [temples]. South Asians often develop a mini *mandir* or altar in their basements, or off of their kitchens. Growing up, I had one such altar. Seeing all these [statues of] Shiva, Ganesh, Krishna all together, it reminds me of my childhood altar. As a South Asian, I did not grow up with a lot of South Asians around me. And so the idea of a place or space where I could be truly myself was nonexistent. Instead, I took refuge in mini pockets of home throughout the world, which brought me back to my heritage and my home. Often it was the sound of a language, a smell of food, a few bars of a song, or the touch of a fabric. Sometimes, it was seeing windows just like this window here."

Just across the street from Singh's, we passed a woman who was making an elaborate design on the sidewalk. Nupur explained that this was a *rangoli*, an Indian art form. Designs are made on the floor or the ground with materials such as dry rice.[3] "My mom had so many stories of doing *rangoli* for holidays. It's something I wished we did here in the States; it seemed like such fun. Being able to do *rangoli* means you have space, you own space, and you are willing to be open about it. It's such a public act, saying 'We're here! We're Indian!'"

In 2010, that two-block stretch was owned by Indians. Some were there to buy useful products—first and foremost groceries, sometimes in bulk for restaurants, or in smaller quantities for home use. After

# Jersey City Scroll, 2010

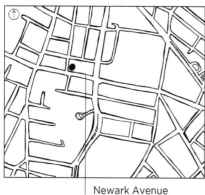

Newark Avenue

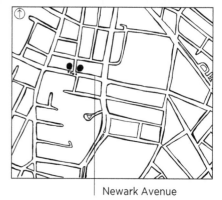

Newark Avenue

We started at the Courthouse. We crossed Kennedy Boulevard and headed into Little India, the densest and most active part of Newark Avenue. The venerable Singh's Department Store, with a variety of statues in the window, clearly dated back to the 1950s, which indicated that for a long period of time this had been a section of town where Indians gathered.

We passed a woman who was making an elaborate design on the sidewalk. I later learned from Nupur Chaudhury that this was a rangoli, an Indian art form. Designs are made on the floor or the ground with materials such as dry rice. "Being able to do rangoli means you have space, you own space, and you are willing to be open about it. It's such a public act, saying 'We're here! We're Indian!'"

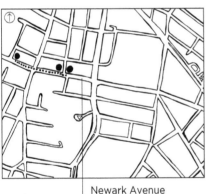

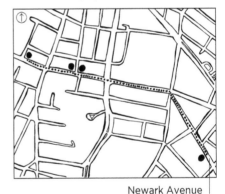

| Newark Avenue | Newark Avenue |

We continued down the hill toward the hulking remains of some of Jersey City's great factories. I pointed out my favorite old-time neon sign, which read STARR'S STEAKS FRYS BURGERS. Hanging just parallel was a bright blue banner, put up by the city, which read WELCOME TO THE NEW JOURNAL SQUARE.

We walked back to the courthouse and went inside. David pointed out that it was built before the invention of fluorescent lights. The courthouse architects, working hard to bring light into the building, used skylights to illuminate a central atrium and placed offices around the outside of the building.

*Photos by David Chapin, used with permission.*

that, saris and jewelry were popular on the street. And restaurants abounded, catering to a variety of tastes and dietary preferences.

Little India had the same diversity of building materials as other parts of the street. David commented that every building had a different surface material; we saw brick, aluminum, asbestos, and wood. The materials were of different colors and textures. "I feel like I'm in a museum of surfaces," David joked. "We don't appreciate the urbanism of motley the way we should. It's like *Learning from Las Vegas*, although that book, for all its strengths, overlooked gangs and other dark truths of that city."

We continued down the hill toward the hulking remains of some of Jersey City's great factories. I pointed out my favorite old-time neon sign, which read STARR'S STEAKS FRYS BURGERS. Hanging just parallel was a bright blue banner, put up by the city, which read WELCOME TO THE NEW JOURNAL SQUARE.

We walked back to the courthouse and went inside. David pointed out that it was built before the invention of fluorescent lights. The courthouse architects, working hard to bring light into the building, used skylights to illuminate a central atrium and placed offices around the outside of the building. We read on a plaque that the courthouse had been threatened with demolition. Theodore Conrad, an architect and model maker, mounted a campaign to save it. He made a model so that people could appreciate its splendor, and got twenty thousand people to sign a petition. It was declared a historic landmark and protected. After our visit, we drove back down the hill to have tea with Molly at a Vietnamese restaurant.

David and I didn't visit the downtown stretch, the last major section of Newark Avenue, but I knew that area well, as I lived nearby at the time, and walked through there to get the train to work. It was a center for shopping for the nearby residents, older communities founded by immigrants and migrants from many nations and places, including Puerto Rico, the American South, and Eastern Europe. They had been joined in more recent decades by artists and "urban pioneers," middle-class people who were venturing into the "inner city" because of cheap and convenient housing. They were adding their own businesses to the mix: restaurants, an art-supply store, and coffee shops among them.

After I moved to West Orange, I would often return to Jersey City to visit family and friends, entering Newark Avenue by the Starr's sign and following the street to downtown. I watched as Little India filled in the few vacant lots that had been there in 2010, saw a set of older buildings in the courthouse area be demolished to be replaced by new, grander ones, and witnessed the downtown transform in audience and form.

In 2019, I asked anthropologist Edgar Rivera Colón to walk with me in downtown. He had grown up in the area, part of its dense Puerto Rican community. At the time of our walk, he was living on Grove Street, several blocks over from Newark Avenue. The first block of Newark Avenue had been made into a pedestrian block a few years before, and the second block more recently, so I parked just beyond the pedestrian plaza and walked to the meeting point. As it was 10:00 A.M. on a Sunday, the walkway was nearly empty. In front of C. H. Martin, a young man was putting up the steel window grates. Edgar was looking around the plaza when I arrived. "None of this was here," he said of the plaza. "It was just a pit for the subway."

We walked north on Grove Street, and he pointed out the buildings and businesses owned by the Latino community, including a small supermarket, La Conga, and a restaurant that used to serve Cuban food but had been rented out to others. At the corner of Grove and Morgan streets, he pointed to a several-story building that had once been a community center run by a Jesuit priest, who loved serving the Puerto Rican community. Edgar's parents had met at a dance in that community center.

Edgar made the first of several points about the meaning of time. "What I see are layers of time. When I go down Newark Avenue or Grove Street, I see what's there, and I see what's been there, and that I'm comparing it in terms of, like, the kind of relationships that I had in the former place, that led me to now. So, time has this relational aspect. It's not linear, right? It's a sort of spiral, but it returns to itself in one sense."

As we walked west on Newark Avenue, looking at what was there, we were able to investigate this idea, as well as begin to examine a second idea: the endurance of the old intermingled with the new. The hardware store and Torico's were old-time businesses, while Porta and the Ashford were new, serving the gentrifying population. C. H. Martin, an old store, served everyone, and would, he thought, survive. The dollar store, 99¢ Dream, was run by merchants who owned their building, protecting them for a while. We passed several markets that had had trouble since traffic had been banned, because it was difficult for them to get their deliveries. In addition, they were burdened, as everyone was, with rising property taxes. It was the property taxes that had forced Molly's landlord to put his building on the market. When it was sold, she would no longer be able to afford to live there, or anywhere in the neighborhood, for that matter, a fact that left her feeling chased from her home.

James Solomon, the area councilman, came by, hurrying to a meeting. He was a fellow professor of Saint Peter's University and stopped to say hello to Edgar. He was pushing for tax protections for small businesses, as well as other interventions that could stop the displacement of people from the neighborhood and the city.

One pattern was clear from our five-block walk. The people who had been able to buy their buildings back in the day when Jersey City was suffering from disinvestment were still in place. Many of their businesses were still viable. Tax increases were a distinct threat, as was the recent evolution, which we could see was far from over. Edgar suggested we go to a unique business, Subia's, where we could have some tea and talk more. That business, Edgar explained, was located in a building a Puerto Rican family owned. They had once operated a bodega, but when the business was transferred to the daughters, they decided to transform it into a vegan restaurant. As it was two blocks from where I had lived in Jersey City, it was a place

I had frequented, without knowing its history, only its delicious food and quiet atmosphere.

One of the co-owners, Yvonne Rodriguez, was there and sat with us for a while to tell the story of the restaurant. She had worked in corporate America for twenty years before taking over her family's business. "I said, 'If I'm going to leave the corporate world, I'm going to do something I believe in.'"

She'd been researching the vegan industry and where she thought the world was going. That made her determined to start the restaurant. "It was rough for several years," she noted, speaking about starting the restaurant sixteen years earlier. "And the world caught up with us finally. It's been a big push, as more documentaries come out, and then the more we see all the stuff that's happening with the environment due to overusage of water, and animals and all that. We have people from all over the world coming here. Vegans who travel find a spot, because they are committed to this."

While her restaurant was serving the world by offering tasty vegan food, it was doing much more for the community than that. Edgar noted that Yvonne and her sister Nilsa took in youth from the neighborhood and helped them get on their feet. Yvonne said it was something she was committed to, and part of her mission on earth. "Sometimes I happen to find souls in the streets that I'm not sure which direction they're going, and I reel them in, and give them a job, train them, make them part of the movement, make them understand that they're part of something bigger than themselves, and that they're useful to society and that they're here for a cause and for a reason. And it seems to help them stay on track and clean up their lives."

Her current chef was an example, a young man just out of high school, who'd recently become a vegan but was confused about his life and lacking direction. Yvonne took him in and her chef taught him to cook. The young man had blossomed and was gaining renown as a vegan chef, with a following of his own, including a podcast.

## Jersey City Scroll, 2019

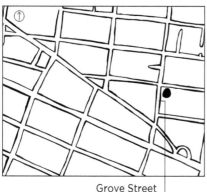

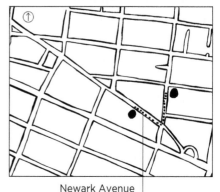

Grove Street

Newark Avenue

We walked north on Grove Street, and he pointed out the buildings and businesses owned by the Puerto Rican community, including a small supermarket, La Conga, and a restaurant that used to serve Puerto Rican food, but had been rented out to others.

The hardware store and the pharmacy were old-time Puerto Rican businesses, while Porta and The Ashford were new, serving the gentrifying population.

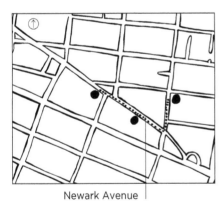

Newark Avenue | | Jersey Avenue

The dollar store, 99¢ Dreams, was run by merchants who owned their building, protecting them for a while.

While we were talking in Subia, I had the chance to take in the painting that was on the wall in front of me. It showed Our Lady in a posture of humble submission, but with her foot firmly on a snake.

We all agreed that it was small, locally owned businesses that had a possibility of caring for youth in this important manner.

While we were talking, I had the chance to take in the painting that was on the wall in front of me. It showed Our Lady in a posture of humble submission, but with her foot firmly on a snake. That seemed emblematic of the role of women in the community, which Edgar described as a strong matriarchal society. His sister, he noted, was the first out lesbian to be the matriarch in their extended family network. People went to her for advice and for help with keeping the young on the right path. Yvonne and Nilsa, by providing connection for the young, were part of this network of women keeping the youth on the straight and narrow.

Yet the intense pressure of gentrification was pushing the poor— and even the not-so-poor, like Molly—out of the neighborhood, disrupting networks that had been built over more than seventy years. Edgar challenged the idea that time was simply time; he thought we had to think of it as spatial, as well. "For me, as a kid growing up, like let's say this ghetto kid, growing up in this world that was black, Puerto Rican, some Cuban, Polish, Irish, Italian, what a sociologist would call 'white ethnics.' Time for me growing up was ten blocks. As I got older, I realized, oh, there was a city, right? And I began to also expand my vision of time, but it also grounded me, because I was from a certain time-place. Right? And I never lost that. And believe me, I think there was a bunch of institutions devoted for me to lose that, right?"

Edgar described the massive forces of big capital that were pushing the change on the macro level, disrupting the grounding of the block. He emphasized, "In the old, old political discourse of traditional Marxism there was a notion that a people is connected to a land. And for us it's not agricultural land; it's the block. It's the block I grew up on. Who wouldn't know you on that block?"

As we talked, it became clear that what he was describing was even larger than displacement from the block; it included the massive displacement that followed deindustrialization. People had moved to Jersey City to work in the factories. Edgar's mother worked in garment factories in Hoboken, his father in a factory in Kearny. Edgar noted, "There was this material underpinning, the Dixon, the Emerson, all these factories, in fact, the culture that went with it. So yeah. And then, my father always said, 'You know, I began on a machine and I ended baking chips in some oven.'

"I can remember my own block. Older couple, Polish couple, had no children. Lived with the grandfather, or the grandfather lived with them. Didn't speak a word of English, just called him 'Papa.' And she worked at the Maxwell House plant over in Hoboken. Other people worked at the Emerson Factory. Other people worked in what they called '*las maletas*,' which is basically suitcase factories. So, that world disappears. It gets sent to the south, less union penetration, except for the case of Allentown, where there was union penetration."

Thus, the disruption of the stable blocks was ungrounding the people, in the largest sense of that word. That some could stay in no way mitigated the disruption of the group. At the same time, this disruption was not a first—Puerto Ricans had been uprooted from Puerto Rico and had come to the mainland in the aftermath of vast changes in the farming systems on the island in the postwar era. They came for work in factories in Jersey City and elsewhere, as had all the other working people who'd made their way to Jersey City, my father among them. The earlier experiences meant that people understood the harms of displacement and, to the extent possible, fought against them. Edgar was concerned that the opposition to all the upheaval, which was everywhere, had not yet articulated a vision of the way forward. Nor had anyone really understood that "gentrifiers" were really the replacement workers. The unskilled were being pushed out to make room for skilled workers, who commanded higher pay but worked under their own dreadful conditions of insecurity and helplessness.

In the midst of this bleak exploration of the effects of time and macroeconomic forces on his community, Edgar paused to tell a story of hope. "I had an interesting encounter when I was in the

Twin Cities in Minnesota. I was sitting with a friend of mine's mom and dad, folks who had been displaced from Laos. Bee, my friend, was going to go to Brown, which would be his first time living on the East Coast. His dad said to me, 'Take care of my son.'

"That kid was more than able to take care of himself, and he had hooked himself up with a bunch of professors at Brown. But I told the dad—and this is all in translation, because the father didn't speak a word of English—'You know, I know you folks are mountain people.'

"He said, 'Yeah, we're mountain people.'

"I said, 'So, my dad's family in Puerto Rico, they were moonshiners in the mountains.'

"The dad replied, 'Oh, really?'

"And he took out this bottle of moonshine and he puts it in front of me. Bee says to him, 'Dad, don't give it to him; he's going to get drunk.'

"And his dad looked at him and said, 'Don't worry about it. His ancestors made moonshine; he has it in his blood.'"

I was struck by the similarity to Michael Lally's ideas on time. One of his books of poetry is entitled *It's Not Nostalgia*. For a conference on nostalgia, I talked to him about his poem and his ideas. Michael told me, "Scientists and researchers have recently confirmed my childhood belief that I had within me not just 'the blood of my ancestors,' as they would say back then before genes were discovered or were common knowledge—or at least common terminology—but their traumas and other experiences. So my grandfather's crossing the Atlantic in a ship belowdecks as a teenager farther and farther from his home—a home I only encountered as an adult but was moved to tears by, as were my older children, despite their never having known him when I took them to the thatched-roof cottage in Ireland where he grew up—not only lived within me but so did that home.

"When I first saw the landscape of the area where he lived as a boy, it was the same as the one I saw in my mind when I needed comforting as a boy and soothed myself with that image! I think most of us have these experiences but are perhaps not as conscious of them as those who are particularly sensitive to them. Anyway, science does seem to continually confirm what poets and other creative folks have been expressing throughout history. And, by the way, that history isn't just our immediate ancestry, obviously, so that the earlier traumas of most so-called ethnic groups converge the further back you go, etc., until you get to Lucy or whoever Eve truly was."

# Part Three

# Naming & Framing
# The Problem

# 8 The Great Mistake

*We are the American heartbreak—*
*The rock on which Freedom*
*Stumped its toe—*
*The great mistake*
*That Jamestown made*
*Long ago.*
—Langston Hughes, "American Heartbreak"

I BELIEVE THAT Main Streets serve us as a net of connections, a source of knowledge about our society, and a tool for naming and framing our problems and fixing them. In this section of the book, I focus on this task of naming and framing our problems, not the "Main Street is dead" problems, but the larger problems facing U.S. society. There are three that I find to be of particular importance: the deep structure of inequality in which we find ourselves; the shifts and threats resulting from ecological damage; and the inertial forces defending the status quo. Here I tackle the sources and structures of inequality.

In 1619, a ship landed at Point Comfort in Virginia and traded twenty or so Africans for provisions. Those Africans were sold into indentured servitude, the beginning of what would become chattel slavery. The *New York Times* special magazine *1619* argued that

1619 is as important a date in U.S. history as is 1776.[1]

Indeed, everything about the development of slavery hinged on asserting that Africans were not fully human and therefore might be stripped of the "natural rights" of people. They belonged to their owners, who had the right of life and death over them, as well as the right to use them as they saw fit. Enslaved people were denied the status of "created equal," which animates the Declaration of Independence and inspires us to this day to struggle toward that ideal. In the many petitions enslaved people wrote to argue for liberty, they constantly challenged the denial of their humanity.

In this example, Benjamin Banneker, astronomer and almanac author, wrote to Thomas Jefferson on the evident contradiction:

> Sir,
>
> I am fully sensible of the greatness of that freedom, which I take with you on the present occasion; a liberty which Seemed to me scarcely allowable, where I reflected on that distinguished and dignified station in which you Stand; and the almost general prejudice and prepossession which is so prevalent in the world against those of my complexion.
>
> I suppose it is a truth too well attested to you, to need a proof here, that we are a race of Beings who have long labored under the abuse and censure of the world, that we have long been looked upon with an eye of contempt, and that we have long been considered rather as brutish than human, and Scarcely capable of mental endowments....
>
> Now Sir if this is founded in truth, I apprehend you will readily embrace every opportunity, to eradicate that train of absurd and false ideas and opinion which so generally prevails with respect to us, and that your sentiments are concurrent with mine, which are that one universal Father hath given being to us all...
>
> [It] is now Sir that your abhorrence thereof was so excited, that you publicly held forth this true and invaluable doctrine, which is worthy to be recorded and remember'd in all Succeeding ages. "We hold these truths to be self-evident, that all men are created equal,

and that they are endowed by their creator with certain unalienable rights, that among these are life, liberty and the pursuit of happiness." Sir, ... as Job proposed to his friends, "Put your Souls in their souls stead[.]" [T]hus shall your hearts be enlarged with kindness and benevolence toward them, and thus shall you need neither the direction of myself or others in what manner to proceed herein. ... And now Sir, I shall conclude and Subscribe my Self with the most profound respect your most Obedient humble Servant,

Benjamin Banneker[2]

The dehumanization of Native Americans, women, Jews, and, later, immigrants, sexual minorities, and other religious minorities parallels that of Africans. One might say that the *concept* of inequality became a *tool* of social control specifically used to prevent working people from joining in unity and demanding a fair share of the profits of their labor. This use of inequality to divide and conquer has clear roots in the American colonial era. Bacon's Rebellion in 1676 involved a thousand people, diverse in race and class. Troubled by the threat of such unity, the colonial authorities created penalties that punished black enslaved people more harshly than white indentured servants or free men. This differential treatment was embedded in the Virginia Slave Codes of 1705.

Danielle Allen, in her book *Our Declaration: A Reading of the Declaration of Independence in Defense of Equality*, pointed out, "The Declaration of Independence matters because it helps us see that we cannot have freedom *without* equality. It is out of an egalitarian commitment that a people grows—a people that is capable of protecting us all collectively, and each of us individually, from domination. If the Declaration can stake a claim to freedom, it is only because it is so clear-eyed about the fact that the people's strength resides in its equality."[3]

Allen's contention—that a people's strength resides in its equality —speaks directly to the sociology of collective consciousness. Scientists have suggested that one of humankind's greatest achievements is to distribute consciousness among people, to embed our thinking in our working groups, not simply in the individual. It is this that has enabled people to make such magnificent achievements as pyramids and dams and railroad tracks. Yet the working group is only as strong as its ability to incorporate the thoughts and knowledge of all its members. The great cost of inequality is that whole portions of the working group are excluded from the process of collective thinking and problem solving.

If inequality is a threat to the survival of our species as we face ecological transitions surpassing any in human experience, then the question arises, "How do we get rid of inequality?" In other words, how do we realize the promise of our Declaration of Independence?

I had worked on an anniversary observance before and knew the contributions it could make. In 2001, after the World Trade Center was destroyed in a terrorist attack, we at the Community Research Group started a project we called "NYC RECOVERS." It was a project to mobilize organizations to attend to the collective recovery of the Greater New York Region. As we approached the first anniversary, it became clear that we all had fear and unresolved emotions that would get worse as we got closer to the dreaded date. Working with the organizations in our network, we developed a plan for managing the anniversary by tucking it inside "September Wellness Month." That provided a wonderful cushion, pointing us away from one terrible day, toward a month of self- and collective caring. During that month, I attended meditation sessions, went to health fairs and concerts, and gathered with people in solidarity. Although we throw the word *healed* around rather too glibly, my terrors were assuaged and I ended the month with a greater confidence in the power of the city to heal us all.[4]

It was this experience that came to mind when I realized, in 2016, that the 400th anniversary of 1619 was three years away. Might we use the occasion of the anniversary and the feelings it would provoke to chip away at the *concept* and *tool* of inequality? This was in the spring of 2016, as Donald Trump was unleashing his racist campaign for president of the nation. Molly and the University of Orange team agreed with my idea, and we launched a call for observance. The first public presentation was at my "job talk" at the New School. Bill Morrish said afterward, "Let's go!"

When I started to work at the New School that fall, Bill created the first architecture of our project. He started with the Constitution's Three-Fifths Compromise but argued that more and more of us—not simply African Americans—were being treated as less than a full person as wealth was concentrated among the few. He expressed this as "<3/5."

He identified our starting point, 2016–2017, as 3/5ths, the next year, 2017–2018, as 4/5ths, and the final year, 2018–2019, as

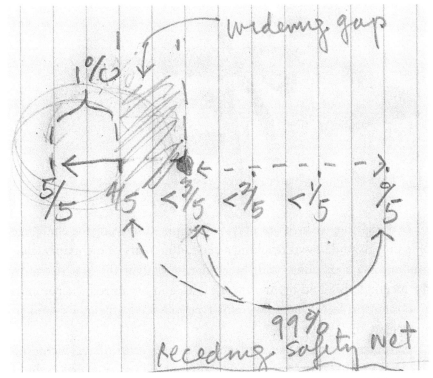

The Architecture of the Project. William Morrish conceived the architecture of the project. *Drawing used with permission.*

5/5ths. In the fall of 2019, we would call for observances all across the nation.

### The 3/5ths' Academic Year, 2016–2017

That fall, the University of Orange reached out to other organizations to recruit a set of "founding" partners. Bill Morrish, Robert Sember, and I represented The New School. Dominic Moulden brought ONE DC into the mix. Roisin Davis, of Voices of People's History, arrived shortly after, as did Bob Fullilove, of Columbia's Mailman School of Public Health. The New School became a gathering place for representatives of our five organizations, and we developed the practice of meeting weekly in a small conference room in the Milano building, where my office was housed.

<3/5 William Morrish made this image to get us started. *Used with permission.*

In the spring, we held our first symposium, discussing the challenge of losing ground. I was teaching a class, 400 Years of Inequality, that was making a timeline, and the students brought the first drafts to the meeting. Bill laid them out on tables and organized the room to give them pride of place. Watching people study them, I began to appreciate their power.

Gathered round those artifacts, a small group of us, including the UofO team, people from other organizations, and New School faculty and students, talked about the project. With a day to reflect

The Draft Timeline.  The draft timeline made by my class, 400 Years of Inequality, on display at our first syposium.

on our situation—Divided We Fall, according to me—and to articulate what we were FOR, we solidified our sense that our project was worthwhile.

As the class finished the first version of the timeline, fellow faculty member Michael Park pointed out that the periods of great advancement had been characterized by the rise of coalitions. My father, Ernest Thompson, emphasized the building of coalitions as a key lesson that he had learned in the union organizing of the 1940s and brought to community organizing in

Orange. We recognized that our project, by lifting up the ubiquitous nature of inequality, laid groundwork for common cause among many disadvantaged groups. Our organizing committee proposed three books for people to study: *Voices of a People's History*, the documentary history that accompanies Howard Zinn's *A People's History of America*; Ernie's book, *Homeboy Came to Orange: A Story of People's Power*; and the Reverend William Barber's book, *The Third Reconstruction: How a Moral Movement Is Overcoming the Politics of Division and Fear*.

## The 4/5ths' Academic Year, 2017–2018

We used the opportunity of a fall "curriculum disruption" to spread the message to the New School community. This is a New School practice of designating a week when faculty can set aside "teaching as usual" and examine a designated topic. The fifty faculty members who shared their plans used their own course material as the starting point for class conversation. They were remarkably inventive. One professor of music played an abolitionist version of "The Star-Spangled Banner," then invited students to write their own anthems. Another professor investigated inequality in the "canon," the artwork deemed most worthy and collected in museums. A third taught about protest songs across many generations. This inspired me to think that the observances we hoped to see in 2019 would be equally unique.

Right: Winning poster. Madhuri Shukla won our contest for a poster to advertise the curriculum disruption.

I was teaching my course 400 Years of Inequality for the second time that semester. The goal of the class was to refine the timeline, which was a hard job, eased by the help of Octavia Driscoll and her remarkable talent for organization. It was also a time to consider my own understanding of the history. Like my students, I had to rethink many stories I'd been told—for example, that John Smith quelled noblemen's laziness in Jamestown by saying, "If you don't work, you don't eat." For us at Tremont Avenue School in Orange, this made perfect sense, as our parents expected us to do our chores. As it turned out, this was profoundly simplistic.

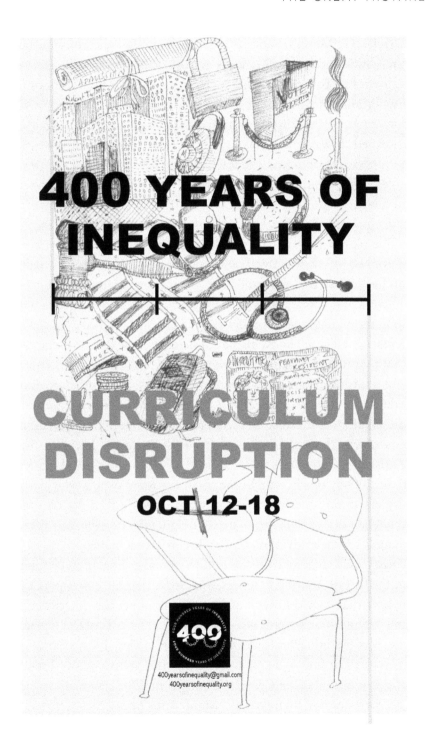

400 YEARS OF
INEQUALITY

CURRICULUM
DISRUPTION
OCT 12-18

400yearsofinequality@gmail.com
400yearsofinequality.org

Charles G. Mann's book *1493*, which tackles the consequences for the New World of Columbus's arrival, ably explores the story of Jamestown in "Tobacco Coast," a chapter devoted to the story of the colony. Mann's central point is that the creation of the colony was an encounter of the European and American ecosystems, which are transformed in ways that make them more homogeneous. He opens with an observation about the lowly earthworm, which did not exist in Jamestown at that time. The creatures were probably dumped with ship ballast, which was exchanged for tobacco. As the earthworms spread, they did their work of turning the detritus of the forest into soil. The plants and animals that had depended on that forest cover were robbed of their habitat and sustenance. Mann quotes worm researcher Cindy Hale, who told him, "Four centuries ago, we launched this gigantic, unplanned ecological experiment. We have no idea what the long-term consequences will be."[5]

While we still don't know all the consequences, we do know that over the past four hundred years, earthworms have reached the polar regions and are releasing greenhouse gases into the atmosphere as they go about their days.[6] And we do know that English colonists destroyed a massive Indian kingdom to make money from tobacco plantations. The Virginia Company sent thousands of people to settle the area. Many of them were aristocrats—the ones Smith scolded to get to work—and many of them died. Only one in eight of the seven thousand people who arrived in Virginia during the first years survived. People died because they arrived ready to live as they had lived in England, not willing to ask the Powhatans for their advice on how to live in Tsenacomoco.

Those who did survive set out to remake England, chopping down the forests, putting in fences, and importing the cows, pigs, and honeybees that they'd known at home. The honeybee, in particular, became a symbol of the process. Mann notes, "So critical to European success was the honeybee that Indians came to view it as a harbinger of invasion: the first sight of a bee in a new territory, the French-American writer Jean de Crèvecoeur noted in 1782, 'spreads sadness and consternation in all minds.'"[7] Mann sums up:

Removing forest cover, blocking regrowth on fallow land, exhausting the soil, shutting down annual burning, unleashing big grazing and rooting animals, introducing earthworms, honeybees and other alien invertebrates—the colonists so profoundly changed Tsenacomoco that it became harder and harder for its inhabitants to prosper there. Meanwhile, it was easier and easier for Europeans to thrive in an environment that their own actions were making increasingly familiar. Despite starvation, disease, and financial meltdown, immigrants poured into Chesapeake Bay. Axes flashing, oxen straining before the plow, hundreds of new colonists planted spreads of tobacco across every accessible river bluff. When they wore out the soil, they gave the fields over to cattle and then moved on.[8]

Mann argues that two of our key social structures were set then: democracy, represented in the Virginia House of Burgess, and slavery, in the arrival of the first Africans in 1619. Both were happening in the context of the third formative structure, that of capitalism. The English were not planting yeoman farmers in the colonies, but, rather, industrial farms designed to produce crops for sale in England, and demanding the cheapest possible labor to maximize profits. From the beginning of their arrival in North America, Africans were slowly stripped of the few rights that were held by indentured servants and forced into a new and lower class of labor, chattel slavery, defined by its being slavery for life, passed on to one's descendants, and with no limits on the rights of owners over their property. The utilization of inequality as a tool of capitalist exploitation is deliberate, slow, and inexorable. It eventually colored all of our institutions. With the pervasiveness of all "great" ideas, the utility of the concept of "not human" is recognized and employed throughout the world. Hitler, for example, studied the American institutions of racism in devising his policies toward the Jews.[9]

The concept that "some people are not fully human" has been applied to many groups of people, including women, Native Americans, working people, religious and sexual minorities, and immigrants—in sum, what Occupy Wall Street named the 99 percent. The people's observance of 400 Years of Inequality was designed to help all people tell their stories of oppression and resistance, deepening our understanding of what had happened and clarifying our ideas about what to do next. In the way that the National Memorial for Peace and Justice had offered counties the opportunity to claim a marker of their part of the grim history of lynching,[10] 400 Years of Inequality offered people the opportunity to reflect on the ways in which the process of history had shaped where they were in their own time and space, what Edgar Rivera Colón called "time-place."

Slowly our 400 Years of Inequality team came to call the system of relationships that emerged from Jamestown an "ecology of inequality." We adopted the phrase "Stolen hands, working stolen lands" as central to our thinking about the anniversary, and realized, in the spirit of Hiro's psychoanalysis of cities, that this complex of harms was "the great mistake" in American history, the deep trauma that we could barely articulate or face. Hiro, writing about the creation of the Hiroshima Peace Park and Monument, described how the builders embraced the call for peace and nuclear disarmament but suppressed the recognition of Japan's militarism and imperialistic ambitions, which had fueled its engagement in World War II.[11] While visiting New York in 2019, Hiro returned to the National Museum of the American Indian, which we had visited as part of our psychoanalysis of Broadway. In the opening galleries, he was disconcerted by an exhibit dedicated to Native American people who had served in the wars. Like the Hiroshima monument, the museum was hiding the deeper story of ecological disaster and genocide that set the course for the history of the United States.

We had learned enough, we thought, to launch our call, and we made that the topic of our 2018 spring symposium. We hung our timeline on the wall, and underneath it, we placed a second roll of paper—to track the conversation and post images of the "ecology of inequality" that we made from "chenille stems," what people used to call "pipe cleaners" before public health recognized that smoking was dangerous for health.

Our call can be summed up in these words:

2019 will be the 400th Anniversary of the arrival of the first Africans to be sold into bondage in North America: in 1619 at Jamestown. We believe that the system established after this defining moment codified inequality in law and custom, and that addressing this legacy of injustice is intimately connected to the struggle for rights of all oppressed people. We are calling on families, organizations, neighborhoods and cities to observe the anniversary by telling their stories of oppression and resistance, and organize for a more just and equal future.[12]

We left the symposium in great spirits. Three participants, Bob Fullilove, Bill, and I, took off for a special visit to Nantes, the city in France that was the nation's leading port in the slave trade. It had suppressed that history for many years, until an eruption of racism forced the residents to look more deeply into their actions and their story. The city then created a memorial and devoted substantial floor space in its museum to the artifacts of the trade. Visiting those sites was a visceral experience for us, as they were designed to convey both the essential truth highlighted by Danielle Allen that equality equals strength *and* the venality of capitalism, the willingness to deny humanity to make a buck, or a franc, as in this case. Seeing how a place might grow from confronting and telling its story made a deep impression on us, creating a touchpoint as we talked to others about the role of observance.

## The 5/5ths' Academic Year, 2018–2019
The more we worked on the project, the more we drew on the experiences we'd had working with NYC RECOVERS from 2001 to 2003.[13] We knew that the fabric of the Greater New York Region had been ripped by the destruction of the Twin Towers, and that this damage needed to be mended. This was not something that could be accomplished by individual therapy, even if that therapy was directed at many, many individuals. As individuals, we are single units. But

as members of a collective, we make a larger whole that is greater than the sum of the parts. This greater collective performs work on behalf of all of us, including the work of rebuilding, protecting the weak and innocent, and solving problems. To repair the collective, people needed to work together on four core tasks of recovery: remember, respect, learn, and connect.

The concept of collective recovery had been put on a shelf for a number of years, until an escalation in violence in Orange called us to pull it out to help the city. Molly and Aubrey had developed a simple pamphlet that explained the principles so that anyone might use them.[14] Remembering Jamestown, and all that had happened since, was squarely in line with this work of collective recovery from the damage of dividing the population—indeed, the world—into greater and lesser pieces and using those differences to justify brutal exploitation for the purposes of piling up profit. Sojourner Truth, speaking at the Women's Rights Convention in Akron, Ohio, in 1851, launched a fundamental attack on the premise that difference justified abuse. She said, "Then they talk about this thing in the head; what's this they call it? [a member of audience whispers, "intellect"] That's it, honey. What's that got to do with women's rights or negroes' [sic] rights? If my cup won't hold but a pint, and yours holds a quart, wouldn't you be mean not to let me have my little half measure full?"[15]

In addition to claiming our own stories, the 400 Years of Inequality observances offered people an opportunity to listen to the stories of others. Ken, a student in my course on 400 Years of Inequality, shared that listening to stories of injustices suffered by white working people had had a deep impact on him. "I always thought of it as a black story, and the suffering related to being black. But they suffered, too."

Listening is a fundamental task in its own right. Murray Nossel and Paul Browde, in their storytelling work, always emphasize that the story is told into the listening of the auditors.[16] The listening is a bowl, and the story is a liquid that is poured into the bowl. In that way, the many kinds of storytelling that emerged in honor of the observance asked us to listen, and listen in new ways so that we could hear and take in the vast array of stories that made up our American mosaic of inequality.

On a visit to Charlottesville, I learned about a pilgrimage local clergy had organized to Jamestown, and they shared a video with me.[17] They stopped at Monticello, the plantation of Thomas Jefferson, where they read the names of the 360 people who had been enslaved there. I was anticipating being bored by the recitation of the names. As it went on, I suddenly realized no one had a last name, and I started to cry. Something about the dehumanization of slavery rocked my understanding and took me to a new and deeper connection with those ancestors and their suffering and endurance.

For those of us who were part of organizing the observance of the 400 Years of Inequality, the several years of work were a constant experience of learning and reckoning with the past. We were deeply touched as our call reached people and they said to us eagerly, "Oh yes, of course we want to be part of that."

We were moved by the creativity that people brought to the task. Even something as simple as being asked to read an essay or speech from the past was met with honor and dignity, with an effort to produce something worthy of the moment. The United States does not have a culture of ancestor worship—quite the opposite, we adore the new. But for this one moment, all those people who tried to realize the promise of the Declaration of Independence—that all of us are created equal—were in our minds and hearts with respect and gratitude.

It was Alice Walker who gave me the language of "the wound and the medicine." She wrote a foreword to *Barracoon: The Story of the Last 'Black Cargo'* by Zora Neale Hurston. Walker said that the story was very hard to read, but it came with medicine. When Lewis Cudjo tired of talking to Hurston, he would tell her, "Go away. I have to take care of my garden."

Walker wrote:

> Here is the medicine:
> That though the heart is breaking, happiness can exist in a
> moment, also. And because the moment in which we live is all the
> time there really is, we can keep going. It may be true, and often
> is, that every person we hold dear is taken from us. Still. From
> moment to moment, we watch our beans and our watermelons
> grow. We plant. We hoe. We harvest. We share with neighbors.
> If a young anthropologist appears with two hams and gives us one,
> we look forward to enjoying it.[18]

We were ready to hold our own observance by the time our third
spring symposium rolled around in 2019, and we reflected on all
the components we'd like to have. As we were inviting a growing
number of interested people to our event, we wanted both elements
of observance and elements of how-to. Singing "Lift Every Voice
and Sing" became a part of our day, which meant that we had to
learn all the words of all the verses and practice singing the complex
melody. We wanted Havanna Fisher and her group to dance,
Margaux Simmons and Doug Farrand to do music, and Angel Acosta
to lead a meditation. While we were thinking what to do, Vivian
Price wrote from California to ask if she might show one of her films
at the New School, and that became the powerful first part of the
day. If the reading of the names at Monticello had helped me feel
more deeply the harms of slavery, Vivian's film about the braceros,
temporary workers from Mexico who came to work in the fields
of the Southwest, taught me about the horrors of another kind of
exploitive labor.

At the end of our own observance, we felt secure in saying to
people, "It is okay to look at the truth. You will feel better at the end."

That word *better* lingered in my mind. What was it I had learned
as a result of the trips and talks and reading and discussions of the
past three years? I came to think of it as what Abraham Lincoln was
talking about at the end of the Gettysburg Address. He wrote:

But, in a larger sense, we can not dedicate—we can not consecrate—we can not hallow—this ground. The brave men, living and dead, who struggled here, have consecrated it, far above our poor power to add or detract. The world will little note, nor long remember what we say here, but it can never forget what they did here. It is for us the living, rather, to be dedicated here to the unfinished work which they who fought here have thus far so nobly advanced. It is rather for us to be here dedicated to the great task remaining before us—that from these honored dead we take increased devotion to that cause for which they gave the last full measure of devotion—that we here highly resolve that these dead shall not have died in vain—that this nation, under God, shall have a new birth of freedom—and that government of the people, by the people, for the people, shall not perish from the earth.

It is in defense of equality, as Danielle Allen taught us, that we look sternly at the past and learn its lessons. We cannot mobilize Main Street as the kind of tool it can be without this work. It was Coach Dave Crenshaw, a leader of youth programs in Washington Heights, who perceived this connection between 400 Years of Inequality and Main Street and decided that he would lead a walk the eight miles from the Audubon Ballroom in Washington Heights to Union Square on Columbus Day, 2019, in a Hike to End Inequality. Crossing the borders of neighborhoods ostensibly divided by race, class, and ethnicity, Coach Dave and his friends and colleagues affirmed, along with Jefferson and Banneker and Lincoln and Allen, that equality is the essence of our strength.

Team Dreamers' Hike to End Inequality.  The Team Dreamers stopped at statues of important African Americans.  Here they paused in front of the Adam Clayton Powell Statue in Harlem.

# 9   Exiting Regularity

*The woman named To-morrow*
*sits with a hairpin in her teeth*
*and takes her time*
*and does her hair the way she wants it*
> —Carl Sandberg, "Four Preludes on
> Playthings of the Wind"

I'VE KNOWN—in the abstract sense and for a long time—that the climate was changing and I should recycle and get a fuel-efficient car. But I felt it as a threatening reality in my own life when Tropical Storm Irene hit in 2011. It was the first named hurricane of that season. It made its way up the East Coast, making landfall in New Jersey on August 27, then gathering power to become a tropical cyclone on August 29, dumping rain over the entire state of Vermont.

With the storm bearing down on us, I was worried about a sickly-looking tree on my property. The local tree surgeon agreed that it was a liability; his crew took it down the day before the storm. Our family decided to leave West Orange, which is near the coast, and go to Warwick, an hour away, and located in the interior.

Little did we guess that the storm had the same idea. Warwick was drenched. We went out in the morning and found scouring of the roads and high water in the local streams. Then we went to see downtown Warwick, where there had been flooding from waters rushing down the mountains after the heavy rains. The water in the stream that passes through downtown Warwick was several feet higher than it had been the day before. Several of the stores with basements near the stream had experienced flooding. We wanted to get home, but many roads were closed. Fortunately, we met a man who knew the back roads and told us how to do it. When I got to my house, I found there was two feet of water in my basement. While other storms, such as Sandy, did damage by pushing water up from the shore, Irene dropped its water in the mountains and it came rushing down to the piedmont, where I live.

Bad as the experience in New Jersey was, in Vermont, as I described in chapter 6, it was really dire. The bravery and solidarity of all really touched me. Yet I did not completely get the message of climate change. I know this because I neither wrote in my notebook nor posted on my Countdown to Main Street blog. I would have done one of those two things if I had understood the implications of what I was seeing. That took some one-to-one tutoring, and more wake-up calls.

My second wake-up call was "Snowtober," the Halloween nor'easter that followed on the heels of Irene. It dumped record amounts of snow all over New Jersey, arriving while the trees still had their leaves and the ground was wet from Irene. Trees lost branches or fell. Electricity was out all over. A second storm so soon after Irene made an impression on me. I wrote a post on my blog, largely focused on Vinnie Mazzirisi's great Halloween costume, but mentioning that Halloween had been officially canceled because there were live wires downed all over.

In 2012 I had help understanding my world and my ecosystem by taking a boat tour around Newark Bay, led by Damon Rich, then city planner for Newark. The tour started by walking through our area's massive sewage-treatment plant to get to the boat dock. From there we descended a five-foot ladder to the tour boat. We went all over the bay and the Passaic River, passing an electric-generating station,

Flooding from Tropical Storm Irene in downtown Warwick, 2011.

toxic-waste sites, including one filled with the carcinogen Agent Orange, train tracks, and homes, all, like the sewage-treatment plant, set five feet above the river. These observations would take on new meaning in the days to come.

Hurricane Sandy started its journey on October 22 that year, gathering strength as it moved up the coast. It arrived in New Jersey on October 29 and took an unprecedented left turn into Atlantic City. It then continued up to New York City, its storm surge putting out all the lights south of 34th Street, pushing masses of water into tunnels and parking garages, and flooding streets and subways. It was a deadly and costly storm.

Sandy did not hit my neighborhood directly, but it did have powerful indirect effects. The electricity was out, which also meant that we couldn't get gas, as none of the stations could pump it out of their tanks. Later we would have gas shortages from problems at the docks. Trees were down all over. The trains that people used to get to work were out of service. Someone had the idea that train cars should be parked in the wetlands, and all of them were swamped by the storm surge. Thoughts of the bay kept flashing in my mind—if Sandy had inundated the train yards, it had also hit all that sewage and toxic waste.

Sandy brought climate change home for me. I wrote in my notebook:

> We are just in the aftermath of Hurricane Sandy, the Frankenstorm—
> part hurricane, part nor'easter—that tore up the coast and then
> walloped NJ and NY City. It has been a trying time. I started
> storm prep on Friday, getting water and canned food and batteries,
> reviewing what we had on hand, going over strategy for the
> basement with Mr. Mark. Sunday we cleared the yard. ... Molly
> settled with us for the duration. Sunday we went to the nail salon,
> Trader Joe's (chocolate-covered pretzels, chips, and salsa), and
> dinner at Arturo's. We came home and settled in for the storm. ...
> As it turned out, we didn't have much rain—thank God!—but the
> surge was horrific. PSE&G said "a wall of water" was pushed up
> the Raritan, Passaic, and Hudson rivers, flooding their generators
> for Hudson, Bergen, and Essex Counties. Our lights went out
> about 8:00 P.M. [Monday]. It could have been wind or could have
> been the flooding. Water flooded Hoboken, Jersey City, and lower
> Manhattan. Downtown Jersey City was "a lake," according to Pam.
> What we lived with was the wind, whining, howling, whistling,
> and getting so strong Monday night that it shook the house. ... As
> to my FEELINGS: I find it hard to concentrate; I feel jittery and
> mildly disoriented. I do not want to leave the Valley—I don't want
> to attempt to get into the city. ... I'm glad Obama and Christie are
> behaving sanely in this crisis.

I could write that there was a surge—a wall of water—that took out the generators. I was not, however, entirely sure what a storm surge was. In November, Molly and I got to go on a visit to the shore with Dennis Hway, a disaster preparation specialist, and Jon Miller, a scientist at Stevens Institute who was studying the dynamics, water, and land of the Jersey shore. Jon's team was doing its work even while we were touring. He knew the shore intimately and had been in and out of all its nooks and crannies since Sandy had hit. He took us through a stretch of towns, from Asbury Park to Sea Bright, and then over to Highlands. We saw some of the worst damage: houses blown out by the storm, stores wracked, roads scoured, beaches eroded.

He kept talking about surge. "Could you explain surge to me? What does 'thirteen-foot surge' mean?" I asked.

"Surge is not just how far the water travels up the beach. It's how high it swells from its usual height." He raised his hand as he said this.

"You mean it was thirteen feet higher than it is now?" I squeaked.

"Exactly."

"But how does that happen?"

"There are several factors," he explained. "There was more water from the rain and the push of the winds, and there was extremely low barometric pressure, which pulls the water up. All of those forces act together to create a surge. You see the water line on that cliff? That's where the surge hit."

That's when my memories of Newark Bay, with its assets and problems set five feet above the normal waterline, clicked into place with the effects I'd experienced from Sandy. I thought of the tower of water washing over the open pits at the sewage-treatment plant. "Yes," said Jon. "That's exactly what happened. All that sewage washed into the bay."

Seen in the light of all Jon showed us that day, a sign on Sea Bright's Main Street, NO SURRENDER, NO RETREAT, has lingered in my mind.

My tutoring in ecological change was part of my annual visits to Martha Stitelman, my medical school classmate, who explained the changing landscape of Vermont. As part of our travels, she undertook

# Post-Sandy Tour Scroll, November 2012

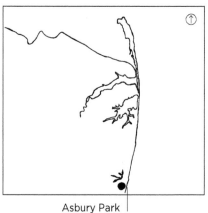

Asbury Park

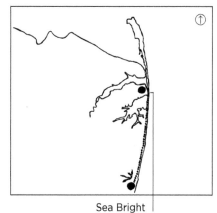

Sea Bright

We gathered at the Asbury Park Boardwalk for the tour. The boardwalk has suffered, as had buildings along the shore.

We drove north from Asbury, stopping at various towns. The power of the water was on display in Sea Bright, where these cabanas were tipped over.

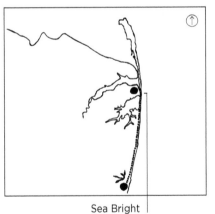

Sea Bright

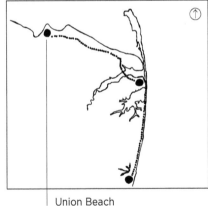

Union Beach

The spirit of New Jersey was manifest in this bright sign on Anjelica's in Sea Bright.

This house in Union Beach was photographed thousands of times. As I was taking a picture, a man drove by and screamed at us to go home.

to show me Irene's damage and Vermont's recovery. Proudly, she took me to see new bridges and reopened roads, including roads through the forest that had been restored for use. She is right to be proud, I thought. The thorough commitment to the recovery of all is testimony to the character of the state, and profoundly different from the ambivalence concerning recovery after Hurricane Katrina or the slow Sandy recovery in New Jersey.

Martha, who is a steward of the forest in Vermont, annually spends many hours on trail maintenance, in addition to her own hiking and boating. Over the twenty-five years she has been doing this, she has seen changes in the flora and fauna due to global warming. She would point out to me how the landscape was evolving, everything from the changes in winter snow and the impact on skiing to the introduction of deer ticks and Lyme disease. "When I first came to Vermont," she noted, "I didn't see any Lyme disease at all. There were no ticks."

The changing climate was to blame for the arrival of deer ticks and other shifts in fauna and flora. "My friends and I think we're seeing more erratic winter weather. The snow doesn't build up as deeply in the woods. When I was doing a lot more backcountry skiing, there would be four feet of snow on the ground, which would get you above the little bushes. It would be nice open woods to ski through, and the streams would be frozen solid, so you could ski right down the middle. Now it tends to snow and then melt and then snow and then melt, so we don't get quite as solid a freeze.

"And that's what's hurting the poor moose, because the ticks don't freeze. Those guys are suffering. When I moved up here, we'd ski and we would regularly see moose tracks and moose poop, and occasionally see the moose. But they were definitely there. The moose population in Vermont has fallen so far that they basically canceled the hunting season."

## The Envelope of Regularity

I met Bill Morrish in 2013. He invited me to lecture in his course at Parsons School of Design, and later that year to coteach with him, which we continued to do in subsequent years. In one of his lectures, he told the story of encountering a chart of the "envelope of regularity." He explained to me how it happened. "I was invited to a conference called Now Urbanism. The first speaker was Lisa Graumlich, a scientist who works with a hundred different interdisciplinary people. They were graphing the development of the political landscape and technology, as the two sides, and then, in the middle of the diagram, the chemistry and biology of the atmosphere, water environment, forestation. They were trying to see the story of urbanization and technology, because technology is the way in which we amplify or protect ourselves to be able to live beyond our capacities.

"And then they showed that chart and I was looking at it and she was talking about this envelope. The concept of the envelope of regularity suggests that the fluctuations—for example, of the weather—stayed within defined limits. We passed through a great acceleration post–World War II, when we blew up the whole planet with our use of gasoline and other chemicals. At a certain point, as the ways in which we lived shifted, the envelope opened up. We now have fluctuations that defy the old norms. We are not looking at climate change as something in the future; we are living in climate change. Our actions have opened the envelope of regularity, and we are living without limits that we can define."[1]

This exit from regularity is what climate experts have been emphasizing for a while, that "global warming" doesn't mean it is warm all the time or doesn't snow anymore. A predictable range of temperatures was the foundation for our established ways of living. As our ways of living changed the environment, the temperature shifted, and with it global patterns of winds, currents, and weather. From a rather stable range of events in those domains—the envelope of regularity—we have moved to an unpredictable and larger range.

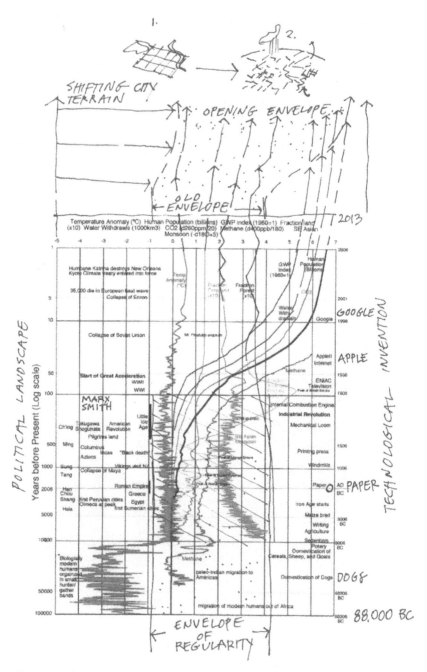

William Morrish saw this diagram during a talk at a conference on Urbanism Now. He added his own ideas to make this version. *Used with permission*

Martha's account of what was happening to ticks and moose and cross-country skiers were the meat-and-potatoes experiences of exiting the envelope of regularity.

Martha sent me a link to an article describing what was happening to maple sugar production, which was published in *Northern Woodlands*, a magazine she subscribes to. She wrote of the author, "Dave Mance lives near where I used to in Shaftsbury—and writes consistently good articles for *Northern Woodlands* magazine. He's the editor, as well as a surveyor, hunter, naturalist, and logger, when it's not maple syrup season."

Reading what he'd written taught me a lot about the process of collecting sap from sugar-maple trees. The heart of the matter is that temperature is critical to the flow of sap. "Perfect" conditions are found when the daily high is about forty-five degrees and the low about twenty-five degrees. That keeps the sap running and the bacterial count low. Historically, March was the month for collecting maple sap in Vermont. But maple sugar makers have been finding conditions far from ideal, with temperatures fluctuating wildly as climate change progresses.

Dave wrote:

> Farmers of all stripes crave consistency, which has been in short supply recently. The sugaring season of 2017 adhered to this rule. Sap ran in January and we could have made syrup then if we had been ready to gather it. We collected 53 percent of our sap in February, racing against the clock to get things processed amidst unprecedented heat. We collected 41 percent of our sap in March— the traditional sugaring month—and fought weather that was colder than historic norms. We collected 6 percent in April, before the season piddled out last week.[2]

Dave compared the numbers over a twenty-year period, which I've made into a chart. He remarked that in the five years previous there had been no consistency, whereas before that, the timing of the sap running was quite consistent. He concluded, "The point here is that 4 out of the last 5 seasons have been statistical outliers. And if you count the bizarre year of 2012, where the season up and ended on March 17 amidst a week of 70- and 80-degree temperatures the likes of which had never been recorded, 5 out of the last 6 years have been weird."

The maple sugar makers are not the only farmers noting climatic changes. Farmers in coastal North Carolina are finding that salt has invaded their fields, making the land inhospitable to standard crops.[3] Fishing towns and villages are finding that the yield from sustainable fishing is falling as the oceans warm and fish populations relocate to more hospitable waters.[4] The insurance industry, tasked with covering losses from more frequent disasters, is at great risk.[5] And real estate along the coasts is losing its value, even in places as precious as Miami Beach.[6]

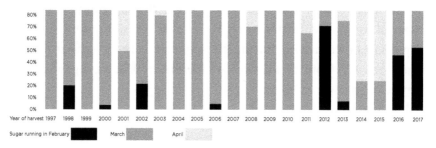

Dave Mance examined the changing collection times and concluded: "The point here is that 4 out of the last 5 seasons have been statistical outliers. And if you count the bizarre year of 2012, where the season up and ended on March 17 amidst a week of 70- and 80-degree temperatures the likes of which had never been recorded, 5 out of the last 6 years have been weird."

## Seeing This on Main Street

Marisela Gomez is a physician and Buddhist renunciate who divides her time between Baltimore, where she organizes for equality, and Havre de Grace, where she retreats to have time to meditate. I got to know her in 2005, when she was organizing to stop Johns Hopkins from usurping land in the Middle East neighborhood of Baltimore. Though the community was not able to stop the project, they were able to stop the spread of toxins during demolition. As to other outcomes, she told me, "We also struggled and won fair compensation for houses and relocation cost. We did not win a right of return because there was no mandate, policy, or funding for this, though we did win some affordable housing in the redeveloped area. But without assistance to help people back and insufficient affordable ownership housing options, well, you know the drill."[7]

On several occasions, she has taken me to see Main Streets throughout that area. In 2016, we went to a contrasting pair: one in Old Town in Baltimore, a failed pedestrian street that was falling into ruins, and one in Ellicott City, an old mill town gaily transformed into a tourist center.

In Old Town, we passed a barbershop whose proprietor Marisela knew. He was considering whether or not to buy the building where his shop was located, but the future of the street was uncertain. At the other end of the block, we were admiring a beautiful old brick building when some youths passed by and made an elaborate joke about our role on the street. We laughed at their brilliance, as they knew we would.

In Ellicott City, we visited various shops. In the bookstore, where there were not very many books, we heard the proprietor complaining bitterly to another woman about the lack of commerce, even in the summer. That second woman turned out to be the head of the local Main Street organization, and she shared with us the challenges of making it work. Summer was fine, but the winters were long and visitors sparse. After that informative conversation, we found our way to good ice cream and sat happily eating our ice cream and looking at a pleasant stream that was flowing by, running into a culvert under the shops on Main Street.

In July 2018 we went back to see the pair of Main Streets. Old Town was even more dissipated, and urban renewal was on its way. But Ellicott City was also in trouble. The area had barely recovered from a devastating flood in 2016, when a second major flood had washed through the city on May 27, 2018, causing major damage to the wonderful Main Street.

Marisela Gomez and I were admiring a beautiful old brick building when some youths passed by, and made an elaborate joke about our role on the street. We laughed at their brilliance, as they knew we would.

Ellicott City had originally developed because people were able to harness the power of the water rushing down the hills. The Main Street sits in the embrace of a set of hills and gracefully ascends them. The hills get even higher and steeper around the area. On our 2018 visit, we had to park by the old train station, then walk back to the bottom of the hill. Several security guards were parked there to keep gawkers from entering the lower half of the street. We chatted with them about the flood.

They explained that it was a flash flood, with five inches of water falling in a few hours. The Hudson, Tiber, and New Cut, three streams that run through downtown, couldn't empty fast enough into the Patabsco River and water backed up onto Main Street. The guards pointed to heights the waters had reached—past the first floor in some instances—and told us about a deputy who had almost been

Above: The historic mill town of Ellicott City became a successful tourist attraction. When we visited in 2016, the street was thronged with people and cars.

Below: When we returned in 2018, we had to take a long detour to see the top of the street, which was blocked off and devoid of life.

washed away but saved himself by grabbing the handrails of a nearby outdoor staircase. A National Guardsman had lost his life in the catastrophe. They also explained that discussions were going on about what to do, but that knocking down the side of the street over the culvert was probably the plan.

We wanted to see the top part of the street, which was open, but they said we couldn't walk there. We had to drive around on a long detour, which took us past the suburban-style houses that were nestled up and down the hills. As some of the problem of flooding is created by our patterns of development, Marisela and I looked closely at the roads, homes, driveways, and other structures that were influencing the permeability of the land in the watershed of the streams and creeks that ran into Main Street. A 2018 article, "Why Does Ellicott City Keep Flooding?" noted development as a contributor to the problem:

> Developers should make sure to consider stormwater runoff when building new projects, said Joe Sexton, the chief scientist at terraPulse and an associate research professor at the University of Maryland's Department of Geographical Sciences.
>
> In severe rain events, stormwater flows faster off impervious surfaces than it would off undeveloped land, he said.
>
> Sexton used computer algorithms to analyze satellite images of roughly 7,700 square miles covering the D.C. and Baltimore metro areas. He examined how much of the area has been paved or built on from 1984–2010.
>
> "We laid down 94 square miles of buildings and pavement," he said. "That's an area the size of Baltimore."
>
> The pace of development about doubled during the period they studied, he said.[8]

We made it to the upper stretch of Main Street. A few of the stores on that stretch had been cleaned up and reopened, but without the integrity of the whole, they were in trouble. We could look down the hill at the part of the street that was cordoned off and empty. As a Main Street, its purpose was to serve tourists. Without freedom to explore the area, tourists would drift off, finding somewhere else to amuse themselves and buy trinkets.

I wanted to know more about the proposals, as I was saddened by the prospect of a major portion of the historic street being demolished. I found the Master Plan onlin: they did indeed plan to remove buildings, replacing them with a park that was to be designed as an "amenity" to keep the historic character of the city intact. The water would be moved through the area by expanded channels. I learned, reading up online, that developers had defeated legislation to control new building or ensure that runoff was managed on-site. I went over it with Bill, who pointed out that the plan did not address either the problems of development on the surrounding hills or the ability of the Patabsco River to absorb the rapid transfer of water. Where would it go next? What would happen to communities downstream?

## Metabolic Rift

I found Jason Moore's article on metabolic rift in a favorite scientific journal, *Organization & Environment*.[9] Metabolic rift is a concept originally proposed by Karl Marx to explain what happens when we fail to return nutrients to the place from which they were extracted. Think of coffee grown in Colombia but entering the waste streams in New York City. All the nutrients that the Colombian soil contributed to the coffee go somewhere to fester in the landfill. Eventually the land is drained. This has happened all over the world, following the pathways of European colonization, which extracted raw materials to send back to factories in the home countries.

I thought of metabolic rift as simply the failure to recycle in place, but Rod argued otherwise. He would come every year to present the Metabolic Rift Award to a student in my class on Urban Space and Health. One year he awarded the prize not to the student who'd worked on recycling, but, rather, to the student who'd studied the differences in investment around the city. I was shocked. I thought that was crucial, of course, but not metabolic rift. "American apartheid is metabolic rift," he insisted when we discussed it later. Looked at that way, Old Town and Ellicott City are not different at all, but, rather, two spaces easily sacrificed for profit elsewhere.

Rod's point—that the metabolism of materials has geography *and* sociology—is essential if we are to understand Bill's assessment that "we blew up the world." The language we use for climate change exonerates us and our way of life. We say, "There's too much carbon in the air." Then we equivocate about whose fault that is, saying, "It's likely that human activity contributed." This view lets us off the hook. There are numerous other sentences that convey the same distancing and minimizing, important human psychological means for keeping the truth at bay. But the truth is that the massive, relentless, and brutal taking of the land, the sea, and the people has punched a hole in the balloon of the ecosystem, and its vitality is leaking out. To Rod's point, when we travel Main Streets, we can see the metabolic rift at work. In this case, acknowledging that truth is the necessary first action.

# 10  The Trap of the Status Quo

*Mr. Wall Street,*
*Do you care about the Main Street?*
*And show some love for the side street...*
　　　　　　　—Gary Nesta Pine, "Mr. Wall Street"

THE STATUS QUO is defined as the "existing state of affairs, especially regarding social or political issues."[1] An example given in the entry in Wikipedia is, "They have a vested interest in maintaining the status quo." That "vested interest" is the inertial force that opposes change and seeks to keep things as they are. The maintenance of the status quo is the opposite of time, which wears at everything and everyone. I learned a lot about this by the confluence of visiting a friend and reading Sinclair Lewis's *Main Street*.

I was honored to receive Nancy Hoving's invitation to see her Main Street in Pawling, New York. Nancy is a forceful and generous woman, with a great welcome and much curiosity. I got to know her when we both served on an advisory committee for a federal substance abuse treatment agency. She was a member of the board of Phoenix House and I was doing research on crack addiction. We had the chance to visit with each other, and had always stayed in touch by email. She is a great reader of Facebook and was always up-to-date on my doings, including my Main Street project.

We first drove around the town and then headed to her house, moving quickly past modest houses into a neighborhood of large mansions with well-tended green lawns and sweeping views. The first thing I learned about her house was that it was for sale. She was quite matter-of-fact about that, more worried about what to do with the dog and how to find new work for her caretaker than with the loss of the house. She'd once told me she was a city person, and regretted that her husband, Tom Hoving, had become more and more fond of passing time in the country.

The story of the house and her family unfolded slowly over the visit. Her father, Elliott V. Bell, was superintendent of banks when Thomas E. Dewey was governor of New York State. The broadcaster Lowell Thomas invited them to join him in a land collective that entitled owners to use a pristine lake, a "barn" that served as a clubhouse, and a golf course. "They were people that had made some money—not a lot of money—enough to send their children to Europe and own a house in the country. They wanted a small colony; 'enough for a poker game' is how they used to put it." They created a land conservancy around the land to protect it from development, maintaining it as a tree-lined respite in the densifying countryside.

That night, we went to a nearby estate for a fund-raiser for the Pawling Farmers Market. The estate was owned by a hedge-fund manager who used the land to raise a rare kind of deer for the Japanese market. The cocktail reception was held in the stables, which had a great view over the hills. The horses were not at home, although each stall was marked with a name. Waiters served roasted slices of the special venison. Nancy, looking around, said wryly, "It's a white crowd."

We got into a conversation with a man who owned the bookstore in town. Somehow we got on the topic of giving. The wealth of the hedge-fund manager was on display for us, but he was hosting us as an act of charity. One of the people we were conversing with suggested that generous donations were a true sign of character, and somehow "fixed" the accumulation of wealth. She smiled at me condescendingly, I thought, and I interpreted her look as saying, "If you had money, you'd understand." The bookstore owner did not take such an extreme view, but he was ambivalent about it.

"Well," I responded, "philanthropy is governed by the decisions of the giver. It ultimately bolsters the position of the well-to-do; it can't challenge their assumptions or our status quo. People don't give money for that."

They looked at me skeptically. Nancy later said, "You don't look like a bomb thrower. People have to listen to you to get it."

I met Nancy's best friend, Liz, daughter of the famous minister Norman Vincent Peale. Liz's family was also there, and we enjoyed their gracious company at dinner. The delicious farm-to-table dinner was served in a tent in the corral by the stables. Dishes had been prepared by various chefs from around the area and celebrated everything that good food could be.

The next day, Nancy and I had a leisurely breakfast at the breakfast bar in her kitchen. I learned more about her life. She'd met her husband, Tom, while they were students—he at Princeton and she at Vassar. She was focused on marriage and children and never set out to have a career. She did, however, marry an inventor and provocateur who shook up the establishment, first as director of the New York City Parks Department and then as head of the Metropolitan Museum of Art. I got the impression that Nancy had thoroughly enjoyed watching him set the establishment on its ear.

Then we went to see the Main Street, two blocks of stunning contrast, one chichi, the other workaday. The latter block was even set back a bit, as if to give precedence to its upscale neighbor. We wandered through the block of high-end stores, where I got some truffle olive oil, and then walked past the Irish bar, Laundromat, and dentist office that occupied the second block. A white woman was coming out of the Laundromat with a basket piled high with her clean clothes. She carried it to her battered car and drove away.

The sharp rise in income inequality is one of the defining social and economic processes of the four decades from 1980 to 2019, and no end is in sight as I write this. While all the social movements were fighting issues of identity politics, the rich people quietly cornered the market on money. The graphs have trouble depicting this shift, as the distance between the bottom and the top shoots off the page.

Having money is considered a privilege. So is having white skin, which, in the minds of many, is closely associated with having money. Without money, it is difficult to survive and really hard to thrive. I've seen too many floundering Main Streets to doubt the ways in which money plays a role in our lives. And I've seen too many people flout their connections to power to doubt that it's who you know, not what you know. Antiracism teaching popularly features explanations of white privilege these days, the articulation of the advantages that accrue to people with white skin, regardless of their own merit or money.

Eating special venison in the untenanted stable was a good moment to appreciate white privilege. Watching the white woman carry her wash to the car was a good moment to consider its limits. But knowing Nancy Hoving makes me consider a third issue, not broached as often: the costs of living inside the privilege. Nancy, by marrying Tom and setting off to be part of the counterculture, left the bubble. Selling her house was simply the dot at the end of the sentence—she liberated herself at a very young age. This enabled her to see the world, and to get the joke, as when she quipped, "It's a white crowd."

This liberation is what Lewis's *Main Street* is all about.

## Carol Went to Gopher Prairie

At a time of massive urbanization, industrialization, world war, and emancipation of women, Carol Milford married into the establishment of a prairie village, anchored in the stores and businesses on Main Street. Arriving from St. Paul and filled with an ineffable longing to make beauty, this clueless young woman stumbled and fumbled in her confrontation with the powers that be. Lewis writes of her, "Carol was, without understanding or accepting it, a revolutionist, a radical, and therefore possessed of 'constructive ideas' which only the destroyer can have, since the reformer believes that all the essential constructing has already been done."[2]

The strength of Lewis's diatribe is his attention to the detail of Carol's defeat, the constant assertion by the establishment of its infallibility, hundreds of pages detailing the process of asserting authority and defeating the future. Once I got what he was describing, it took my breath away. Reading in 2015 what Sinclair Lewis had seen in 1915, it was obvious that the world the doctor, the grocer, and the banker were ruling with such assurance would be swept away by the currents of the times.

Although World War I spelled the beginning of the end of the small town, the small town of Gopher Prairie could still defeat Carol. A snippet will illustrate how Lewis shows us this process. Carol, who has a master's degree in library science, gets into a conversation with the local librarian at a coffee klatch.

"We haven't seen you at the library yet," Miss Villets reproved.

"I've wanted to run in so much but I've been getting settled and— I'll probably come in so often you'll get tired of me! I hear you have such a nice library!"

"There are many who like it. We have two thousand more books than Wakamin."

"Isn't that fine? I'm sure you are largely responsible. I've had some experience in St. Paul."

"So I have been informed. Not that I entirely approve of library methods in these large cities. So careless, letting tramps and all sorts of dirty persons practically sleep in the reading-rooms."

"I know, but the poor souls—Well, I'm sure you will agree with me in one thing: The chief task of a librarian is get people to read."

"You feel so? My feeling, Mrs. Kennicott, and I am merely quoting the librarian of a very large college, is that the first duty of the conscientious librarian is to preserve the books."

"Oh!" Carol repented her "Oh." Miss Villets stiffened, and attacked.

"It may be very well in cities, where they have unlimited funds, to let nasty children ruin books and just deliberately tear them up, and fresh young men take more books out than they are entitled to by the regulations, but I'm never going to permit it in this library!"

"What if some children are destructive? They learn to read. Books are cheaper than minds."

"Nothing is cheaper than the minds of some of these children that come in and bother me simply because their mothers don't keep them home where they belong. Some librarians may choose to be so wishy-washy and turn their libraries into nursing-homes and kindergartens, but as a long as I'm in charge, the Gopher Prairie library is going to be quiet and decent, and the books well kept!"

Carol saw that the others were listening, waiting for her to be objectionable.[3]

Carol, completely flustered, makes her excuses and flees. That happens on page 83—the book has 323 pages to go, all filled with Carol's sincere efforts to be kind to others and bring some beauty into life. She is countered each time by the ethos of Main Street: Don't be friendly with your maid; don't patronize people who don't patronize you; don't put on airs or try to change anything; don't reach for the sublime, just stick with the ordinary; don't try to bring outcasts into society; don't think we will spend our money on the public good; don't do anything different. Toward the end of the book, she reflects on the "humdrum inevitable tragedy of the struggle against inertia."[4]

One of my teachers, Dr. Michael Smith, liked to read the opening and closing sentences of books. *Main Street* opens with the narrator's observations:

On a hill by the Mississippi where Chippewas camped two generations ago, a girl stood in relief against the cornflower blue of Northern sky. ...

It is Carol Milford, fleeing for an hour from Blodgett College. The days of pioneering, of lassies in sunbonnets, and bears killed with axes in piney clearings, are deader now than Camelot; and a rebellious girl is the spirit of that bewildered empire called the American Middlewest.[5]

And the book concludes with Carol saying,

> "But I have won in this: I've never excused my failures by sneering at my aspiration, by pretending to have gone beyond them. I do not admit that Main Street is as beautiful as it should be! I do not admit that Gopher Prairie is greater or more generous than Europe! I do not admit that dish-washing is enough to satisfy all women! I may not have fought the good fight, but I have kept the faith."[6]

To which Kennicott, who has no understanding of the woman he married, responds,

> "Sure. You bet you have. Well, good night. Sort of feels to me like it might snow tomorrow. Have to be thinking about putting up the storm-windows pretty soon. Say, did you notice whether the girl put that screwdriver back?"[7]

*Main Street* is a frustrating book. Carol is perfectly good and perfectly inept. She marries the wrong man, lives in the wrong place, fights with the wrong tools. Who wants to read 406 pages about that? Even the narrator is ambivalent, liking her one minute and impatient with her constant catastrophes the next. But the narrator's deeper impatience is with the status quo and its ability to suck the life out of good people who want to make things better.

*Main Street* is the book that introduced the metonym "Main Street" into the language. Lewis uses the term derisively, defining the place as an interchangeable part and its petit bourgeois leaders as so self-involved that they can't see their own irrelevance. As Lewis writes in his ironic prologue:

> Main Street is the climax of civilization. That this Ford car might stand in front of the Bon Ton Store, Hannibal invaded Rome and Erasmus wrote in Oxford cloisters. What Ole Jenson the grocer says to Ezra Stowbody the banker is the new law for London, Prague, and

the unprofitable isles of the sea; whatsoever Ezra does not know and sanction, that thing is heresy, worthless for knowing and wicked to consider.[8]

The book was a best-seller in its time and Lewis was voted winner of the Pulitzer Prize, though the trustees of Columbia University "decided the book failed the 'wholesome' requirement in the Pulitzer Plan of Awards and gave the prize to *The Age of Innocence* by Edith Wharton."[9]

That denial does clarify what the novel is: a kaleidoscope of accusations, each more damning than the last. Lewis holds out some hope for us. We get to the end and learn that salvation lies in the next generation. Pointing to her young child, asleep in the nursery, Carol says to her husband:

> "Do you see that object on the pillow? Do you know what it is? It's a bomb to blow up smugness. If you Tories were wise, you wouldn't arrest anarchists; you'd arrest all these children while they're asleep in their cribs. Think what that baby will see and meddle with before she dies in the year 2000! She may see an industrial union of the whole world, she may see aeroplanes going to Mars."
>
> "Yump, probably be changes all right," yawned Kennicott.[10]

*Main Street* has few dates, but Martin Bucco, in the introduction to the Penguin Classics edition, said that when Carol returned to Gopher Prairie in 1920, "her second baby was stirring within her." My mother, Margaret Brown Thompson, was born in Ohio in 1919, grew up in the small town of Chippewa Lake, and went on to live the life that Carol predicted for her child: seeing change and meddling with the status quo. She left the Gopher Prairie of her youth, and flung herself at the conventions of Main Street, identifying racism as one of the great issues of our time, and dedicating her life and energy to fighting it. When Maggie died in 2012, she had not seen a worldwide industrial union or aeroplanes to Mars, but she had seen the triumph of the civil rights movement and the lunar landing. And she had participated in remaking Main Street.

## Homeboy Came to Orange

My mom bought a small house in Orange in 1953. Dad was busy running the Fair Employment Practices program of the United Electrical, Radio and Machine Workers of America (UE) and this took him all around the country. He was involved in struggles against all kinds of employment discrimination. One time, he told me, a man said to him, "You just got to this city. How can you know if we're racist?"

"I don't have to live here to know that—I know racism when I see it," he countered.

The work he accomplished was important and contributed to lasting changes. The reactionary forces of the country, seeking to derail progress toward equality for all, struck back, using the weapon of anticommunism. UE was one of the progressive unions that was labeled "Communist" and viciously attacked. Eventually, the union split, and my father lost his job. He looked for work everywhere, but without luck. Unemployed and suffering from the blows of McCarthyism, he fell into a depression. My mother racked her brain to find a solution. When she learned that the schools were segregated, she demanded that my father act for the sake of my brother Josh and me.

In 1957, Mom went to the Board of Education, then located at the Colgate School on Main Street in Orange, and asked for the map of school districts, ostensibly on behalf of her employer, Morton Stavis, Esq. Because she was white and the lawyer was white, they gave her the map. My dad knew that what it showed was that the school districts had been illegally gerrymandered to create all-white and all-black schools. When the map was released to the press, it raised great commotion in the city.

This fight against school segregation was the first time that the African American community in Orange had stood up for itself and entered the political fray. The authorities immediately let loose a campaign of intimidation, and many cowered in fear. But Dad had what Carol didn't: deep political savvy. He had been involved in politics from his youth in Jersey City, at the time a famously corrupt place led by Mayor Frank Hague. Dad was always organizing in the teeth of that powerful machine. He often had fun. He loved to tell me about putting out a rumor that there would be a big picket line one day. A huge police force arrived, only to find one lone black woman walking with a sign. And he often lost. He told many stories of trying to run candidates without enough political strength to get the votes he needed. But from those experiences, he became a crafty master politician. When he entered the school fight, he was at the top of his game.

From his work at UE, he knew that the school gerrymander was illegal and the New Jersey Division Against Discrimination would find against it. All he had to do was reveal the map to create change. It didn't matter that people were afraid.

Having won that round, people emerged from their fear, excited to do more. An election campaign, running the popular pediatrician Dr. John Alexander for mayor, followed that spring. That, Dad knew, was a hopeless endeavor, as blacks made up only 20 percent of the population and wouldn't get support from the white community. Nevertheless, it was a thrilling experience for all involved, including me, then seven and very enthusiastic about the buttons, shiny leaflets, and cavalcade.

The expected defeat opened a new era, one in which constant organizing by the new Citizens for Representative Government slowly led to substantial changes. At the heart of the work was a strategy that Dad articulated: building power in the Democratic machine, and working toward a reorganization of city government that would allow the black community to elect a representative, someone who would speak for them in the halls of government.

In thinking of Carol's tribulations, it is the early years of this organizing that come to mind for me. One of the first victories that my dad registered was in 1959.[11] The Democratic Party was fighting for control of Essex County. Dad knocked on every door throughout the East Ward, explaining the issues and getting out the vote. The Democrats won by a margin that was smaller than the plurality of the East Ward. This contribution to victory earned Citizens a place at the table in Democrats' conversations.

The second fight in that period was for change of government.[12] This involved building a coalition across the political spectrum. The mayor-council system was a form of government that had been endorsed by many, including the League of Women Voters and other "good government" groups. Republicans, as well as Democrats, were in favor. Still, the black community was held in disdain. A careless remark to the press by Citizen's Preston Grimsley set off alarm bells that change of government was a grab by the black population for power. This disrupted the emerging coalition and set back the organizing. Dad and his colleagues had to go back to the drawing board to find their way out of that situation, and it took years. It was not until 1963 that change of government was completed and the East Ward elected a black man, Ben Jones, as its council representative.

The concrete knowledge of every aspect of the political process—how to map out a long-range plan for social change, how to build an organization, how to write a leaflet, how to knock on doors—all of this was what Dad had learned in union and political organizing. It is a massive set of skills that he used to create people's power in Orange.

*Main Street*'s hapless Carol, with a vague dream of making Gopher Prairie more beautiful, more cosmopolitan, has none of these. Her life is just short of tragic; she sees in her daughter the realization of her hopes. But perhaps she is right to put her faith in the future. She is living before the great movement to build the Congress of Industrial Organizations. It was in that movement that my dad became a formidable organizer. The working class had not, in Carol's time, learned to overcome differences and build the great coalitions that were necessary if industrial unions were to win. And Carol, though living just as women were getting the vote, was still expected to live within the very limited possibilities offered for women's lives. Keeping the faith is a fundamental part of winning in the long run.

## Love Trumps Hate

I am sure all mothers look to their daughters in this same way, hoping that they will fulfill the dreams their mothers could not. In 1920, Carol's vision of wonders was shared by many. The bright hope of invention was everywhere, and the breaking apart of old strictures was in progress. The men who went to Europe to fight in World War I, after all, were the same ones who went to Paree and had their lives changed.

But by 2016, in the United States, the inevitability of progress was called into question. While several generations of financial progress had fueled the belief that people would earn more than their parents, in fact, people were earning less, largely due to the massive concentration of wealth in the hands of a very small number of wealthy people. In June, as the presidential election was heating up, an upsurge in racism, endorsed by the Republican candidate, Donald Trump, began to make inroads into the confidence that we had made progress in rooting out racism. Indeed, the conservatism and nativism that led to Carol's torment were morphing into new, pernicious forms, startling in their ferocity as they bounded back.

The night of November 8, 2016, was horrifying for me as I watched Donald Trump march on to garner the 270 electoral votes required to become president of the United States. It represented the endorsement by fellow Americans of a man who had attacked Pope Francis, a sitting judge, all Mexican immigrants, and a Gold Star mother. His constant bullying of anyone in his way had put on display the ugliest side of American masculinity. How do you show so much disdain for so many people and get elected president? Our leader was to be a man who lied and cheated, and was endorsed by the KKK, heralded by the alt-right, and celebrated with swastikas, liberally strewn around the landscape. His call to "Make America Great Again" implied "when white supremacy and patriarchy reigned." It carried all the force of the status quo putting itself in the way of time.

I was stunned and disoriented. Before that night, I knew that our country had very serious problems. My daily work as a social psychiatrist has taken me into the heart of our social fracture. Rod Wallace had predicted that the Right would take over soon, given the extent of that breakage and its twin products, intergroup hostility and insecurity. Yet to see racism and hatred given free rein was a shock to my body and my heart. I had, in some deep sense, lost my place.

In my scientific work, I had spent a lot of time talking to people who had lost their neighborhoods as a result of various urban policies. What they had described to me was a wrenching feeling of disconnection, accompanied by disorientation at first, followed by alienation and nostalgia. This last was nostalgia in the psychiatric sense, a profound and even life-threatening grief caused by the loss of home. I labeled this "root shock," borrowing the term from gardeners, who use it to describe the threat to the life of a plant caused by moving it from one place to another and in the process disconnecting the roots from the soil with which they are bonded. Careless transplantation can kill a plant; some plants will not tolerate it all. It was a regular part of people's stories that old people died when the neighborhood was uprooted. They couldn't take the move.

And so I knew, from my informants' descriptions, that I had root shock. Like them, I had lost part of my emotional ecosystem, "my America." In my America, we were emerging from a racist past, becoming a multicultural, multiethnic, democratic society. The election of Trump turned us away from that goal, empowering instead a white supremacist oligarchy, which used racial hatred as a narcotic to win over white voters, while planning to steal everything from most of us, to give it all to the powerful few.

I was as stunned by the success of the con as I was by the dread of the future to which we were now committed. I took comfort from President Lincoln's witty comment on deception: "You can fool all the people some of the time, and some of the people all the time, but you cannot fool all the people all the time."

As my head cleared, I knew that two tasks were paramount if we were to defeat the con and get back on track. The first was to refine what I knew about our society's sickness, given the new data emerging from the election. The election turned on a few percentage points and was hacked by James Comey and Vladimir Putin, but why was Trump that close?

The answer was that President Obama and the Democrats had not turned around the growing inequality in wealth, the terrible job situation facing former industrial workers, or the constant sorting of communities by race and class. The combination of these three troubles left too many outside the system. Those troubles had also shattered the limited unity that had existed in the United States, a unity that had made it possible to win World War II, to distribute polio vaccines quickly and universally, and even to pass civil rights legislation. Spatial and economic upheavals had broken social bonds, creating many small groups, each fighting for its own issues and causes, what we call "identity politics" but which is really the internecine warfare of a shattered body politic. The strong ties had triumphed, to the detriment of the nation.

While Rod had predicted that the fractured society was ripe for exploitation by right-wing ideologues, what made it happen in 2016? Looking at Main Streets suggested to me that the terrible July that year—marked by the nominating conventions and murders, especially the terrible murders in Dallas—aggravated the intergroup anxiety and tipped the scales.

While these were my reflections, I knew that "naming the moment" was a key task for groups to do together. The University of Orange, for example, dedicated its January term seminar to the work of naming the moment, pulling together our observations and other kinds of data so that we could delineate where we stood. It was only from a place of utmost clarity that we could then move forward. We were guided in this by Deborah Barndt's eponymous book.

I had a class in situation analysis in the spring of 2017 that examined the election of Donald Trump. It was a great experience to get a group of very smart policy students to work on the story behind the election so that we might name the situation and begin to find a way forward. For my part, I remained awed by how important social division was for Trump's ascendance. In the spirit of Abraham Lincoln, who reminded us that a house divided cannot stand, I named the situation, "Divided, we have fallen."

The second task, as Dad had taught me, was to "Find what you're FOR," which became the second element of urban restoration in my book, *Urban Alchemy*. This is partly pragmatic: Obviously, security, stability, and employment are what we're FOR. But this is also partly philosophical. Ernie always scolded me when I would say I hated something, and as a teenager, I hated pretty much everything. "Hate," he would say, "won't get you anywhere."

Dr. Martin Luther King, Jr., at that time, was teaching people that they had to love their enemies. "The white man needs our love," he would say to the people of Montgomery.

This seemed outrageous to me at that time, and I think such ideas still seem outrageous to many. I have become convinced, however, that those two wise men were right about love as an orientation. How can we create a democratic, inclusive society if we do not start from love? This is a stern discipline. Father Richard Rohr, who also preaches about the fundamental role of love, says, "You have to work to live in love, to develop a generosity of spirit, a readiness to smile, a willingness to serve instead of to take."[13] Yet it works: As many protest signs have said, LOVE TRUMPS HATE.

Therefore, knowing what we're FOR is an action of *love*. It places us in the position of thinking and working for one another's welfare, and from a psychological, social, and spiritual place of *love*. There is much more to do to come from a place of love. That is why, during the long Montgomery bus boycott, there were mass meetings every Monday night at which the Reverend King and other ministers took turns delivering the message. This spiritual work sustained people as they walked miles every day. So, too, did the shipments of shoes, the donations of money, and the messages of hope that arrived from around the United States and around the world. My father, then head of Fair Employment Practices for the UE, organized the women at the 1956 UE Women's Conference to send a message of solidarity signed by all the delegates at the meeting, as shown in the photo. When we express what we are FOR, we show our *love*.

In the complex landscape of conflict that exists in the United States, the cacophony of identity politics and the fight for hegemony have posed challenges for those seeking positive change. This is inevitable— it should not be a distraction. If we have a firm understanding of the actual crisis—the profound insecurity and shattered unity of the working class—and a practice of love, we can fight for what is right. The new multicultural, multiethnic, just society that we hope for will emerge, as its time has come. Once, as a medical student, I found myself alone with a woman whose baby suddenly crowned, the top of its little head appearing between her legs. I tried to push it back in until more senior staff arrived. Birth, I learned in that futile effort, cannot be delayed. It is a determined process. My America is in the process of being born—it is the emerging reality. Trump's election was a delaying tactic, but it cannot work. Therefore, let us use this time of root shock as a wake-up call to name the deep problems and get on with building democracy.

In 1956, UE women signed this message of solidarity and sent it to the Montgomery Improvement Association, which was in the middle of the historic bus boycott.

# Part Four

# The Factory of Invention

# 11  Planning to Stay

*Stay, the card you're drawing*
*is the only world you'll win.*
—Ingeborg Bachmann, "Stay"

I LEARNED ABOUT the concept of "planning to stay" from Bill Morrish, whose idea it was. But I got to reflect on the life process of planning to stay as a result of a television series. As Miles Orvell's Main Street book demonstrates, we can see many of the issues of Main Street taken up in popular culture.[1] "Planning to stay" came up in the television series *The Good Witch*, which is centered on the lives and Main Street businesses of three women, two of them witches. Abigail Pershing, the "not-so-good" witch arrives in Middleton powered by jealousy of her cousin, Cassie Nightingale, the "good" witch. Gradually, Abigail comes to feel welcomed and secure. While helping to make a "wish quilt" for her cousin's wedding, she says, "I guess what I want the most right now is to settle in, meet people who feel the same way about Middleton that I do. People who look at Middleton like it's their home and actually want to stay here."

Because of the magical properties of the quilt, her wish comes true. She is invited to join a regular card game and becomes mayor of the town. Sam Radford, the local doctor and her cousin's intended, notes, "It's weird."

"Once I decided to embrace being a Middletonian, this happened."
He observes, "I didn't realize you were just visiting."
She replies, "I was sort of living my life like that. But now I'm here to stay. I even put an offer on a house—your house!"[2]

## Bill and Catherine's Insight

Bill Morrish and landscape architect Catherine Brown, who was his wife and partner, were working with old suburbs of Minneapolis. He was tired of the usual urban-planning conversation that typically started with listing people's problems. He wanted something different, a new starting point. What, he thought to himself, if we started with the affirmation that we're planning to stay? Then we can ask, "What do we need to make that possible?"

Planning a neighborhood is a participatory act of community membership and an expression of belief about the future of one's community. Before residents and merchants can begin planning for their neighborhood, participants must make a sincere declaration about themselves: "We're planning to stay." Planning to stay in a neighborhood can be a transforming experience in which participants discover new dimensions of being a good neighbor and a good citizen. When coupled with planning, "to stay" becomes an active verb. Once this active role is embraced, two questions need to be addressed:
1. What is it about this place that draws us here?
2. What could we add to this place that will keep us here?

"Planning to stay" became the starting point for community planning.[3] This affirmation of belonging, Bill and Catherine proposed, was the real starting point of taking a sagging suburban city into the future. Having met Bill shortly after I'd published a paper on serial forced displacement in the American city, I experienced this concept as an antidote to the poison of constant root shock. This was the essence of health: affirming commitment to a place. Deborah Tall, author of *From Where We Stand: Recovering a Sense of Place*, urged us to make a commitment to a known and loved bioregion.[4] That is the only way we can move forward from where we are to a stable future.

Bill and Catherine suggested that people look around their cities, taking into account the existing resources in the domains of homes and gardens, community streets, neighborhood niches, anchoring institutions, and public gardens. Through this survey of what they had, people were able to make comprehensive plans for building on their assets and solving their deficits.

Main Streets were part of the category "neighborhood niches." In rich prose, Bill and Catherine described the crucial role of commerce set in the neighborhood and part of its functioning. The neighborhood niche was not only a place to buy goods and services but also a setting of encounter and pleasure. Built to human size, and functioning throughout the seasons, these neighborhood niches were critical spaces for connection and community building.

In technical terms, neighborhood niches played a role in building "weak ties." It was sociologist Mark Granovetter who pointed out the paradox that "weak ties" are what make society strong.[5] This was a surprise to me when I first heard it. His argument was that the myriad casual connections, like those of a storekeeper, are connecting ties, while the strong ties of family and religion create partition, or separation, among groups. While both strong and weak ties are important, it is the weak ties that make the parts into a whole that is greater than their sum, what we call "society." Neighborhood niches build weak ties par excellence.

## Cherokee Street

In September 2017, I went to St. Louis to give a talk at the Pulitzer Arts Foundation, as part of an exhibition by Chicago-based artists Amanda Williams and Andres L. Hernandez titled "A Way, Away (Listen While I Say)." It was planned to honor the demolition of a building, and I was asked to talk about root shock and displacement.

# Cherokee Street Scroll

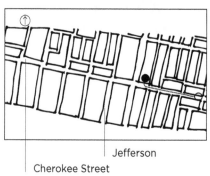

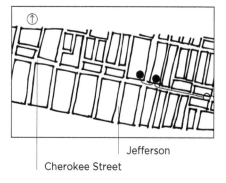

Jefferson

Cherokee Street

Jefferson

Cherokee Street

We encountered a store with take-a-number posters on the window. One had a photo of Lionel Ritchie, and it read HELLO, IS IT ME YOU'RE LOOKING FOR? The words of the song occupied the pieces that you could tear off and take with you. Another offered love and said of the tear-off pieces, TAKE AS MUCH AS YOU NEED.

I was, therefore, in the right mood to arrive at Jefferson Street and look up at the giant Indian statue on the northwest corner. Such a statue is not an everyday sight where I come from. It seemed so profoundly politically incorrect, I had to ask. So far, the Indian was considered an integral part of the area's history; he was planning to stay, too.

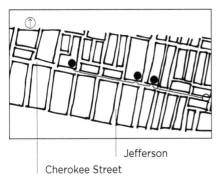

Jefferson

Cherokee Street

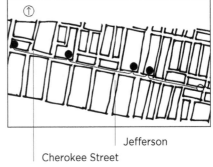

Jefferson

Cherokee Street

On Cherokee west of Jefferson, where there had been department stores in the days of trolley cars and heavy industry, the street was lighter and larger. The street had fallen on hard times forty years earlier with deindustrialization and white flight, but it had been reanimated by the arrival of Hispanic businesses.

At the end of the commercial center of the street was a vacant lot that had been transformed into Love Bank Park, a basketball court for local young people. This was something I'd never seen before. We sat on one of the benches and talked about the importance of making young people part of Main Street.

While there, Sophie Lipman, a community engagement leader at the Pulitzer, organized a walking tour of Cherokee Street with Anne McCullough, Amanda Colón-Smith, and Pacia Anderson.

We met at the Mud House, gathered drinks, and went to the back garden to sit, a place walled with warm old brick and filled with plants and wooden benches. The women were a powerful set. Anne was Executive Director of the Cherokee Street Community Improvement District (a business district) and the non-profit Cherokee Street Development League. Pacia was an artist and cofounder of Cherokee Street Reach. Amanda was a somewhat new transplant to St. Louis who had recently taken a position as head of the Dutchtown South Community Corporation, a community development corporation that bordered Cherokee Street. All were connected to Sophie, who was an activist in addition to her work at the Pulitzer.

The conversation bubbled, because each had a piece of the puzzle of how to make a Main Street work and they were deeply engaged with one another. They would take detours to discuss the protests over the death of Michael Brown, murdered by a policeman in Ferguson, or to worry about the engagement of local teens. These would circle back to the work of making a street come alive. By the time we'd finished our coffee, I was in love with all of them and with their street.

The Cherokee Main Street section that we walked extended for 12 blocks. We started in the part east of Jefferson Avenue, which had a number of antique shops. The antique shops were politically reactionary, displaying pro-police flags. The dealers resented the multiethnic, all-ages-welcome place these leaders were creating. Toward the major intersection with Jefferson Avenue, the tone lightened. We encountered a store with take-a-number posters on the window. One had a photo of Lionel Ritchie, and it read HELLO, IS IT ME YOU'RE LOOKING FOR? The words of the song occupied the pieces that you could tear off and take with you. Another offered love and said of the tear-off pieces, TAKE AS MUCH AS YOU NEED.

I was, therefore, in the right mood to arrive at Jefferson Street and look up at the giant Indian statue on the northwest corner. Such a statue is not an everyday sight where I come from. It seemed so profoundly politically incorrect, I had to ask. So far, the Indian was considered an integral part of the area's history; he was planning to stay, too.

On Cherokee west of Jefferson, where there had been department stores in the days of trolley cars and heavy industry, the street was lighter and the buildings larger. The street had fallen on hard times forty years earlier with deindustrialization and white flight, but it had been reanimated by the arrival of Hispanic businesses. Now a center of Hispanic culture, the street had been given the honorary name "Calle Cherokee." The street had, more recently, welcomed a more diverse array of artists' stores, featuring punk and other ideas of what to wear and what to do. All along the way on this side of Jefferson, I noticed signs: WE PAY THE FAIR WAGE; RIP KATT-15 YEAR; and one of Hello Kitty in her pink pussy hat, with HELL NO, GRABBY! written on the bottom of her shoe.

At the end of the commercial center of the street was a vacant lot that had been transformed into Love Bank Park, a basketball court for local young people. This was something I'd never seen on a Main Street. We sat on one of the benches and talked about the importance of making young people part of Main Street. The engagement of the organizations Pacia, Anne, and Amanda represented struck me as vital to making a successful Main Street. In a follow-up meeting by phone, we got to go into more detail about the work they were doing, independently and together.

I said to them, "Walking with all of you on Cherokee Street was a very powerful experience on three dimensions: the physical, the commercial, which is mainly what people talk about when they talk about Main Streets, and the social.

"The physical was just gorgeous; the commercial was very interesting and very attractive; and the social, there's so much that you were describing that's going on to animate the street. I don't know if you think about it in those three dimensions for work, or if you think about it in a different way, but I just wanted to share that that was what has stayed with me."

Pacia responded, "I absolutely think about it in those three dimensions. I've actually been thinking about it a lot, because there's so much that's changing on this street. There's a narrative that's being put out that there's a heightened sense of—I don't want to call it social unrest, but you know—crime and the unhoused. There's the dynamic with the street becoming a community improvement district, so businesses and properties on this street are being taxed a little more and that money's going into a pool for street improvements, things like that.

"And then a lot of businesses are closing and Cherokee Street used to be like one in, one out, and now it's like one out, and then there's a long wait for another one to come in. So those three areas are specifically where my brain is at, and I think I'm the thorn in the side because I'm always the one talking about a need for a process and standard and direction. And acknowledgment of the history. You know? So yeah, absolutely."

"For me," Anne said, "I always thought of the street really on a social level. A big part of my job was building relationships with different nodes. To me, that's really what makes Cherokee Street what it is—the people—and that's what I focused on in my work."

"And I was going to say economic," Amanda added. "I can never think about Cherokee Street truly without thinking about the neighborhoods, like the residential context that sits on either side. I just refuse to separate the two. A lot of investment has been coming to this area. Permit activity is way up. We did this comprehensive neighborhood planning effort to try to make sure that things were thought about in a holistic manner, and even in terms of, like, the physical rehab of vacant buildings."

The street was, it developed, touched by four neighborhoods, two of which had been examined in the planning effort that Amanda had led.[6] She was, in my view, justly proud of the plan, which had used a racial-equity lens to look at the densely inhabited neighborhoods, which included many people of color, youth, and households in poverty. The triptych shown below was included in the plan a number of times, helping to keep the focus on the needs of the most vulnerable.

Equity lens from Amanda's neighborhood plan. *Used with permission.*

The people in the neighborhoods had varying relationships to Cherokee Street. Pacia, who lived a block from Cherokee, in Gravois Park, said her neighbors never went to the street. One said, "Ain't nothing up there for me." The area had a high concentration of artists, and much about the street in the iteration I saw was made by and for them. Another adjacent neighborhood was wealthier and whiter, arguably more interested in Cherokee Street. But the street was also a regional draw, with its magnificent special events, like Cinco de Mayo, and its specialty bars, like Whiskey Ring and Fortune Teller. Similarly, the Hispanic eateries were a draw for Hispanics throughout the area, as well as for others who wanted to enjoy Hispanic food and culture.

This meant that while Cherokee Street was embedded in the surrounding neighborhoods and benefited from their functionality, there was an ongoing insider-outsider tension. It's possible that this had long been the situation with respect to Cherokee Street, which had historically been a regional shopping area because a trolley stop at Cherokee and California drew shoppers from around the city.

I asked about the basketball court, and this brought out many of the issues the women were managing. I pointed out that I hadn't, in all my Main Street visits, seen a basketball court. Anne explained,

"The basketball court was an idea from a business owner, William Porter, who has since moved out from Master Pieza. He saw an empty lot across from his business and wanted to put in a basketball hoop. So myself, Will Porter, and a board member, some kids from the neighborhood, and somebody who generously donated the equipment to put it in just did it without getting a permit or thinking about anything other than just doing it. It was kind of like a 'Do it yourself' urbanism kind of experiment.

"The park had been utilized previously by Pacia for Cherokee Street Reach and other activities, so the idea kind of was already there for it to be utilized as a space for youth. But the basketball court was something that we put in with the intention of having a space for everyone on this street. And it's been host to a lot of really great events—a basketball tournament, the trick or treat on Cherokee Street, Cherokee Street Reach Camp—and a lot of activities, but it's a really interesting case study, because we did it without really thinking about how we would manage it. How safe it would be. If it was really something that the residents that live around it would want. Who would use it. How we could make space for everyone. And there's been a lot of problems with the park, unfortunately, and trying to manage that was really difficult. I'm assuming it's still really difficult. Not something we really thought one hundred percent through. You know, a lot of times, those DIY projects don't really last. They're just temporary, and it's still there, with the intention of building out a greater, a better, more functional park. But from what I understand, there're some safety concerns more as of late. Am I right, Pacia?"

Pacia agreed. "It's really interesting because you think about caregivers and caretakers and just how really important they are. Anne has gone, and Master Pieza is closed, and Street Reach is really busy. So within a couple months' period, the primary people who have been the caregivers of the park are gone, and that's everything from picking up the trash to just being present to, you know, breaking up conflicts or trying to manage some kind of programming or renting basketballs."

As the conversation about the basketball court continued, what surfaced was another problem: the opposition of some Hispanic business owners, some of whom thought the basketball court was bad for the image of the street and might deter their customers. Amanda interjected, "I'm trying to figure out how to not frame it as an accusation, but I think personally—I grew up in New York—I identify as Afro-Latina, and I would say that culturally within a lot of Latino communities, there is a specific antiblack racism. I mean, there's an anti-youth culture that maybe is present across—I don't want to say anti-youth, but in terms of seeing the social development piece as a part of business owners' responsibility is like, 'It's not our job to raise those children.'

A photo of Love Bank Park in use, with a helpful admonition. *Photo by Anne McCullough, used with permission.*

"Maybe it's not just the Latino business owners. Maybe it's everyone, but, like, anti-black racism is a very specific thing that has been very difficult within Latino communities to bring up. I think that just overall, the question about, like, safety and youth is encoded in a much bigger conversation about racism in St. Louis."

For a group of women profoundly engaged with the Michael Brown protests that had rocked the region, the conversation about racism was front and center in their minds. How to balance the many demands was obviously not straightforward, but making a neighborhood plan using a racial-equity lens was profoundly important.

As the time for our conversation was running out, I wanted to close by asking what they were proud of. On this topic, they were just as expansive as on the others, and that represented the ways in which their constant engagement with the contradictions permitted them to make and celebrate a remarkable space. Anne said she was really proud of Love Bank Park. Pacia was really proud that even when people didn't see eye-to-eye on everything, they could work together to make magic. Amanda was really proud of the comprehensive neighborhood plan she helped produce, which would strengthen and protect the vulnerable of the area. Sophie, who didn't work on the street and had been quiet through much of the conversation, added that she was proud of them all. She singled out Anne, who had moved to Seattle since I'd first met her, to laud her bridge-building across all the different groups.

A few months later, the *Cherokee Street News* arrived in my email. In it was a call:

> We are calling YOU—the broken-hearted Prince entourage, David Bowie impersonators, Mexican dancers, moving vehicle rock bands, bike brigades, cardboard Bricoleurs, art cars, performance artists, motorcycle crews, Volvo devotees, dancing troupes, Bombastic Marching Bands, dancing grannies, lawn chair performers, kazoo groups, breakdancers, kinetic sculpture builders, gigante artisans, Frida Kahlo and Mermaid Wannabees, and any other lost members of the Cherokee Street tribe... We are inviting you to join us on May 5th at 1:15 pm during the People's Joy Parade as part of the Cherokee Street Cinco de Mayo Celebration.[7]

I had heard there was such a celebration, but I hadn't heard about the Joy Parade. Happily, the Internet has everything, here's a photo.

## Beyoğlu I Will Survive

On the heels of learning about Cherokee Street, I learned of the work of the Center for Spatial Justice, in Istanbul, a group which is also planning to stay. I had started dreaming of a visit to Istanbul about a decade before I actually got there. It was Jason Goodwin's detective novels starring Yashim the Ottoman that captured my imagination.

Cherokee Street, en fête. *Photo by Bob Crowe, used with permission.*

Yashim, confronted with a terrible dilemma and no time to spare, did what anyone wishes they would do: He started to cook dinner with fresh vegetables that he prepared with care and a very sharp knife. He also took ferries across the Golden Horn, which seemed to me like the height of romance.

Of course, Yashim had a Main Street: "... Kava Davut was his kind of street. Ever since he'd found this café, where the proprietor always remembered how he liked his coffee—straight, no spice, a hint of sugar—he'd been happy in the Kara Davut. The people all knew him... He paid his bills. In return he asked for nothing more than to be left in peace over his morning coffees, to watch the street show, to be waved over by the fishmonger with news of an important haul or to visit the Libyan baker for his excellent sprouted-grain bread."[8]

In June 2019, my dream finally came true. I landed at the new Istanbul airport, miles outside the city, and got whisked to town by a luxurious van. We drove through the countryside for many minutes, until the first vision of the city appeared on the horizon, some tall buildings in the distance. Cantal's lessons in how to approach a city flashed through my mind: start from the outside and arrive at the center.[9] This vision on the horizon was the first step. Soon we entered the city, but on highways that were perched above the fray. Getting off the highways took us onto the streets, but still the noise and action seemed at a distance. We crossed a bridge and saw people fishing. We drove down narrow streets, dodging other vehicles. Eventually we got to Hotel Turkoman, in the neighborhood called Sultanahmet, in honor of the sultan who built the Blue Mosque and is buried near it.

Dumping my bags and walking on the streets was finally a full immersion in Istanbul. As I walked down the hill to the nearby Main Street, a kitten poked its head out of a crack in an abandoned building. Someone had left food on the sidewalk, which the kitten ate enthusiastically and then scuttled back into the safety of its home.

I would never want to say that, as a result of a short trip, I understood any place, and perhaps especially not Istanbul, which is a massive city, 2,109 square miles, home to approximately seventeen million people. It is nearly twice the size of Rhode Island, which is 1,212 square miles, with a population of one million, and nearly as large as Delaware, which occupies 2,489 square miles and has 967,171 residents.

Yet places offer clues, and that kitten was one. There were cats everywhere. At first, I thought of them as "feral," meaning suspicious of people and living near but not with them. The cats of Istanbul were not feral in the way I meant. Most looked expectantly and benevolently on people. One jumped up and twined itself around Molly's legs in eager anticipation of some food. A man explained to me, "Ah cats! Cats are just cats. Turkish people love cats." The city also had numerous dogs and birds. A waiter in a restaurant showed me how he fed the seagulls that occupied a nearby roof, his face suffused with pleasure as they grabbed for the leftover pizza he threw to them. One night, walking back to my hotel, I saw a woman in a hijab kneel down and pet a cat she was passing.

City pets and monuments. Hagia Sofia was just around the corner from my hotel. On the way there, I was shanghaied by a carpet salesman, and only managed to free myself by explaining I was in Istanbul for work, not rugs. Then I set off again for Hagia Sofia, erected in A.D. 537. I kept doing the math—1,482 years ago the residents of the city had built a church that surpassed all the other buildings of its time. Time was everywhere, peeking out in layers of habitation.

Molly joined me two days into the visit. Two tours and her entrepreneurial spirit, like the twin foci of an ellipse, opened windows on this clever and kind old city. The tours first.

## Two Tours

Our first tour demonstrated the ways in which the same forces that were tearing at Orange and Jersey City were at work to destroy the centuries-old social systems that were keeping Istanbul—and maybe the world—together. That tour was led by Yaşar Adnan Adanalı and Sinan Erensü, his colleague from Mekanda Adalet Derneği (MAD), the Center for Spatial Justice. Our tour focused on Istiklal Caddesi, a pedestrian street in the heart of Beyoğlu, a neighborhood on the European side of Istanbul, across the Golden Horn from the historic district where we were staying.[10] They handed us a glossy map they'd made of the area, *Beyoğlu I Will Survive*, which detailed the losses that were taking place on the street.[11] It was easy to tour on the pedestrian street, as the limited number of cars allowed us to pause while Yaşar explained what we were seeing: the old enterprises on the street usurped to make room for multinationals—Pandora instead of a business that had local meaning and history. The bookstores, music shops, pastry shops, and others were being rudely elbowed out so that global capital could dominate the street and capture the money of the two million people who sauntered the precinct every day. Yaşar explained the cabal between the government and developers that allowed big business to seize the land and use it for the profit of the few, rather than the habitat of the many.

In the United States, this same collusion was enabled by the 1949 federal urban renewal legislation. When the urban renewal program was canceled by President Richard Nixon, the protocols for seizing the land from private citizens and giving it to developers were not eliminated; rather, they continued to serve the purposes of taking desirable land occupied by the poor or unworthy and delivering it to the wealthy and powerful for "higher uses," deemed progress. I had heard this many times in my studies of urban renewal, yet I was shocked when, in 2003, I heard Columbia University's president, Lee Bollinger, evoke the tired old urban renewal propaganda to justify the seizure of a chunk of Harlem to expand the campus. "This means progress," he told a group of Dominican leaders, "and we can't stand in the way of progress."

Yaşar explained that many groups had used the street and its squares for protest. One of these was a group of Kurdish mothers whose sons had disappeared. They were known as Saturday Mothers (*Cumartesi Anneleri* in Turkish) because they organized a vigil every Saturday for years, until repressed by the government. As we stood in the square, temporary fences and massive police vehicles reinforced the prohibition on demonstrating for any reason. One of my students had shared photos with me of Istiklal Caddesi during protests that were violently suppressed. "I was injured," he said, "and two of my friends were lost."

To help us gain an even deeper understanding of the processes changing the neighborhood, Yaşar took us to see the Greek quarter, showing us a school that still served Greek children, though few were left in the city. The erasure of the Greek population had resulted from a pogrom in 1955, in which Greeks, Armenians, and Jews were attacked.[12] Nine people died in nine hours of rioting. Many ethnic minorities fled the city at that time, forced to give up their businesses and their property. One of the abandoned buildings was taken over by rural migrants; Yaşar had rented from them and lived there until evicted by a developer. The developer let the building sit empty for many years, selling it at a huge profit as gentrification penetrated the neighborhoods surrounding Istiklal Caddesi.

We also went to the other side of Istiklal, where a high-speed boulevard cut off the poor neighborhood Tarlabaşı to the north. Our guides told us that the neighborhood had been studied so much, they were sick of visitors and had posted signs saying NO PHOTOGRAPHS. Peering at the neighborhood from across the giant boulevard, we could see the laundry hanging across the buildings, a symbol of the solidarity of social networks and social processes that enabled survival. Urban renewal was quickly eating up that area, displacing the residents. Some were being moved many kilometers from the center of the city—perhaps to the towers that I had passed as I entered the city from the airport. Left in a desolate habitat a long distance from work and social support, the former residents found themselves in much more dire straits than before.

Having shown us the distress of Istanbul, Yaşar and Sinan took us to a rooftop terrace of the Grand Hotel de Londres, where we could watch the sun set over the Golden Horn, and then to a *meyhane* where those who wished could have some raki and all of us could share mezes.

We were up early the next morning for our second tour. Friends had recommended Culinary Backstreets; our tour was led by Senem Pastoressa.[13] Senem took us into nooks and crannies of the city, and, while constantly feeding us, explained how the city worked. We started by walking through the hardware district in Pera, along the shore of the Golden

All the food we ate:
1. Han: We had çay, simit, kaymak, and honey.
2. Çay house: We had pastrami, ezme, cheese, rose jam, and eggs with tomatoes and peppers.
3. Baklava place: We had borek with mincemeat and cheese and two kinds of baklava.
(We then took the ferry to the Asian side.)
4. Café: We had Turkish coffee and lemonade and read our futures in the coffee grounds.
5. Gözde: We had mezes, accompanied by sardines from the stand across the way.
6. Nut shop: We tried nuts, apricots, and Turkish delight.
7. Pickle shop: We tried pomegranate molasses, pickles, and pickle juice.
8. Tantuni place: We had tantuni and lahmacun (pizza) from the shop around the corner.
9. Manti restaurant: We had dumplings, cibörek.
(cheese-filled bread), and semolina cake with Turkish ice cream.
10. Dessert place: We had knafeh (shredded dough with cheese and honey).

# Istanbul Scroll, 2019

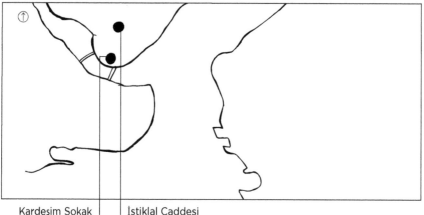

Kardeşim Sokak | İstiklal Caddesi

It was easy to tour on the pedestrian street, as the limited number of cars allowed us to pause while Yaşar explained what we were seeing: the old enterprises on the street usurped to make room for multinationals—Pandora instead of a business that had local meaning and history.

Senem sat us down at a table covered with newspaper [CE2]. She brought out a container filled with cheese made from water buffalo milk and covered with honey, and a bag full of round bread that she called simit. Then she explained about the system of tea, which lubricated the day and was made and delivered by "çay men" (çay is Turkish for tea and is pronounced chai).

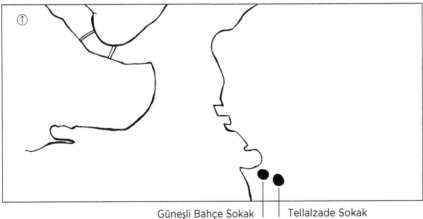

Güneşli Bahçe Sokak | Tellalzade Sokak

The cats of Istanbul were not feral in the way I meant. Most looked expectantly and benevolently on people. One jumped up and twined itself around Molly's legs in eager anticipation of some food. A man explained to me, "Ah cats! Cats are just cats. Turkish people love cats."

Chef Musa Dağdeviren (left) with his maitre d'. He is a man who has total devotion to his work, helping us understand that food is about people's history in a place, not nations or race.

Horn. We turned into a building she called a *han*, which, she explained, was once a caravansary, the last stop along the Silk Road from China. As if all that weren't romantic enough, we entered a well-worn, vine-draped, and sunlit courtyard, with balconies all around and corridors going off in front of us. People were moving in every direction, carrying out the day's tasks.

Senem sat us down at a table covered with newspaper. She brought out a container filled with cheese made from water buffalo milk and covered with honey, and a bag full of round bread that she called simit. Then she explained about the system of tea, which lubricated the day and was made and delivered by "çay men" (çay is Turkish for tea and is pronounced chai). There was a çay man installed in the han. He came over, smiling, and brought us all tea. "If you're doing business," Senem said, "and you want to offer your client a drink, you call the çay man. You take one of the chits you've purchased beforehand and you leave it out for him. He gives you the tea, takes the chit, and you go on with your meeting."

The çay man brought over an old coffee can and showed us the plastic chits—the "money"—that were used in his business. He also showed us his small and spotlessly clean kitchen, tucked into a corner of the *han*. While we sat and ate our delicious breakfast, Senem pointed out a pedestal of a Roman column that had been turned into a fountain. "We have so much stuff like that," she said, "we can't put it all in a museum. And they needed a fountain, so it's put to use."

Every place we stopped, she explained what we were seeing, not just what we eating. We went to a small çay spot for second breakfast and she told us the story of the man who operated the place. He'd come from the country and worked in restaurants. Finally, he was able to get this place. His mother sent him food from the country, like the sausages we were eating, which she'd made herself. "Although it's a small place, he's a success story," she concluded.

Even the table settings could be decoded. One set of tables had white tablecloths and two glasses by every place. She explained,

"That place is a *meyhane,* and the glasses are for drinking raki while eating mezes, while the place next to it, with plain wooden tables, is for drinking beer."

Raki is Turkey's signature drink, accompanied by ceremony and legend.[14] "Once a month," Senem said, "my friend and I go to a *meyhane* where we buy a bottle of raki and put our names on it. We have one or two drinks; then they put the bottle in the refrigerator for our return—and *we will be back*! One time I looked in their refrigerator and it was full of bottles with names on them."

The next evening, Molly and I went to the *han* where MAD had its offices. Yaşar and Sinan had invited me to speak about U.S. urban renewal at MADacademy #20. I shared my impression of Istanbul as a kind of clockwork, the people working extremely hard to keep it together, even in the face of mounting challenges from urban growth, repressive government, and gentrification. Part of what they were holding together, I thought, was East and West. The capitalists' callous disregard for the people's work put all of us at risk.

Indeed, in my thinking about Main Streets, Istiklal Caddesi was a world street, and the fate of the world was teetering as its old shops were displaced. The people of Istanbul were not simply fighting for themselves but for all of us, whether we knew it or not. After the talk, a physician-scientist told me that it made him feel hopeful. Turkey struggled with a sense of inferiority, he said, but my emphasis on the critical nature of their struggle offered him a new way to look at his work and his setting.

## Molly's Explorations

Now for Molly's entrepreneurial spirit, the second foci of the ellipse, and the way I got to walk the circle of Main Street, Bill's "shed," and to see the city's bazaars, market streets, and Main Streets. Some of places we wanted to go, we could find from our guidebooks, like the Blue Mosque, Hagia Sophia, and Topkapi Palace, all near our hotel. Left to my own devices, I would have gone to all the museums and sites, and missed the other things to do, like shopping at the bazaars, visiting Gabrielle Reeves, an American artist living in Turkey and working on the Asian side, and taking a boat ride up the Bosporus, a Main Street in its own right.

After the boat trip, at the top of our list was to eat at Çiya Sofrasi, a restaurant we'd seen on *Chef's Table*.[15] This involved taking the ferry to the Asian side and finding the market streets. We went without a reservation and were lucky to get in. When we walked in, there was the chef, Musa Dağdeviren, a man I admired for the total seriousness of his work, helping us understand that food is about people's history in a place, not nations or race. Molly said she'd never seen me so starstruck. I actually said to him, "I saw you on TV."

There were lots of other meals, too. One recommendation came from George Jevremovic, founder of Philadelphia's Material Culture, which takes its name from Henry Glassie's classic book. I'd met George through Jake, whose wedding venue had fallen through at the last minute. He and his bride, Julie Flynn, found Material Culture, which welcomed them in. George was there the night of the wedding, and he saw me at the end of the evening as I waited for a taxi to get back to 30th Street Station. He gave me a ride—"Taxis are very unreliable out here," he said—and I learned about his deep connections to Turkey. He recommended Hotel Turkoman and *Strolling Through Istanbul*, as well as Henry's book on Turkish folk art.[16]

When I arrived in Istanbul—years later—George sent a restaurant recommendation, Balikci Sabahattin. Molly got us there, helped by her phone's unlimited international data plan, which gave us access to maps. We had a great meal, and enjoyed the majestic presence of a seagull that sat on an awning and watched the proceedings.

Molly collected recommendations for restaurants, *hammams*, and places to shop. We sorted through them to find the perfect set of places to visit. That is how we got to Karakoy Lokantasi for dinner on Molly's last night in Istanbul and to the Çemberlitaş Hamami the next morning. That *hammam* was designed by Sinan, one of the world's greatest architects. I wouldn't have appreciated him as much if I hadn't had that personal experience of the delicacy and attentiveness of his work. As it was, I rushed back to the local English-language bookstore on Divan Yolu Caddesi, where I'd seen a nicely illustrated book on his work. The proprietor snatched the book out of my hand, saying, "If you're only going to read one book on Sinan, it's this one."[17] I looked at the massive volume he thrust at me and tried to imagine getting it into my suitcase and then carrying it home. He also wanted me to buy the *best* history of the Byzantine era.[18] I drew the line at that, as, published by Penguin, I could get that one from Amazon.

## Paradox of the Banal

After three days in Istanbul, Molly and I had gotten in the habit of getting freshly squeezed orange juice down the hill from our hotel. Two young men worked the stand; both smiled broadly when we arrived. Within five days, they were moving us up in the line, ahead of the "tourists." I felt profoundly included in Istanbul, wherever I turned. This is the essence of Main Street, but it has to do with simple things, like buying juice. The paradox of the banal is that the quotidian is too familiar to notice. We have to stop and look more closely in order to get it.

That is what Yaşar and his colleagues had attempted to do in creating a map of Istiklal and its surroundings. They collected stories of places using online and in-person surveys and interviews. From these, they annotated the map of the street, indicating where the stories had unfolded. Istiklal Caddesi was and is an extraordinary Main Street, yet the stories are grounded in those everyday events that we all experience on our own Main Streets: getting a kiss, finding our way, going to movies, demonstrating, researching a paper.

Here are a few of the stories that are included on the map[19]:

- "Beyoğlu was my second home when I was studying in Austrian High School. I first drank in Nevizade, kissed on all the backstreets of Beyoğlu, with a booklet in my hand toured around the 9. Istanbul Biennale all by myself, went to all the exhibitions, festivals and theatres in Beyoğlu, I watched a gay movie alone in Out Istanbul LGBT Film Festival organized for the first and the last time in Alkazar Cinema and as a result of all this, decided that I wanted to work on the field of arts and culture."

- "Back in the day as I was walking on the streets of Beyoglu, I used to feel safe being a part of this diversity, which for some people could be frightening. It was inevitable to come across with acquaintances and friends once you were out on the street. For a while, it was like everyday we were in a demonstration. Today we can't walk collectively on the streets. Shouting slogans is unimaginable. Feeling of belonging gave way to loss and mourning due to the changes in the space."

- "I spent a lot of time in the first place of IkinciKat in Olivia Han between 2012–2014, when I was writing a master thesis on alternative theaters in Bogazici University Ataturk Institute. Later on they had to move from there (because the place would be converted into a hotel), and they opened the theaters 8. Kat in Aznavur Passage and Karakoy IkinciKat where they still continue. In academic year 2013–2014, I was going to Aznavur Passage almost every day, chatting with friends in the ticket office, meeting directors andactors, wiping the floors if necessary and wanderin around. Nobody told me 'get you gone' or anything. I wrote the whole thesis on that way."

The work of the map is to enshrine these memories and to present them to the public so that people realize what they have and what they are losing as the street is simplified, its complexity eliminated, its relationship to the tensions of modern life dampened, and its ability to offer a hand up to the people destroyed. The map will motivate them to plan to stay.

## Taking the Pledge

At the end of *Planning to Stay,* Bill and Catherine offered a pledge.[20] I think that every group that is starting to address the problems of its city would do well to begin with these words:

We, the citizens, have been given a great physical legacy. The gift of our city has been built block by block, layer by layer, for more than one hundred years by those who came before us. Spreading outward from our downtown core—and helping to sustain it—are homes, infrastructures, services, and the diverse social fabric, which is our commonwealth. But we recognize that our city is at a turning point. Therefore, we declare our stewardship of this legacy and pledge our efforts to ensure safe neighborhoods, stable schools, affordable housing, amenable streets, resourceful development, equitable access to goods, services, and jobs, and an integration of the natural environment. Let our acts not diminish this gift, but leave it greater, better, and more beautiful than it was given to us. This ground—our common ground—is a good place to start.

# 12 What Happens Next

*I don't pretend to know what happens next.*
—Ethan Hawke, "I Know Annie"

MAIN STREETS, when they can, bring us together and delight us. They anchor our society, providing spots of much-needed welcome in a troubled world. But the Main Street forces of gathering are not the only forces at work. Diverse centrifugal forces—those of racism, capitalism, and climate change—are working against our gathering in solidarity to make the world we are FOR.

On a sobering trip to Memphis, Tennessee, in 2019, I heard from residents that their neighborhoods were being stripped of all assets, and I saw what they were describing: neighborhoods consigned to the scrap heap, ravaged by the forces of contagious housing destruction, and left without jobs or stores.

At that time, a new master plan, Memphis 3.0, had been announced.[1] Its cheerful photographs of prosperous people participating in planning meetings were emblematic of a deeper truth buried in its pages. There I found a map of "anchor" Main Streets deemed worthy of support. Those anchors were clustered in the well-to-do center, ignoring the beleaguered Main Streets in the north and south parts of the city, where the most desperate neighborhoods were to be found.

The night I left, a black man was killed by a federal officer, and the people of the neighborhoods rose up in protest. That they had reached a limit I could well understand. Memphis was renewing its commitment to exclusion of the poor, the absolutely wrong direction at this point in time.[2]

If we are serious about justice, on the one hand, and making it through the upheavals caused by climate change, on the other, we have to fight for our Main Streets. On Wednesday, January 10, 2018, I read in my morning paper that Coogan's, a restaurant/pub in Northern Manhattan, was to close.[3] I had worked for twenty-six years at the New York State Psychiatric Institute, and during all that time, Coogan's was an anchor of my life.[4] Located on Broadway at West 169th Street, it was a welcoming place and "real" in the best sense of the world. When city connoisseur Phil Hallen would visit from Pittsburgh, he'd say, "Let's go to Coogan's; that place has soul!" It was the site of many special events, among them the promotion party for Bob Fullilove when he became the first African American man to be made a full professor in the School of Public Health at Columbia University. His photo is one of dozens that hang on the walls in Coogan's, celebrating the life of the neighborhood.

When I first arrived in Washington Heights in 1990, Coogan's was a unique Main Street spot in a neighborhood that was leading the city in drug-related violence. My offices, several blocks away, were opposite the biggest drug dealer in Washington Heights, and my walk to the office was accompanied by the crunch of little plastic vials in which crack cocaine was sold.

Coogan's was part of turning that situation around. It was a place that welcomed the working people of the neighborhood: African American, Hispanic, and white. People of all ethnic backgrounds were the hosts, waiters, and bartenders there. Coogan's went beyond that, opening its doors for every celebration, joyous or sad, that was going on in the neighborhood. They sponsored a 5K Blues, Salsa, Shamrock run through the neighborhood, helping reclaim it from violence. They always supported Hike the Heights, our annual parks event. When my students were raising money for Coach Dave Crenshaw's Dreamers project, they talked to Coogan's and got the back room for our event.

Though I had moved downtown to the New School in 2016, the news of the closing hit me hard, and the reason made me mad. Jim Dwyer reported:

> Coogan's will be closing this spring for the usual horrible reasons, the end of a lease and impossible rent demands for a new one. Its space is owned by the neighborhood's dominant institution, New York–Presbyterian Hospital, which once was delighted to have any legitimate business running in a neighborhood that was a headquarters of the city's drug trade and its collateral murders. Now, in more peaceful and prosperous times, the hospital's leadership has emptied out nearly an entire block of commercial real estate along upper Broadway.[5]

I started calling and emailing all my friends. The news was rippling—literally—through the world. Lin-Manual Miranda, author of the musical *Hamilton*, tweeted that the restaurant is "one of the true Washington Heights mainstays, and has embraced every wave of neighborhood changes. I love Coogan's. My stomach hurts from this news."[6]

I signed an online petition from change.org, which quickly garnered fifteen thousand signatures, and learned about a demonstration to be held Sunday. Emails were flying back and forth when the news broke that the hospital had backed down and Coogan's was saved!

Bob got the backstory from co-owner Dave Hunt, who told him they'd been in negotiations with the hospital for three years. The hospital's representative said it was his mandate to get the highest-possible commercial rent. Dave warned him there would be blowback when the news came out, and asked if they were prepared. "You might pay four hundred thousand dollars in public relations fees," he told the man.

The representative laughed. "You may be right, but that's not my department."

THE FACTORY OF INVENTION

Dave and fellow owners Tess O'Connor McDade and Peter Walsh put their heads together to prepare to close in May. They knew the *New York Times* was doing a story. When they realized it would be posted online on Tuesday, January 9, they hurriedly called the staff together. Dave recalled what transpired then. "We have about forty people who work for us. There's a lot of families that depend on this income, a lot of students who go to school, and they depend on this income, right? But every single one, one hundred percent, said they would stay with us till the end. They wouldn't jump ship and say, 'Oh, I have an opportunity now.' By the same token, we called some people in the restaurant industry and said, 'Listen, at the end of May, we're out. I'm going to bring you two guys in my hands,' I said. 'Will you take them?'

"Every single person said, 'If they work for you, we'll make a spot for them immediately.' So everybody was taken care of. Now I'm thinking, I better make sure they at least get a week or two off, but everybody in the restaurant industry was right on and all our employees, one hundred percent, said, 'We're there until the end. We'll work until the very end.'"

That night, when the *Times* posted the story, all hell broke loose. Coogan's was getting phone calls from around the world. Dave told Bob, "A woman from Colombia was in here and said that her daughter was in Kenya and emailed her, saying, 'What is this I hear about Coogan's closing?'"

The following night, Wednesday, local political leaders gathered at Coogan's to form a task force. On Friday morning, Congressman Adriano Espaillat and Luis Miranda, Lin-Manuel's father, had a meeting with the CEO of New York–Presbyterian Hospital. The congressman called Dave after the meeting and said, "They told me they would revise their thinking and make you an offer that you can live with."

Dave said, "So four o'clock in the afternoon, two guys from the real estate department came over, a very, very simple change to the lease terms and with a small rate of rent increase on an annual basis that we could handle. And we were able to sign it and it took twenty-eight minutes of negotiation at that point to make the deal."

The fifteen thousand signatures on the petition, collected in forty-eight hours, alerted the hospital that they had stepped in a hornet's nest. Dave reflected, "We knew we would be missed by people. We knew that people would be disappointed. But I have to tell you the love that came out of this community was incredible."

Bob asked what he thought made people so passionate about the place.

Dave responded, "Tess, Peter, and I treat everybody who walks in the door like a friend. You're going to have to work at it not to be welcome here. One of the people that made a beautiful, beautiful Facebook posting was an African American bishop, Darren Ferguson, who we have known—well, let's put it this way, we've known Darren since before religious life was on the agenda. I said, 'I was so impressed and so heart-warmed by the outreach from the African American community to Coogan's. I hope in the future we'll continue to earn the respect and love of the black community.'

"He came back at me, 'You've already done that.'"

Dave added, "And Mindy was interested in the Spanish people—the Puerto Ricans and the Dominicans saved the Irish! This is what they did."

Dave described going to a local school filled with Hispanic children. He asked them, "How many of you come from, or your loved ones come from, a small island surrounded by water?"

They all raised their hands. After a little pause, Dave raised his, too. "Ireland. They think we're part of the mainstream, that our immigration was a long time ago, but my family came over in the 1920s and '30s. My mother immigrated when she was sixteen."

Dave, Peter, and Tess are Main Street people, running a Main Street place on one of America's greatest Main Streets. They earned the support of people around the world, and we, in turn, saved them with our readiness to leap to our feet in protest. Twenty-nine years after my first visit as an anxious new recruit, I can still walk into

Coogan's, take in all the photos and memorabilia on the walls, and know that I am at home.

That, in sum, is what Main Street is all about and how it works to support our mental health.

Coogan's has a table waiting for you!

# May I Have the Envelope, Please?

> *Might and Main, with:*
> *Strenuously, vigorously, as in* She pulled on the rope
> with all her might and main. *This expression is*
> *redundant, since the noun main also means "strength"*
> *or "power." It survives only in this phrase, which may*
> *also be dying out.*
>
> —Dictionary.com

THIS IS WHAT you've been waiting for: the Main Street awards!

I've been thinking about them for years, wondering what to call them. One day I remembered the expression "might and main," as in "I fought with all my might and main." People rarely use the expression these days, and Dictionary.com said it may be dying out. I love the expression and would hate to see it go. Therefore, I'm putting it back to work as the name of the Main Street awards.

I am bestowing one Might and Main Award for Best Main Street, two to places that are working with all their might and main to keep to it going, and many M&Ms (you saw that coming, right?) for main things. Here we go.

## Might and Main Award for Best Main Street:
## Burlington, New Jersey

I knew at the end of my visit there that Burlington had won. It has impeccable charm, lots of history, and people there who knew the story of their ancestors rescuing a free black man who'd been snatched by fugitive slave hunters. It has, hands down, my favorite Main Street statue. And at the end of Main Street, there's the Delaware, which Washington crossed to win the Revolution.

## Might and Main Awards for Keeping It Going:
## Sauk Centre and Asbury Park

Obviously, Sauk Centre, Minnesota, gets an M&M for tenacity. It is fighting the forces of the mall, the highway, and the collapse of the family farm, yet it had the ability to commission an exceptional mural to celebrate its long past, going back to the Native people who once lived there. That little city, having inspired Sinclair Lewis to write his great book, has much more to tell us, I believe.

I'm also giving an M&M to Asbury Park, New Jersey, which has struggled with segregation, urban renewal, disinvestment, Hurricane Sandy, and gentrification, among other traumas. I was there days after the hurricane and then again eight months later to stroll on the rebuilt boardwalk. Asbury Park has more than one great ice-cream place, the best mural in an abandoned building, and dedicated citizens who never quit. May they keep their city a "working class town with a beach"!

## Might and Main Awards for Main Things (open category):
## Many Winners!

- Best "Love My Hood!" Restaurant/Pub: Coogan's. Of course.
- Best Gospel Choir in the Circle: Ebenezer Baptist Church in Orange, New Jersey. What can I say? Orange is my hometown, true, but, under the adept leadership of Winston Nelson, Sr., that choir rocks the house. Its members come

to honor Rosa Parks every year on December 1st at the University of Orange's Remembering Rosa concert. They're good people and great singers!

- Best Pastrami with Fortitude: Bragman's on Hawthorne Street in Newark, New Jersey! Go there!
- Best Beach Breakfast: Reynaldo's Mexican Bakery on Linden Avenue in Carpenteria, California. And you can stroll down the street, pick up a bathing suit at one of the cute shops, and discover the Pacific Ocean at the end of the street. What, you say, there are a thousand people on the beach, so how can I discover it? Tell that to Christopher Columbus is all I have to say.
- Best Party Invitation: Cherokee Street, St. Louis, for its invitation to its Cinco de Mayo party and parade! Best Party is an award you have to give for yourself, as there's no accounting for taste.
- Best Doggy in the Window: New Orleans! Extremely cute little guy with an orange tuft.
- Best Shrine at the End of a Four-Hundred-Year-Old Market: Kyoto. Though my son died, I remain grateful for the chance to pause and ask the heavens for succor. Bobby was bathed in love in his last days, so I think my prayers were answered.
- Best Poached Eggs on Rye Toast: Baked on Grant, Grant Street, Johannesburg. I had forgotten how much I loved poached eggs on rye toast until I went there. I had a hotel room overlooking Grant Street, and dreamed of writing this book while sitting on the little balcony, watching life pass by.
- Best Parade with a Presidential Candidate: 2015 Strolling of the Heifers. These parades are a dime a dozen as I finish this book and twenty-two people are competing for the Democratic nomination. But hands down best, 2015 Strolling of the Heifers on Main Street in Brattleboro,

Vermont. Bernie Sanders, candidate. Which reminds me of the M&M for best spirit animal!

- Best Spirit Animal: CLIMB's Giraffe. You might call this favoritism, but I have to give this award to CLIMB's giraffe. I thought Strolling of the Heifers had the edge, because they had people in heifer costumes. But artist Tony Gonzalez turned his fierce imagination to the task, and now CLIMB has won. City Life Is Moving Bodies has invited children of all ages to envision our giraffe. These giraffes have come in all sizes. When CLIMB was honored in 2019 by the *Manhattan Times*—along with Lin-Manuel Miranda, I might add—we took our massive giraffes with us, and they were the hit of the party! There are a lot of spirit animals out there—moose in Bennington, Vermont, heifers in Brattleboro, crabs in Baltimore—so maybe this award should be for all the places that have found their spirit animal. If yours hasn't, keep searching! And I will give another M&M to the rococo United Palace on Broadway as "Best Place to Honor CLIMB." Lin-Manuel Miranda already has a lot of awards, but I will add to his stack and give him "Most Famous Playwright to Stand up for the Heights." Why not?

- Best Reminder of a Novel I Loved: Lake Ohrid, North Macedonia. Albania was across the lake from the hotel where I was staying. In *The Unexpected Mrs. Pollifax*, Emily Pollifax gets to Albania, which, in the book, is "behind the Iron Curtain" and impossible to enter. I asked people in North Macedonia if it was hard to go to Albania back in the day. They looked at me as if they didn't understand the question. "No, it's Albania. You just went," they all said. Was I a victim of Cold War propaganda? Of course, Lake Ohrid had tough competition from Istanbul and the Yashim books. But I wouldn't give Istanbul an award for that.

- Best Nooks and Crannies on Main Street: Istanbul. It is this complexity that is so powerful for making Istanbul the pivot of the world. These places are threatened, as all complexity is threatened, by the demands of global capitalism. Wishing the people of Istanbul—and all of us—the strength we need to battle simplification in all its forms. Life is not simple.

Those are the Might and Main Awards I want to give at the end of my eleven years of seeing Main Streets. I could keep on, but you get the idea. Here's what I really want to say about Might and Main Awards: You can give them out, too! That's why there's a blank copy on page 255.

If you find a place or a person you admire, hand out an award. We get too little recognition that we're working with all our might and main to keep it together. Let people know you see and appreciate the effort they're putting in. Without all the people who are making Main Street for us, we'd just fly apart, and who knows what might happen then. We are so fortunate to have their work, which is one of the great centripetal forces holding our universe together.

Here's to all the people working with all their might and main to keep our world going!

*Mitakuye Oyasin*
—Lakota prayer, which means
"We are all related."

# Acknowledgments

OVER THE ELEVEN YEARS I've been working on this book, I have benefited from the kindness of dozens of people who have walked Main Street with me, talked about urban process, commented on my writing, and given permission for their materials to be used. Strangers in airport lines, store owners, and passersby have lent a hand so that I could get this work done. My gratitude to people known and unknown knows no bounds.

I am grateful to the following people who walked and talked with me: David Chapin, Hirofumi Minami, Martha Stitelman, Anne McCullough, Amanda Colón-Smith, Pacia Anderson, Sophie Lipman, Edgar Rivera Colón, Yaşar Adnan Adanalı, Sinan Erensü, Senem Pastoressa, Martin Kohn, Marisela Gomez, Haruko Takasaki-Fullilove and her family, Patricia Fulliove, Michael Lally, Nupur Chaudhury, Wing Young Huie, the Reverend Tom Goldsmith, Tyler Stovall, Nancy Hoving, Yvonne Rodriguez, Dave Hunt, Jon Miller, and Dennis Hway.

The department of social psychiatry at New York State Psychiatric Institute—especially my chair, Bruce Dohwenrend and colleague Bruce Link—supported the project from its inception. Members of my writing group, Maura Speigel, Ann Burack-Weiss, Kelli Harding, Jim Gilbert, and Simon Fortin, kindly read many versions of this book and encouraged me to keep going. Scientific colleagues, Robert Sember, Robert Fullilove, William Morrish, and Rodrick Wallace, have been very helpful in honing the ideas presented here. Urbanism colleagues, especially Ron Shiffman, Michel Cantal-Dupart, and Xavier Cantal-Dupart, have been similarly unflagging in their support. My Main Street collaborator Jacob Izenberg's work on the basic model, and then extending our first model to include the tangle and time, was essential to taking this project from nice vistas to solid ideas. My colleagues in Orange, Molly Rose Kaufman, Aubrey Murdock, and Doug Farrand of the University of Orange, and Charles Wirene of the HUUB, led work that offered many opportunities to think about Main Streets. Molly, who is also my daughter, joined me in many Main Street trips, some described here, as well many others; I benefited from her vast expertise. My granddaughter Lily Johnson retraced the steps of her middle school science project on shopping in Englewood, New Jersey, and worked tirelessly to create endnotes and a bibliography for this book.

My agent, Angela Miller, is not only a great literary agent but also a great urbanist who understands the role of the market in city making. Publisher Lynne Elizabeth believed in this book way before I did. Rich Brown supported the graphic design and artistry of the book. Aditi Nair and Jacqueline Castaneda created the line drawings and assembled the scrolls. Carol Hsiung created the certificate for the Might and Main Award as well as the cover and the four-part "Tangle" diagram. Conceptual editor Susan Hasho helped me smooth out the story. Publication coach Daphne Gray-Grant, organizer of Get it Done, cheered me over the finish line. Jay Goss, of Village Copier in New York City, managed printing and binding of many drafts and added encouraging smiles.

Michael Lally and Martin Kohn gave me permission to reprint their poems. Molly Kaufman, Wing Young Huie, David Chapin, Anne McCullough, Aditi Nair, and Pierre Perron gave me permission to reprint their photographs. I am grateful to the archives of the United Electrical, Radio and Machine Workers of America for the photo of the women's convention from their collection. Amanda Colón-Smith gave permission to reprint a graphic from her planning report. William Morrish gave permission to reprint his drawings. Charles Billings supplied the map of Ripton, Vermont. The American Psychiatric Association gave me permission to adapt my chapter on liberation psychiatry, first published in *Black Mental Health: Patients, Providers, and Systems,* as the introduction to this book and to adapt diagrams from George Engel's seminal paper, first published in the association's journal. The chief priest of the Nishiki Tenmangu Shrine gave permission to reprint their goshuin, the red stamp given to visitors.

Pam Shaw, who designed covers for three of my books and the logo for 400 Years of Inequality, died in September 2019, before she had a chance to design the cover for this book. I am grateful for her guidance and for introducing me to her colleague Keith Kinsella, who is carrying on her legacy of brilliant design in the service of the people. She lives on in our hearts and memories.

Many generations of my family have stood by me through the years. I am grateful to my parents, Ernie and Maggie, my children, Bobby, Kenny, Dina, and Molly, my grandchildren, Gil, Lily, Christina, Hope, and Javier, and my great-grandson, Apollo. They remained steadfast through the travails of writing this book and I am grateful to all of them!

That errors may remain in spite of all this help is astonishing. Any errors are entirely mine.

# Endnotes

## Introduction

1. Engel, "The Clinical Application of the Biopsychosocial Model."
2. Fullilove and Reynolds.
3. Ibid., 590
4. Ghose.
5. Rodrick Wallace, "A Synergism of Plagues."
6. See Bowlby; Granovetter; Barker; Anthony F. C. Wallace; Leighton; and Erikson.
7. Fullilove, "Psychiatric Implications of Displacement."
8. Harvey.
9. Martin Luther King, Jr., *Stride Toward Freedom*.
10. Fullilove, *Root Shock*.
11. National Advisory Commission on Civil Disorders.
12. Fullilove, *Root Shock*.
13. Fullilove and Wallace, "Serial Forced Displacement in American Cities, 1916–2010."
14. Bluestone and Harrison.
15. Granovetter.
16. Rodrick Wallace and Deborah Wallace, "Emerging Infections and Nested Martingales."
17. Wallace and Fullilove, *Collective Consciousness and Its Discontents*, 18.
18. Fullilove, *Urban Alchemy*.
19. News Story Hub Contributors.

## Chapter 1. Weather Permitting

1. Demarco.
2. Fullilove, *Root Shock*, 180–81.
3. Hendrix.

4.  Geronimus et al.
5.  "Nishiki Tenmangū."
6.  Kepner.
7.  See Izenberg; Fullilove, Izenberg, Golemeski, Stitelman, and Wallace.

### Chapter 2. Synmorphy

1.  Schoggen, 42.
2.  Ibid., 20.
3.  Ibid, 142.
4.  Dyckman Farmhouse Museum Alliance.
5.  Ohno.
6.  "13th Century Picture Scroll Depicting the Mongolian Invasions."
7.  Von Simson, 167.
8.  This quotation was found on the Duke University website for a course, but the page was deleted before I accessed the full citation information. This unknown professor's summary was so excellent, I am keeping it and hope to identify the author eventually.
9.  Wikipedia, Ladies' Mile.
10. Peterson.
11. Janofsky.
12. *First Unitarian Church v. Salt Lake.*
13. Ganga.

### Chapter 3. Box

1.  De La Baume.
2.  For a history of Ripton, Vermont, see Billings.
3.  Johnson, 7.
4.  LaToya Ruby Frazier might have said, "To see black people [or just people], look at my photos." As an example, see Frazier.
5.  Hoffman.
6.  Field Museum, "Looking at Ourselves."
7.  Bulteau.
8.  Bulteau, iv.
9.  Ibid., 50.
10. Ibid., 53.

### Chapter 4. Circle

1.  Fullilove, *Root Shock*, 200–203.
2.  David Chapin shared these thoughts with me on the Churchill quote. "I'm a firm believer that our behavior, our point of view, and how we interact with others are greatly shaped by the buildings, the streets, and the neighborhoods we occupy. What I didn't know until recently

was the context behind the quote. Churchill was not making a general statement when he said this; he had a particular building in mind. The House of Commons, which had been badly bombed during World War II, was in the process of being reconstructed. Some MPs wanted to expand the building to accommodate more seats as the number of MPs had grown since the original building was constructed. Churchill's statement was made when Parliament was deciding how to proceed—to keep the building as it was, or make it larger to accommodate more seats. Churchill was against "giving each member a desk to sit at and a lid to bang" because, he explained, the House would be empty most of the time. At critical votes and moments, it would fill beyond capacity, with MPs spilling out into the aisles, in his view, a suitable "sense of crowd and urgency." Here is the full quote: "On the night of May 10, 1941, with one of the last bombs of the last serious raid, our House of Commons was destroyed by the violence of the enemy, and we have now to consider whether we should build it up again, and how, and when. We shape our buildings, and afterwards our buildings shape us. Having dwelt and served for more than forty years in the late Chamber, and having derived very great pleasure and advantage therefrom, I, naturally, should like to see it restored in all essentials to its old form, convenience and dignity."

3. Azimi and Baena-Tan, 2.
4. Robert King
5. Nishuane.
6. Fullilove, *Root Shock*.
7. Ibid., 83–91.

## Chapter 5. Line

1. Janofsky.
2. Wallace, Golembeski, and Fullilove.
3. Ibid., 6.
4. Blow.
5. Craven.
6. Fernandez, Pérez-Peña, and Bromwich.
7. Huie, *Lake Street*.
8. See for example, Carnegie Museum of Art, Harris Archive, and Historic Pittsburgh, Photographic Library.
9. Harding.
10. Huie, *Chinese-ness*.
11. Kensey.
12. Stovall.

## Chapter 6. Tangle

1. Lally, *South Orange Sonnets.*
2. Ibid., 1.
3. Lally, *Another Way*, 438.
4. Ibid, 332.
5. McKibben.
6. Winerup.
7. Ibid.
8. Ring.
9. Pierre-Louis.
10. Wikipedia Contributors, "Vermont."
11. McGeehan.
12. Orvell, 139–148.
13. Paul.
14. Fulllilove, Izenberg, Golembeski, et al.

## Chapter 7. Time

1. Cantal-Dupart, 27.
2. Capuzzo.
3. Wikipedia Contributors, "Rangoli."

## Chapter 8. The Great Mistake

1. "The 1619 Project," *New York Times.*
2. This excerpt was prepared by Ken Hardin from the text in Howard Zinn and Anthony Arnove, 58–61.
3. Allen, 21.
4. See Fullilove, Hernandez-Cordero, Madoff, and Fullilove; Fullilove and Hernandez-Cordero; and Hernandez-Cordero and Fullilove.
5. Mann, 41.
6. Pidcock. Martha Stitelman noted that invasive earthworms from Japan had reached her backyard in Vermont. Just as earthworms were carried in ship ballast in the 1600s, now they are carried as fish bait, in compost and soil, and in the root balls of transplanted shrubs and trees.
7. Mann, 72–73. The story of the honeybees has echoes in 2019. A Philadelphia councilperson proposed a law to prohibit adding a bay window in gentrifying neighborhoods, as the windows, like the honeybees, signaled change and made people anxious.
8. Mann, 73.
9. Whitman.
10. Equal Justice Initiative.
11. Minami and Davis.
12. 400 Years of Inequality Educational Materials Team.

13. See the following publications on collective recovery: Saul; Hernandez Cordero.
14. University of Orange Urbanism Department.
15. Truth.
16. Nossel.
17. Charlottesville Clergy Collective.
18. Walker.

## Chapter 9. Exiting Regularity

1. Morrish.
2. Mance.
3. Roberson.
4. Pierre-Louis, "The World Is Losing Fish to Eat as Oceans Warm, Study Finds."
5. Duva.
6. Olick.
7. Gomez.
8. Cioffi.
9. Moore.

## Chapter 10. The Trap of the Status Quo

1. Definition taken from Google Dictionary.
2. Lewis, 231.
3. Ibid., 83.
4. Ibid., 405.
5. Ibid., 1.
6. Ibid., 406.
7. Ibid., 406.
8. Ibid., i.
9. Weissberg.
10. Lewis, 406.
11. Thompson and Fullilove, 70–74.
12. Ibid., 75–82.
13. Rohr.

## Chapter 11. Planning to Stay

1. Orvell.
2. Bell.
3. Morrish and Brown.
4. Tall, 216.
5. Granovetter.
6. St. Louis Planning Commission.

7. Cherokee Street News.
8. Goodwin, 33–34.
9. Cantal-Dupart , 27.
10. Wikipedia, "Beyoğlu."
11. Bourli, Dadaş, and Lira.
12. Wikipedia, "Istanbul Pogrom."
13. Mullins and Schleifer.
14. Arditi.
15. Şatana.
16. See Glassie, *Material Culture*; Summer-Boyd and Freely; and Glassie, Turkish Art.
17. Necipoğlu.
18. Norwich.
19. Bourli, Dadaş, and Lira.
20. Morrish and Brown.

Chapter 12. What Happens Next
1. Memphis Office of Comprehensive Planning.
2. Martinez.
3. Dwyer, "Coogan's, an Uptown Stalwart, Makes Its Last Stand." See also Robert Synder for an opinion piece.
4. "Coogan's Restaurant."
5. Dwyer, "Coogan's, an Uptown Stalwart, Makes Its Last Stand."
6. Fox and Pereira.

# Bibliography

Acosta, A. Contemplating 400 Years of Inequality. In D. Hucks (Ed.), *Purposeful Teaching and Learning in Diverse Contexts*. Charlotte, NC: Information Age Publishing, 2020.

Adanali, Yaşar Adnan. "De-spatialized Space as Neoliberal Utopia: Gentrified Istiklal Street and Commercialized Urban Spaces." Red Thread, December 18, 2018. http://red-thread.org/en/de-spatialized-space-as-neoliberal-utopia-gentrified-istiklal-street-and-commercialized-urban-spaces/ (accessed September 23, 2019).

———, ed. Gecekondu Conversations: Archive, Memory, Imagery, Space, Architecture. Istanbul: Center for Spatial Justice, 2018.

Adanali, Yaşar Adnan, Vasiliki Bourli, Merv Dadaş, Mateus Lira, and Deniz Öztürk. *Beyoğlu: I Will Survive Map*. Istanbul: Center for Spatial Justice, 2018.

Allen, Danielle. *Our Declaration: A Reading of the Declaration of Independence in Defense of Equality*. New York: W. W. Norton, 2014.

Arditi, Talya. "How to Drink Raki: A Crash Course in Turkey's Signature Drink." CNN Travel. https://www.cnn.com/travel/article/turkey-signature-drink-raki/index.html (last modified December 29, 2015).

Artson, Rabbi Bradley. "Justice, Justice You Shall Pursue." www.myjewishlearning.com. https://www.myjewishlearning.com/article/justice-justice-you-shall-pursue/ (accessed April 19, 2016).

Azimi, Rehanna, and Monique Baena-Tan. *Anchoring the City of Orange: A Community Report*. New York: New School, 2015.

Bachmann, Ingeborg. "Stay." GYSPYSCARLETT's Weblog. https://gypsyscarlett.wordpress.com/2010/10/25/ingeborg-bachmanns-stay-a-poem/ (accessed September 2, 2019).

Bacon, John, and Christal Hayes. "Stunning Videos, Photos Reveal Enormity of Ellicott City Flood Devastation." *USA Today*, May 29, 2018. https://www.usatoday.com/story/news/nation/2018/05/29/ellicott-city-flood-devastation-stunning-videos-photos/650489002/.

Bagli, Charles. "Resurrecting a Village by Buying Up Main Street." *New York Times*, November 11, 2010. https://www.nytimes.com/2010/11/12/nyregion/12morris.html.

Barber, Reverend Dr. William J., II, and Jonathan Wilson-Hartgrove. *The Third Reconstruction: How a Moral Movement Is Overcoming the Politics of Division and Fear*. Boston: Beacon Press, 2016.

Barker, Roger Garlock. *Ecological Psychology: Concepts and Methods for Studying the Environment of Human Behavior*. Stanford: Stanford University Press, 1968.

Barndt, Deborah. *Naming the Moment: Political Analysis for Action: A Manual for Community Groups*. Toronto: Jesuit Centre for Social Faith and Justice, 1989.

Bell, Catherine. *Good Witch*, Season 4, Episodes 9 and 10, 2019. https://www.hallmarkchannel.com/good-witch/videos/good-witch-season-4-preview.

Belluck, Pam. "Warm Winters Upset Rhythms of Maple Sugar." *New York Times*, March 3, 2007. https://www.nytimes.com/2007/03/03/us/03maple.html.

Bergman, Meghan Mayhew. "Florida Is Drowning. Condos Are Still Being Built. Can't Humans See the Writing on the Wall?" *The Guardian*, February 15, 2019. https://www.theguardian.com/environment/2019/feb/15/florida-climate-change-coastal-real-estate-rising-seas.

Biesecker, Michael, Jason Dearen, and Angeliki Kastanis. "Toxic Trouble Swamps Jersey: N.J. Has Most Superfund Cleanup Sites Located in Flood-Prone Areas—a Lethal Mix for Residents." *The Star-Ledger*, December 23, 2017.

Billings, Charles A. *A History of Ripton, Vermont*. Vol. 1. Ripton, VT: Niche Arts, 2019.

Blow, Charles M. "A Week from Hell." *New York Times*, July 11, 2016. https://www.nytimes.com/2016/07/11/opinion/a-week-from-hell.html (last modified July 8, 2016).

Bluestone, Barry, and Bennett Harrison. *The Deindustrialization of America: Plant Closings, Community Abandonment, and the Dismantling of Basic Industry*. New York: Basic Books, 1982.

Bourli, Vasiliki, Merve Dadas, and Mateus Lira. "Beyoglu I Will Survive! Collective Memory and Radical Urban Transformations in Istanbul." Beyond. Istanbul. https://beyond.istanbul/beyoglu-i-will-survive-collective-memory-and-radical-urban-transformations-in-istanbul-2049fb60e5a5 (last modified November 4, 2018).

Bowlby, John. *Attachment and Loss: Volume I: Attachment*. London: The Hogarth Press and the Institute of Psycho-Analysis, 1969.

Bulteau, Marcel Joseph. *Monographie de la cathédrale de Chartres*. Vol. 2. Chartres, France: R. Selleret, 1891.

Cantal-Dupart, Michel. *Merci la Ville*. Bordeaux, France: Investigations Le Castor Astral, 1994.

Capuzzo, Jill P. "Maplewood, N.J.: If Brooklyn Were a Suburb." *The New York Times*, October 8, 2014. https://www.nytimes.com/2014/10/12/realestate/maplewood-nj-if-brooklyn-were-a-suburb.

Carnegie Museum of Art. "Teenie Harris Archive." Carnegie Museum of Art. https://cmoa.org/art/teenie-harris-archive/ (accessed September 10, 2019).

Charlottesville Clergy Collective. "Charlottesville to Jamestown Pilgrimage." Cville2Jtown. https://cville2jtown.weebly.com/ (accessed August 23, 2019).

Cherokee Street Development League. Invitation to Cinco de Mayo on Cherokee Street. The text used in this book was edited by Mindy Fullilove.

Cioffi, Chris. "Why Does Ellicott City Keep Flooding? And What Other Local Areas Are at Risk?" WTOP. https://wtop.com/howard-county/2018/06/ellicott-city-keep-flooding-local-areas-risk/(last modified July 4, 2018).

Ciraulo, Graham. "Petition to Steven J. Corwin: Save Coogan's Irish Pub and Restaurant," 2018. Change.Org The version used in this boook was edited by Mindy Fullilove.

———. "Victory! We Saved Coogan's!!!!!!!!" 2018. Change.Org. The version used in this text was edited by Mindy Fullilove.

City of St. Louis Planning Commission. Gravois-Jefferson Historic Neighborhoods Plan. https://gravoisjeffersonplanning.org/ (accessed September 7, 2019).

Conte, Michaelangelo. "No Car, Just Foot Traffic, on Newark." *Jersey Journal*, June 6, 2014 .

"Coogan's Restaurant." http://www.coogans.com/ (accessed August 22, 2019).

Craven, Julia. "More Than 250 Black People Were Killed by Police in 2016 [Updated]." *Huffington Post*, July 7, 2016. https://www.huffpost.com/entry/black-people-killed-by-police-america_n_577da633e4b0c590f7e7fb17.

Cronon, William. *Changes in the Land: Indians, Colonists, and the Ecology of New England*. New York: Hill and Wang, 2003.

De La Baume, Maïa. "August in the City of Lights: Beyond the Paris Plage." *New York Times*, August 6, 2008. https://intransit.blogs.nytimes.com/2008/08/06/august-in-the-city-of-lights-beyond-the-paris-plage/?_r=0.

DeMarco, Laura. "A Look Back at Big Fun: 27 years of toys and memories." *Cleveland Plain Dealer*. https://www.cleveland.com/entertainment/2018/05/post_207.html (accessed December 15, 2019).

Dickinson, Emily. "Look Back on Time." Famous Poets and Poems. http://famouspoetsandpoems.com/poets/emily_dickinson/poems/9285 (accessed September 15, 2019).

Doyle, Martin W., Emily H. Stanley, David G. Havlick, Mark J. Kaiser, George Steinbach, William L. Graf, Gerald E. Galloway, and J. Adam Riggsbee. "Aging Infrastructure and Ecosystem Restoration." *Science* 319, no. 5861(2008): 286–87. https://www.jstor.org/stable/20052009.

Duva, Nicholas. "7 Industries at Greatest Risk from Climate Change." CNBC. https://www.cnbc.com/2014/10/22/7-industries-at-greatest-risk-from-climate-change.html?slide=2 (last modified October 22, 2014).

Dwyer, Jim. "Coogan's, an Uptown Stalwart, Makes its Last Stand." *New York Times*, January 9, 2018. https://www.nytimes.com/2018/01/09/nyregion/coogans-washington-heights-closing.html.

———. "To New Yorkers' Delight, Coogan's Says It Isn't Closing After All." *New York Times*, January 12, 2018. https://www.nytimes.com/2018/01/12/nyregion/coogans-bar-staying-open.html.

Dyckman Farmhouse Museum Alliance. "Farm." http://dyckmanfarmhouse.org/farm/ (accessed September 1, 2019).

Economopoulos, Aristide. 2015. "Union Beach 3 Years After Sandy: Then and Now." *NJ.Com*, October 29, 2015. https://www.nj.com/news/2015/10/union_beach_3_years_after_sandy_then_and_now.html.

Eddy, Melissa. "German Chancellor 'Feels Solidarity' for Four Congresswomen Targeted by Trump." *New York Times*, July 20, 2019.

Engel, G. L. "The Clinical Application of the Biopsychosocial Model." *American Journal of Psychiatry* 137, no. 5 (1980): 535–44. http://dx.doi.org/10.1176/ajp.137.5.535.

Engel, George L. "The Need for a New Medical Model: A Challenge for Biomedicine." *Science* 196, no. 4286 (1977): 129–36.

Erikson, Kai. *Everything in Its Path*. New York: Simon & Schuster, 1976.

Equal Justice Initiative. The National Memorial for Peace and Justice, https://museumandmemorial.eji.org/memorial (accessed September 15, 2019).

Fernandez, Manny, Richard Pérez-Peña, and Jonah E. Bromwich "Five Dallas Officers Were Killed as Payback, Police Chief Says." *New York Times*, July 9, 2016. https://www.nytimes.com/2016/07/09/us/dallas-police-shooting.html (accessed September 10, 2019).

Field Museum. "Looking at Ourselves: Rethinking the Sculptures of Malvina Hoffman." https://www.fieldmuseum.org/exhibitions/looking-ourselves-rethinking-sculptures-malvina-hoffman (accessed August 23, 2019).

*First Unitarian Church v. Salt Lake*, 308 F.3d 1114 (10th Cir. 2002).

Foster, John Bellamy. "Absolute Capitalism." *Monthly Review: An Independent Socialist Magazine*, May 1, 2019.

400 Years of Inequality Class, Spring 2019. *A Reading for the Anniversary*. New York: 400 Years of Inequality, 2019.

400 Years of Inequality Educational Materials Team. *Observance Starter Kit 2: A Guidebook to Planning Your Place-Based Observance*. New York: 400 Years of Inequality, 2019.

Fox, Alison, and Ivan Pereira. "Coogan's in Washington Heights Slated to Close After 32 Years in May Due to Rent Hike." *AM New York*, January 10, 2018. https://www.amny.com/eat-and-drink/coogan-s-closing-washington-heights-1.16066640.

Frazier, LaToya Ruby. "The Last Cruze." *New York Times Magazine*, May 5, 2019, 36–53.

Freedman, Samuel. "In the 2020 Elections, American Jews Must Decide: Will We Become White, or Not?" *Haaretz*, September 2, 2019. https://www.haaretz.com/us-news/.premium-in-2020-american-jews-must-decide-will-they-become-white-or-not-1.7776610 (accessed September 17, 2019).

Fullilove, Mindy Thompson. "Death and Life in a Great American City." *International Journal of Mental Health* 28, no. 4 (1999): 20–29. http://www.tandfonline.com/doi/abs/10.1080/00207411.1999.11449469.

———. *The House of Joshua: Meditations on Family and Place.* Lincoln: University of Nebraska Press, 2002.

———. "Psychiatric Implications of Displacement: Contributions from the Psychology of Place." *American Journal of Psychiatry* 153 no.12 (1996): 1516–23. http://dx.doi.org/10.1176/ajp.153.12.1516.

———. *Root Shock: How Tearing Up City Neighborhoods Hurts America, and What We Can Do About It.* 2nd ed. New York: New Village Press, 2016.

———. "Toward a Liberation Psychiatry: Contributions from a Psychology of Place." In *Black Mental Health: Patients, Providers, and Systems*, edited by Ezra E. H. Griffith, Billy E. Jones, and Altha J. Stewart, 283–296. Washington D.C.: American Psychiatric Association Publishing, 2018.

———. *Urban Alchemy: Restoring Joy in America's Sorted-Out Cities.* New York: New York University Press, 2013.

Fullilove, M., and L. Hernández-Cordero. "What Is Collective Recovery?" In *9/11: Mental Health in the Wake of Terrorist Attacks*, edited by Y. Neria, R. Gross, and R. Marshall, 157–63. Cambridge: Cambridge University Press, 2006.

Fullilove, Mindy Thompson, Lourdes Hernandez-Cordero, Jennifer Stevens Madoff, and Robert E. Fullilove III. 2004. "Promoting Collective Recovery Through Organizational Mobilization: The Post-9/11 Disaster Relief Work of NYC RECOVERS." *Journal of Biosocial Science* 36, no. 4 (2004): 479–89.

Fullilove, Mindy Thompson, and Rodrick Wallace. "Serial forced displacement in American cities, 1916–2010." *Journal of Urban Health* 88.3 (2011): 381-389.

Fullilove, Mindy Thompson, Jacob M. Izenberg, Cynthia Golembeski, Martha Stitelman, and Rodrick Wallace. 2020. "Main Streets and Disaster." *City*: 1-12. doi:10.1080/13604813.2020.1739452. https://doi.org/10.1080/13604813.2020.1739452.

Furchgott, Roy. "The Coal Is Gone: It's Time to Get Creative." *New York Times*, October 7, 2018.

Ganga, Maria L. "An Embrace That Swayed the Mormon Church on Gay Rights." *Los Angeles Times*, January 31, 2015. https://www.latimes.com/nation/la-na-mormon-talks-20150131-story.html#page=1.

Gardner, Jennifer. "Community Planning in Mt. Morris, NY." *MultipliCITY*, Spring 2012, 13–14.

Geronimus, Arline T., Margaret Hicken, Danya Keene, and John Bound. "'Weathering' and Age Patterns of Allostatic Load Scores Among Blacks and

Whites in the United States." *American Journal of Public Health* 96, no. 5 (2006): 826–33. https://www.ncbi.nlm.nih.gov/pubmed/16380565 https://www.ncbi.nlm.nih.gov/pmc/articles/PMC1470581/.

Ghose, Tia. "Man with Hole in Stomach Revolutionized Medicine." www.livescience.com. https://www.livescience.com/28996-hole-in-stomach-revealed-digestion.html (last modified April 24, 2014).

Glassie, Henry H. *Material Culture*, Bloomington: Indiana University Prekss, 1999.

Glassie, Henry. *Turkish Traditional Art Today*, Second Edition, Turkish Ministry of Culture and Indiana University Press, 2002.

Goodwin, Jason. *The Janissary Tree*. London: Faber and Faber, 2007.

Google Dictionary. "Definition of Amalgam." (accessed July 11, 2019).

———. "Definition of Status Quo." (accessed July 11, 2019).

Granovetter, Mark S. "The Strength of Weak Ties." *American Journal of Sociology* 78 (1973): 1360-80.

Guthrey, Molly. "Wing Young Huie, Chronicler of St. Paul's University Avenue, Is First Photographer to Win McKnight Award." www.twincities.com (last modified August 20, 2018).

Harding, Kelli. *The Rabbit Effect: Live Longer, Happier, and Healthier with the Groundbreaking Science of Kindness*. New York: Atria Books, 2019.

Harris, Fred, and Alan Curtis. "The Unmet Promise of Equality." *New York Times*, March 1, 2018.

Harvey, David. *A Brief History of Neoliberalism*. Oxford University Press, USA, 2007.

Hendrix, Steve. "He Always Hated Women." *Washington Post*, June 7, 2019. https://www.washingtonpost.com/graphics/2019/local/yoga-shooting-incel-attack-fueled-by-male-supremacy/.

Heon-Klin, Veronique, Ericka Sieber, Julia Huebner, and Mindy Thompson Fullilove. "The Influence of Geopolitical Change on the Well-Being of a Population: The Berlin Wall." *American Journal of Public Health* 91, no. 3 (2001): 369–74. http://ajph.aphapublications.org/cgi/content/abstract/91/3/369.

Hernández-Cordero, L. J., and M. T. Fullilove. "Constructing Peace: Helping Youth Cope in the Aftermath of 9/11." *American Journal of Preventive Medicine*, 34, no. 3 (2008): S31–S35.

Historic Pittsburgh. "Pittsburgh Photographic Library Project." Historic Pittsburgh: Hosted by the University of Pittsburgh Library System. https://historicpittsburgh.org/collection/pittsburgh-photographic-library-collection (accessed September 10, 2019).

Hoffman, Malvina. *Sculpture Inside and Out*. New York: W. W. Norton, 1939.

Howard County Planning and Zoning. "Ellicott City Watershed Master Plan." Howard County, Maryland. https://www.howardcountymd.gov/Departments/Planning-and-Zoning/Community-Planning/Community-Plans/EC-Master-Plan (accessed July 11, 2019).

Hughes, Langston. "Theme for English B." https://bookriot.com/2019/01/11/langston-hughes-poems/.

———. "Langston Hughes: 'We Are the American Heartbreak.' Langston Hughes Reads Langston Hughes." Speakolo. https://speakola.com/arts/langston-hughes-we-are-the-american-heartbreak (accessed August 23, 2019).

Huie, Wing Young. Chinese-Ness: *The Meanings of Identity and the Nature of Belonging*. Minneapolis: Minnesota Historical Society Press, 2018.

———. *Lake Street, USA*. Minneapolis: University of Minnesota Press, 2001.

Hurdle, Jon. "A College Town That Works, for the College and the Town." *New York Times*, May 30, 2018.

Izenberg, Jacob M., and Mindy Thompson Fullilove. "Hospitality Invites Sociability, Which Builds Cohesion: A Model for the Role of Main Streets in Population Mental Health." *Journal of Urban Health* 93, no. 2 (2016): 292–311.

Jackson, John Brinckerhoff. "The Stranger's Path." In *Landscape in Sight: Looking at America*, edited by Helen Lefkowitz Horowitz, 19–29. New Haven: Yale University Press, 1997.

James, C. L. R. et al. *Fighting Racism in World War II*. New York: Monad Press, 1980. http://catalog.hathitrust.org/Record/000098698.

Janofsky, Michael. "Salt Lake City Journal; Plaza Division Goes Past Main Street." *New York Times*, April 20, 2001. https://www.nytimes.com/2001/04/20/us/salt-lake-city-journal-plaza-division-goes-past-main-street.html.

Johnson, A'Lelia. "The Other Side: Eastside, Westside, Are the Prices the Same?" Englewood, New Jersey, 2009.

Kazin, Alfred. *A Walker in the City*. New York: Harcourt, 1946.

Kensey, Porscha. Letter to Wing Young Huie. https://www.wingyounghuie.com/reactions (accessed February 28, 2019).

Kepner, Tyler. "The Home for the Hall of Fame, Nestled in the Past." *New York Times*, July 21, 2019. https://www.nytimes.com/2019/07/21/sports/baseball/the-home-for-the-hall-of-fame-nestled-in-the-past.html?searchResultPosition=2.

Kilmer, Joyce. *Main Street and Other Poems*, Project Guttenberg Ebook 264, 2008.

Kimmelman, Burt. "I Might Die of Love for You: Michael Lally's Poetry Is Experimental and Unabashedly Romantic." www.poetryfoundation.org.https://www.poetryfoundation.org/articles/148631/i-might-die-of-love-for-you (last modified January 2, 2019).

Kimmelman, Michael. "A Sports Complex Shows Its Brains and Brawn." *New York Times*, March 5, 2013. https://www.nytimes.com/2013/03/06/arts/design/columbia-universitys-new-campbell-sports-complex-in-inwood.html.

King, Martin Luther, Jr. *Stride Toward Freedom: The Montgomery Story*. London: Souvenir Press, 2011.

King, Robert. "Death and Resurrection of an Urban Church." Faith and Leadership. https://faithandleadership.com/death-and-resurrection-urban-church

(last modified March 24, 2015).

Korzybski, Alfred. *Science and Sanity: An Introduction to Non-Aristotelian Systems and General Semantics.* Vol. 27. Brooklyn, NY: Institute of General Semantics, 1993.

Kyushu University. "13th Century Picture Scroll Depicting the Mongol Invasions." (accessed September 1, 2019).

Lally, Michael. *Another Way to Play: Poems 1960–2017.* New York: Seven Stories Press, 2018.

———. *It's Not Nostalgia.* Santa Rosa, CA: Black Sparrow Press, 1999.

———. *South Orange Sonnets.* Washington, D.C.: Some of Us Press, 1972.

Leighton, Alexander Hamilton. *Governing of Men.* Princeton: Princeton University Press, 2015.

Lewis, Sinclair. *Main Street: The Story of Carol Kennicott.* New York: Penguin, 1995.

Leydet, François. *Time and the River Flowing: Grand Canyon.* San Francisco: Sierra Club, 1964.

Mance, Dave, III. "Dispatch from the Sugarwoods Part 4." Northern Woodlands. https://northernwoodlands.org/editors_blog/article/dispatch-from-the-sugarwoods-part-4 (accessed July 11, 2019).

Mann, Charles C. *1493: Uncovering the New World Columbus Created.* New York: Alfred A. Knopf, 2011.

Martinez, Gina. "'They're Traumatized.' Why a Police Shooting in Memphis Turned into a Violent Protest." *Time,* June 13, 2019.

Mather, Michael. *Having Nothing, Possessing Everything: Finding Abundant Communities in Unexpected Places.* Grand Rapids, MI: Wm. B. Erdman, 2018.

McKibben, Bill. "Vermont Town Seeks a Heart." *New York Times,* March 31, 2018.

Memphis Office of Comprehensive Planning. "Memphis 3.0." https://www.memphis3point0.com/ (accessed July 11, 2019).

Merkel, Jayne, and Julia Wertz. "New York's Disappearing Storefronts." *New York Times,* August 27, 2016.

Merrifield, Andy. *The Wisdom of Donkeys: Finding Tranquility in a Chaotic World.* Vancouver: Greystone Books, 2008.

Minami, Hirofumi. "Place Philosophy and Psychoanalysis of Cities as a Possible Project." New York: Environmental Design Research Association, 2019.

Minami, Hirofumi, and Brian R. Davis.. "Mirrored Reflections: (Re)Constructing Memory and Identity in Hiroshima and New York." In *New York After 9/11,* edited by Susan Opotow and Zachary Baron Shemtob, 41–66. New York: Fordham University Press, 2018.

Moore, Jason W. "Environmental Crises and the Metabolic Rift in World-Historical Perspective." *Organization & Environment* 13, no. 2 (2000): 123–57.

Morrish, William. "13,001 A Waste Odyssey." In *Now Urbanism: The Future City Is Here*, edited by Jeffrey Hou, Benjamin Spencer, Thaisa Way, and Ken Yocom, 61–77. New York: Routledge, 2014.

Morrish, William R., and Catherine R. Brown. *Planning to Stay: A Collaborative Project*. Minneapolis: Milkweek Editions, 2000.

Mullins, Ansel, and Yigal Schleifer. *Istanbul Eats: Exploring the Culinary Backstreets*. 8th ed. Istanbul: Boyut, 2019.

National Research Council. *Deadly Lessons: Understanding Lethal School Violence*. Washington, D.C.: National Academies Press, 2002.

Necipoğlu, Gülru. *The Age of Sinan: Architectural Culture in the Ottoman Empire*. London: Reaktion Books, 2005.

News Story Hub Contributors. "It Will Take Cathedral Thinking." Greta Thunberg's Climate Change Speech to European Parliament, April 16, 2019. newsstoryhub.com. http://newsstoryhub.com/2019/04/it-will-take-cathedral-thinking-greta-thunbergs-climate-change-speech-to-european-parliament-16-april-2019/ (last modified April 17, 2019).

"Nishiki Tenmangū | 錦天満宮." discoverkyoto.com. https://www.discoverkyoto.com/places-go/nishiki-tenmangu/ (accessed August 23, 2019).

Nishuane Group. *Area in Need of Redevelopment Investigation with Condemnation*. http://www.ci.orange.nj.us/Main_Street_AINS_Draft_2.pdf (accessed July 12, 2019).

Norwich, John. *A Short History of Byzantium*. New York: Vintage, 1998.

Nossiter, Adam. "Rejected Honor Reflects Hardships of 'the Other France': Michelin Star Brings Too Many Expenses." *New York Times*, December 28, 2017.

Ohno, Ryuzo. "Re-Examination of 'Cultural Difference.'" New York: Environmental Design Research Association, 2019.

Olick, Diana. "Rising Risks: 'Climate Gentrification' Is Changing Miami Real Estate Values— for Better and Worse." CNBC. https://www.cnbc.com/2018/08/29/climate-gentrification-is-changing-miami-real-estate-values.html (last modified May 17, 2019).

Orvell, Miles. *The Death and Life of Main Street: Small Towns in American Memory, Space, and Community*. Chapel Hill: University of North Carolina Press, 2012.

"Our Story." https://www.ingebretsens.com/about/ourstory (accessed July 12, 2019).

Paul, Dereck W., Jr. "Ghosts of Our Collective Subconscious—What Blackface in a Yearbook Photo Means for Medical Education." *The New England Journal of Medicine* 381, no. 5 (2019). https://www.nejm.org/doi/full/10.1056/NEJMp1902650.

Peterson, Eric S. "Kiss Off: A Gay Couple Cited for Holding Hands on Main Street Plaza." *Salt Lake City Weekly*, July 10, 2009. https://www.cityweekly.net/utah/kiss-off-a-gay-couple-cited-for-holding-hands-on-main-street-plaza/

Content?oid=2139048.

Pidcock, Roz. "Global Worming: Are Earthworms Contributing to Climate Change?" Carbon Brief. https://www.carbonbrief.org/global-worming-are-earthworms-contributing-to-climate-change (last modified February 4, 2003).

Piercy, Marge. "The Seven of Pentacles." Famous Poets and Poems. http://famouspoetsandpoems.com/poets/marge_piercy/poems/19240 (accessed August 23, 2019).

Pierre-Louis, Kendra. "Syrup Is as Canadian as a Maple Leaf. That Could Change with the Climate." *New York Times*, May 3, 2019. https://www.nytimes.com/2019/05/03/climate/climate-change-maple-syrup.html.

———. "The World Is Losing Fish to Eat as Oceans Warm, Study Finds." *New York Times*, February 28, 2019. https://www.nytimes.com/2019/02/28/climate/fish-climate-change.html.

———. "Five Years After Hurricane Irene, Vermont Still Striving for Resilience." 2016. https://insideclimatenews.org/news/31082016/five-years-after-hurricane-irene-2011-effects-flooding-vermont-damage-resilience-climate-change.

Pine, Gary Nesta. "Mr Wall Street," *Revelations*, 2016.

Pollock, Sarah. "A Norwegian Valley Struggles for Cultural Survival." *New York Times*, July 28, 2019.

Renaldi, Joseph T. "A Penny Candy Store." poemhunter.com. https://www.poemhunter.com/poem/a-penny-candy-store/ (accessed August 23, 2019).

Ring, Wilson. "Vermont Marks Start of Last Irene Recovery Project."*AP News*, October 24, 2018. https://www.apnews.com/50386432fcef44a18b254051e19c91d1.

Roberson, Roy. "Saltwater Intrusion Threatens Eastern North Carolina Crops." Farm Progress. https://www.farmprogress.com/management/saltwater-intrusion-threatens-eastern-north-carolina-crops (last modified December 27, 2012).

Rohr, Richard. "Love Never Fails." Center for Action and Contemplation. https://cac.org/love-never-fails-2016-12-29 (last modified December 29, 2016).

Rosenthal, Elisabeth. "It's Time to Set Broadway Free." *New York Times*, December 11, 2016.

Sanders, Topher. "Only White People." ProPublica. https://www.propublica.org/article/only-white-people-said-the-little-girl (last modified October 13, 2016).

Şatana, Tuba. "Musa Dağdeviren: The Food Pioneer on Chef's Table." Istanbul Food Tour. https://istanbulfood.com/musa-dagdeviren-the-food-pioneer-on-chefs-table/ (accessed August 22, 2019).

Schneier, Matthew. "Holiday Windows Still Matter." *New York Times*, November 25, 2018.

Schoggen, Phil. *Behavior Settings: A Revision and Extension of Roger G. Barker's Ecological Psychology*. Stanford: Stanford University Press, 1989.

Sengupta, Somini. "From an 'Invisible Girl' to an Outspoken Climate Crusader." *New York Times*, February 20, 2019.

Sengupta, Somini, and Kendra Pierre-Louis. "Warning of Cascading Health Risks from the Rapidly Changing Climate." *New York Times*, November 29, 2018.

Simmons, Melody. "10 Historic Buildings to Be Razed on Ellicott City's Main Street." *Baltimore Business Journal*, August 23, 2018.

Snyder, Nancy. "10 Poems from Langston Hughes." Book Riot. https://bookriot. com/2019/01/11/langston-hughes-poems/ (accessed September 2, 2019).

Snyder, Robert. "Amazing Things Have Happened Here: The Shared Mission of a Bar and a Hospital." The Uptown Collective. https://www.uptowncollective. com/2018/01/12/amazing-things-have-happened-here-the-shared-mission-of-a-bar-and-a-hospital/ (accessed July 30, 2019).

Southall, Ashley. "A Celebration of Survival in Brownsville, Marred by Violence." *New York Times*, July 31, 2019.

Stovall, Tyler. *Paris Noir: African Americans in the City of Light*. Boston: Houghton Mifflin, 1996. Chapter 1 available at http://www.washingtonpost. com/wp-srv/style/longterm/books/chap1/parisnoir.htm.

Sumner-Boyd, Hilary, and John Freely. *Strolling Through Istanbul: A Guide to the City*. 2nd ed. Istanbul: Redhouse Press, 1972.

Tall, Deborah. *From Where We Stand: Recovering a Sense of Place*. New York: Alfred A. Knopf, 1993.

Tavernise, Sabrina. "A Dimly Flickering Light in a Darkened Downtown." *New York Times*, January 8, 2012.

"The 1619 Project." *New York Times Magazine*, August 14, 2019.

Thompson, Ernest, and Mindy Thompson Fullilove. *Homeboy Came to Orange: A Story of People's Power*. New York: New Village Press, 2018.

Traverso, Amy. "Barnard General Store: How One Vermont Hamlet Saved the Heart of its Community—and Got the World's Best Pancakes in the Bargain." *Yankee*, May 2017, 64.

Truth, Sojourner. "Ain't I a Woman?" In Zinn, Howard, and Anthony Arnove, *Voices of a People's History of the United States*. 10th Anniversary ed. New York: Seven Stories Press, 2014.

National Advisory Commission on Civil Disorders. *Report of the National Advisory Commission on Civil Disorders*. New York: Bantam Books, 1968.

University of Orange Urbanism Department. *Building Collective Recovery into What You Do*. Orange, NJ: University of Orange, 2008.

Venturi, Robert, Steven Izenour, and Denise Scott Brown. *Learning from Las Vegas: The Forgotten Symbolism of Architectural Form*. Rev. ed. Cambridge: MIT Press, 1977.

von Simson, Otto. *The Gothic Cathedral*, 2nd ed. Princeton: Princeton University Press, 1962.

Walker, Alice. "With Our Grief: Reading *BARRACOON: The Story of the Last 'Black Cargo.'*" Alice Walker: The Official Website. https://alicewalkersgarden. com/2018/03/with-our-grief-reading-barracoon-the-story-of-the-last-black-cargo/ (accessed September 2, 2019).

Wallace, Anthony F. C. 1957. "Mazeway Disintegration: The Individual's Perception of Socio-Cultural Disorganization." *Human Organization* 16, no. 2 (1957): 23.

Wallace, Deborah, and Rodrick Wallace. *Politics, Hierarchy, and Public Health: Voting Patterns in the 2016 Presidential Election.* New York: Routledge, 2019.

Wallace, Rodrick. 1988. "A Synergism of Plagues: 'Planned Shrinkage,' Contagious Housing Destruction, and AIDS in the Bronx." *Environmental Research* 47, no. 1 (1988): 1–33.

Wallace, Rodrick. *Computational Psychiatry: A Systems Biology Approach to the Epigenetics of Mental Disorders.* New York: Springer International Publishing, 2017.

Wallace, Rodrick, and Mindy T. Fullilove. *Collective Consciousness and Its Discontents: Institutional Distributed Cognition, Racial Policy, and Public Health in the United States.* New York: Springer Science+Business Media, 2008.

Wallace, Rodrick, Mindy Thompson Fullilove, and Alan J. Flisher. "AIDS, Violence and Behavioral Coding: Information Theory, Risk Behavior and Dynamic Process on Core-Group Sociogeographic Networks." *Social Science & Medicine* 43, no. 3 (1996): 339–52.

Wallace, Rodrick, Cynthia Golembeski, and Mindy Thompson Fullilove. *Forced Displacement of African-Americans in Newark NJ, 1970–2000: How "Urban Renewal" Triggered an Advancing Glacier of Collapsing Public Order and Public Health.* New York: New York State Psychiatric Institute, 2005.

Wallace, Rodrick, and Deborah Wallace. "Emerging Infections and Nested Martingales: The Entrainment of Affluent Populations into the Disease Ecology of Marginalization." *Environment and Planning A*, 31, no. 10 (1999): 1787–1803.

Wallace, Rodrick, Deborah Wallace, John E. Ullmann, and Howard Andrews. "Deindustrialization, Inner-City Decay, and the Hierarchical Diffusion of AIDS in the USA: How Neoliberal and Cold War Policies Magnified the Ecological Niche for Emerging Infections and Created a National Security Crisis." *Environment and Planning A*, 31, no.1 (1999): 113–39. https://doi-org.libproxy.newschool.edu/10.1068/a310113.

Wallace-Wells, David. 2019. "Go Ahead and Panic." *New York Times*, February 17, 2019.

Weissberg, Claudia S. "Sinclair Lewis, 'the Main Street Burglary' and a Rejection Notice." The Pulitzer Prizes. https://www.pulitzer.org/article/sinclair-lewis-main-street-burglary-and-a-rejection-notice (accessed July 11, 2019).

Whitman, James. *Hitler's American Model: the United States and the Making of Nazi Race Law.* Princeton: Princeton University Press, 2017.

Whitman, Walt. "Song of the Open Road." Poetry Foundation. https://www.poetryfoundation.org/poems/48859/song-of-the-open-road (accessed September 15, 2019).

Wikipedia Contributors. "Beyoğlu." Wikipedia. https://en.wikipedia.org/wiki/

Beyo%C4%9Flu (accessed August 22, 2019).

———. "Chartes Cathedral." Wikipedia. https://en.wikipedia.org/wiki/Chartres_Cathedral (accessed August 23, 2019).

———. "Emakimono." Wikipedia. https://en.wikipedia.org/wiki/Emakimono (accessed September 1, 2019).

———. "Ganglia." Wikipedia. https://en.wikipedia.org/wiki/Ganglion (accessed February 23, 2019).

———. "Istanbul Pogrom." Wikipedia. https://en.wikipedia.org/wiki/Istanbul_pogrom (accessed August 22, 2019).

———. "Ladies' Mile Historic District." Wikipedia. https://en.wikipedia.org/wiki/Ladies%27_Mile_Historic_District (accessed September 1, 2019).

———. "Rangoli." Wikipedia. https://en.wikipedia.org/wiki/Rangoli (accessed July 10, 2019).

———. "Valerie Solanas." Wikipedia. https://en.wikipedia.org/wiki/Valerie_Solanas (accessed July 9, 2019).

———. "Vermont." Wikipedia. https://en.wikipedia.org/wiki/Vermont (accessed July 9, 2019).

Winerup, Michael. "Just Try Topping This 'When I Was Your Age' Tale." *New York Times*, September 12, 2011. https://www.nytimes.com/2011/09/12/us/12winerip.html.

Zinn, Howard, and Anthony Arnove. *Voices of a People's History of the United States*. 3rd ed. New York: Seven Stories Press, 2004.

# Index

Page references followed by p indicate a photograph; followed by fig indicate an illustrated figure.

Lightning Source UK Ltd.
Milton Keynes UK
UKHW021834260920
370441UK00019B/543